This Book Comes With a Website

Nolo's award-winning website has a page dedicated just to this book, where you can:

KEEP UP TO DATE – When there are important changes to the information in this book, we'll post updates

READ BLOGS – Get the latest info from Nolo authors' blogs

LISTEN TO PODCASTS – Listen to authors discuss timely issues on topics that interest you

WATCH VIDEOS – Get a quick introduction to a legal topic with our short videos

You'll find the link in the introduction.

And that's not all. Nolo.com contains thousands of articles on everyday legal and business issues, plus a plain-English law dictionary, all written by Nolo experts and available for free. You'll also find more useful **books, software, online services,** and **downloadable forms.**

Get updates and more at
www.nolo.com

NOLO

The Trusted Name

(but don't take our word for it)

"In Nolo you can trust."

THE NEW YORK TIMES

"Nolo is always there in a jam as the nation's premier publisher of do-it-yourself legal books."

NEWSWEEK

"Nolo publications... guide people simply through the how, when, where and why of the law."

THE WASHINGTON POST

"[Nolo's]... material is developed by experienced attorneys who have a knack for making complicated material accessible."

LIBRARY JOURNAL

"When it comes to self-help legal stuff, nobody does a better job than Nolo..."

USA TODAY

"The most prominent U.S. publisher of self-help legal aids."

TIME MAGAZINE

"Nolo is a pioneer in both consumer and business self-help books and software."

LOS ANGELES TIMES

2nd Edition

The Real Estate Agent's Tax Deduction Guide

Stephen Fishman, J.D.

SECOND EDITION	JANUARY 2013
Editor	DIANA FITZPATRICK
Cover Design	JALEH DOANE
Book Design	TERRI HEARSH
Proofreading	NICOLE THOMAS
Index	ELLEN SHERRON
Printing	BANG PRINTING

Fishman, Stephen.
The real estate agent's tax deduction guide / Stephen Fishman. -- 2nd ed.
p. cm.
Includes index.
ISBN 978-1-4133-1764-0 (pbk.) -- ISBN 978-1-4133-1765-7 (epub ebook)
1. Tax deductions--United States--Popular works. 2. Real estate business--Taxation--Law and legislation--United States--Popular works. 3. Real estate agents--Taxation--Law and legislation--United States--Popular works. 4. Real estate agents--United States--Handbooks, manuals, etc. I. Title.
KF6385.F57 2012a
343.7305'23--dc23
2012028762

This book covers only United States law, unless it specifically states otherwise.

Please note

We believe accurate, plain-English legal information should help you solve many of your own legal problems. But this text is not a substitute for personalized advice from a knowledgeable lawyer. If you want the help of a trained professional—and we'll always point out situations in which we think

icensed to practice in your state.

About the Author

Stephen Fishman is a San Francisco-based attorney and tax expert who has been writing about the law for over 20 years. He is the author of many do-it-yourself law books, including *Deduct It! Lower Your Small Business Taxes, Home Business Tax Deductions, Every Landlord's Tax Deduction Guide*, and *Working for Yourself: Law & Taxes for Independent Contractors, Freelancers & Consultants*. All of his books are published by Nolo.

He is often quoted on tax-related issues by newspapers across the country, including the *Chicago Tribune, San Francisco Chronicle*, and *Cleveland Plain Dealer.*

Table of Contents

Your Tax Deduction Companion for Real Estate Agents

This is a book about tax deductions for real estate agents. In this book, the term "real estate agent" includes both real estate salespeople (also called sales associates) and real estate brokers—in other words, all people licensed by their state to sell real estate. Sometimes we refer to them as real estate professionals.

With the real estate market the way it is, real estate professionals need to reduce their expenses as much as possible. The biggest expense for most real estate pros is taxes. Every year, thousands of agents and brokers pay more taxes on their income then they have to. Why? Because they fail to take advantage of all the tax deductions that are available to them.

Regardless of whether you're a real estate salesperson or broker, you are a business owner. The government has decided that business owners don't have to pay tax on income they spend for certain business purposes. So, the trick to paying lower taxes—and keeping more of your hard-earned dollars—is to take advantage of every tax deduction available to you. To do so, you'll have to figure out which deductions you are entitled to take and keep proper records documenting your expenses. The IRS will never complain if you don't take all the deductions available to you—and it certainly doesn't make a point of advertising ways to lower your taxes.

That's where this book comes in. It shows you how you can deduct all or most of your real estate business expenses from your federal taxes. This book is not a tax preparation guide—it does not show you how to fill out your tax forms. (By the time you do your taxes, it may be too late to take deductions you could have taken if you had planned the prior year's business spending wisely and kept proper records.) Instead, this book gives you all the information you need to maximize your deductible expenses—and avoid common deduction mistakes. You can (and should) use this book all year long, to make April 15th as painless as possible.

Even if you work with an accountant or another tax professional, you need to learn about tax deductions. No tax professional will ever know as much about your real estate business as you do; and you can't expect a hired professional to search high and low for every deduction you might be able to take, especially during the busy tax preparation season. If you do your taxes yourself, your need for knowledge is even greater. Not even the most sophisticated tax preparation program can decide which tax deductions you should take or tell you whether you've overlooked a valuable deduction.

The information in this book will help you provide your tax professional with better records, ask better questions, obtain better advice—and, just as importantly, evaluate the advice you get from tax professionals, websites, and other sources.

Get Updates and More Online

When there are important changes to the information in this book, we'll post updates online, on a page dedicated to this book: **www.nolo.com/back-of-book/DEAR.html**. You'll find other useful information there, too, including author blogs, podcasts, and videos.

CHAPTER 1

Tax Deduction Basics for Real Estate Agents and Brokers

The tax code is full of deductions for real estate agents and brokers —from automobile expenses to wages for employees. Before you can start taking advantage of these deductions, however, you need a basic understanding of how businesses pay taxes and how tax deductions work. This chapter gives you all the information you need to get started. It covers:

- how tax deductions work
- how to calculate the value of a tax deduction, and
- what real estate agents and brokers can deduct.

How Tax Deductions Work

A tax deduction (also called a tax write-off) is an amount of money you are entitled to subtract from your gross income (all the money you make) to determine your taxable income (the amount on which you must pay tax). The more deductions you have, the lower your taxable income will be and the less tax you will have to pay.

Types of Tax Deductions

There are three basic types of tax deductions: personal deductions, investment deductions, and business deductions. This book covers only business deductions—the large array of write-offs available to business owners, including real estate agents and brokers.

Personal Deductions

For the most part, your personal, living, and family expenses are not tax deductible. For example, you can't deduct the food that you buy for yourself and your family. There are, however, special categories of personal expenses that may be deducted, subject to strict limitations. These include items such as home mortgage interest, state and local taxes, charitable contributions, medical expenses above a threshold amount, interest on education loans, and alimony. This book does not cover these personal deductions.

Investment Deductions

Many real estate professionals try to make money by investing money. For example, they often invest in real estate or play the stock market. They incur all kinds of expenses, such as fees paid to money managers or financial planners, legal and accounting fees, and interest on money borrowed to buy investment property. These and other investment expenses (also called expenses for the production of income) are tax deductible, subject to strict limitations. Investment deductions are not covered in this book.

Business Deductions

Because a real estate agent's sales activity is a profit-making enterprise, it is a business for tax purposes. People in business usually must spend money on their business—for example, for office space, supplies, and equipment. Most business expenses are deductible, sooner or later, one way or another. And that's what this book is about: How real estate professionals (agents and brokers) may deduct their business expenses.

You Pay Taxes Only on Your Profits

The federal income tax law recognizes that you must spend money to make money. Virtually every real estate agent or broker, however small his or her business, incurs some expenses. Even an agent or broker who works from home must pay for business driving and insurance.

If you are a sole proprietor (or owner of a one-person LLC taxed as a sole proprietorship), you are not legally required to pay tax on every dollar your real estate sales business takes in (your gross business income). Instead, you owe tax only on the amount left over after your business deductible expenses are subtracted from your gross income (this remaining amount is called your net profit). Although some tax deduction calculations can get a bit complicated, the basic math is simple: the more deductions you take, the lower your net profit will be, and the less tax you will have to pay.

EXAMPLE: Karen, a sole proprietor real estate broker, earned $100,000 in commissions this year. Fortunately, she doesn't have to pay income tax on the entire $100,000—her gross business income. Instead, she can deduct from her gross income various business expenses, including a $10,000 office rental deduction (see Chapter 8) and a $5,000 deduction for insurance (see Chapter 13). These and her other expenses amount to $20,000. She can deduct the $20,000 from her $100,000 gross income to arrive at her net profit: $80,000. She pays income tax only on this net profit amount.

The principle is the same if your business is a partnership, limited liability company, or S corporation: Business expenses are deducted from the entity's profits to determine the entity's net profit for the year, which is passed through the entity to the owners' individual tax returns.

EXAMPLE: Assume that Karen is a member of a three-owner real estate brokerage organized as a limited liability company (LLC), and is entitled to one-third of the LLC's income. She doesn't pay tax on the gross income the LLC receives, only on her portion of its net income after expenses are deducted. This year, the LLC earned $400,000 and had $100,000 in expenses. She pays tax on one-third of the LLC's $300,000 net profit.

If your business is organized as a C corporation, it too pays tax only on its net profits. (See Chapter 2 for details on choice of business entity for real estate agents.)

You Must Have a Legal Basis for Your Deductions

All tax deductions are a matter of "legislative grace," which means that you can take a deduction only if it is specifically allowed by one or more provisions of the tax law. You usually do not have to indicate on your tax return which tax law provision gives you the right to take a particular deduction. If you are audited by the IRS, however, you'll have to provide a legal basis for every deduction the IRS questions. If the IRS concludes that your deduction wasn't justified, it will deny the deduction and charge you back taxes, interest, and, in some cases, penalties.

You Must Be in Business to Claim Business Deductions

Only businesses can claim business tax deductions. This probably seems like a simple concept, but it can get tricky. Even though you might believe you are running a business, the IRS may beg to differ. If your real estate business doesn't turn a profit for several years in a row, the IRS might decide that you are engaged in a hobby rather than a business. This may not sound like a big deal, but it could have disastrous tax consequences: People engaged in hobbies are entitled to very limited tax deductions, while businesses can deduct all kinds of expenses. Fortunately, this unhappy outcome can be avoided by careful agents. (See Chapter 3 for a detailed discussion on how to beat the hobby loss rule.)

The Value of a Tax Deduction

Most taxpayers, even sophisticated real estate professionals, don't fully appreciate just how much money they can save with tax deductions. A deduction represents income on which you don't have to pay tax. So the value of any deduction is the amount of tax you would have had to pay on that income had you not deducted it. A deduction of $1,000 won't save you $1,000—it will save you whatever you would otherwise have had to pay as tax on that $1,000 of income.

Federal and State Income Taxes

To determine how much income tax a deduction will save you, you must first figure out your marginal income tax bracket. The United States has a progressive income tax system for individual taxpayers, with six different tax rates (often called tax brackets) ranging from 10% of taxable income to 35% (see the chart below). The higher your income, the higher your tax rate.

You move from one bracket to the next only when your taxable income exceeds the bracket amount. For example, if you are a single taxpayer in 2012, you pay 10% income tax on all your taxable income up to $8,700. If your taxable income exceeds that amount, the next tax rate (15%) applies to all your income over $8,700—but the 10% rate still applies to the first $8,700. If your income exceeds the 15% bracket amount, the next tax rate (25%) applies to the excess amount, and so on until the top bracket of 35% is reached.

The tax bracket in which the last dollar you earn for the year falls is called your marginal tax bracket. For example, if you have $150,000 in taxable income, your marginal tax bracket is 28%. To determine how much federal income tax a deduction will save you, multiply the amount of the deduction by your marginal tax bracket. For example, if your marginal tax bracket is 28%, you will save 28¢ in federal income taxes for every dollar you are able to claim as a deductible business expense (28% × $1 = 28¢).

The following table lists the federal income tax brackets for single and married individual taxpayers.

2012 Federal Personal Income Tax Rates

Tax Bracket	Income If Single	Income If Married Filing Jointly
10%	Up to $8,700	Up to $17,400
15%	$8,701 to $35,350	$17,401 to $70,700
25%	$35,351 to $85,650	$70,701 to $142,700
28%	$85,651 to $178,650	$142,701 to $217,450
33%	$178,651 to $388,350	$217,451 to 388,350
35%	All over $388,350	All over $388,350

Income tax brackets are adjusted each year for inflation. For current brackets, see IRS Publication 505, *Tax Withholding and Estimated Tax.*

You can also deduct your business expenses from any state income tax you must pay. The average state income tax rate is about 6%, although seven states (Alaska, Florida, Nevada, South Dakota, Texas, Washington, and Wyoming) don't have an income tax. (New Hampshire residents pay tax on gambling winnings and income earned through interest and dividends only.) You can find a list of all state income tax rates at the Federation of Tax Administrators website at www.taxadmin.org.

Higher Income Taxes for 2013?

The tax rates in effect in 2012 are scheduled to expire at the end of the 2012 calendar year. These rates were enacted in 2001 and 2003 as part of the so-called "Bush tax cuts," when income tax rates were reduced across the board. Starting in 2013, the tax rates are scheduled to go back to the higher tax rates in effect prior to 2001. If this happens, the 10% rate will be eliminated and the rates will be 15%, 28%, 31%, 36%, and 39.6%. Most people believe Congress will not allow rates to return to their pre-2001 higher levels. However, as this book went to press it was unclear what the income tax rates would be for 2013 and later.

Social Security and Medicare Taxes

Everyone who works—whether a business owner or an employee—is required to pay Social Security and Medicare taxes. The total tax paid is the same, but the tax is paid differently depending on whether you are an employee of an incorporated real estate business or a self-employed owner of a partnership or LLC. Employees pay one-half of these taxes through payroll deductions; employers must pony up the other half and send the entire payment to the IRS. Self-employed professionals must pay all of these taxes themselves. These differences don't mean much when you're an employee of a business you own, since the money is coming out of your pocket whether it is paid by the employee or employer.

These taxes are levied on the employment income of employees, and on the net self-employment income of business owners. Ordinarily they consist of a 12.4% Social Security tax on income up to an annual ceiling; however, for 2012, this amount has been reduced to 10.4%. In 2012, the annual Social Security ceiling was $110,100. Medicare taxes are not subject to any income ceiling and are levied at a 2.9% rate. For 2012, this combines to a total 13.3% tax on employment or self-employment income up to the Social Security tax ceiling. However, the effective self-employment tax rate is somewhat lower because (1) you are allowed to deduct half of your self-employment taxes from your net income for income tax purposes, and (2) you pay self-employment tax on only 92.35% of your net self-employment income. Like income taxes, self-employment taxes are paid on the net profit you earn from a business. Thus, deductible business expenses reduce the amount of self-employment tax you have to pay by lowering your net profit.

Higher Medicare Taxes in 2013

Starting in 2013, Medicare taxes for high-income taxpayers will go up by 0.9% to 3.8%. The increase applies to self-employed people with net self-employment income over $200,000. If a taxpayer is married and files a joint return, the increase kicks in at $250,000. Thus, for example, a single person with self-employment income of $300,000 would pay a 2.9% Medicare tax on the first $200,000 in income and 3.8% on the remaining $100,000.

Unlike the other self-employment taxes discussed above, you can't deduct the increased Medicare payments from your income taxes.

The increase applies to employees as well as to the self-employed. Employees will have to pay the entire increase out of their own pockets. Thus, employers will continue to pay a 1.45% Medicare tax on their employees' wages. Employees will continue to pay 1.45% until their wages reach the $200,000 or $250,000 ceiling. Then they will pay the additional 2.35%.

In addition, starting in 2013, Medicare taxes will have to be paid by high-income taxpayers on investment income as well as on wages and self-employment income. A 3.8% Medicare contributions tax will be imposed on the lesser of (1) the taxpayer's net investment income, or (2) any excess of modified adjusted gross income over $200,000 ($250,000 for married taxpayers filing jointly). Net investment income consists of net income from interest, dividends, royalties, or any other gain from a passive trade or business, and taxable gains from the sale or other disposition of investment property.

Total Tax Savings

When you add up your savings in federal, state, and self-employment taxes, you can see the true value of a business tax deduction. For example, if you're single and your taxable business income (whether as an employee of an incorporated real estate business or a self-employed owner of a partnership or LLC) is below the Social Security tax ceiling, a business deduction can be worth as much as 28% (in federal taxes) + 12.3% (in self-employment taxes) + 6% (in state taxes). That adds up to a whopping 43.3% savings. (If you itemize your personal deductions, your actual tax savings from a business deduction is a bit less because it reduces your state income tax and therefore reduces the federal income tax savings from this itemized deduction.) If you buy a $1,000 computer for your business and you deduct the expense, you save about $433 in taxes. In effect, the government is paying for almost half of your business expenses.

Additional business deductions are worth less if your income is above the Social Security tax ceiling, because you don't have to pay the Social Security tax. For example, if you're in the 33% income tax bracket, an additional deduction will be worth 33% (in federal taxes) + 6% (in state taxes) + 2.9% (in Medicare taxes). This adds up to 41.9%. Still not bad.

This is why it's so important to know all the business deductions you are entitled to take and to take advantage of every one.

CAUTION

Don't buy things just to get a tax deduction. Although tax deductions can be worth a lot, it doesn't make sense to buy something you don't need just to get a deduction. After all, you still have to pay for the item, and the tax deduction you get in return will only cover a portion of the cost. For example, if you buy a $3,000 computer you don't really need, you'll probably be able to deduct less than half the cost. That means you're still out over $1,500—money you've spent for something you don't need. On the other hand, if you really do need a computer, the deduction you're entitled to is like found money—and it may help you buy a better computer than you could otherwise afford.

What Real Estate Agents and Brokers Can Deduct

Real estate agents and brokers are business owners, and as such they can deduct three broad categories of business expenses:

- start-up expenses
- operating expenses, and
- capital expenses.

This section provides an introduction to each of these categories (they are covered in greater detail in later chapters).

CAUTION

You must keep track of your expenses. You can deduct only those expenses that you actually incur. You need to keep records of these expenses to (1) know for sure how much you actually spent; and (2) prove to the IRS that you really spent the money you deducted on your tax return, in case you are audited. Accounting and bookkeeping are discussed in detail in Chapter 17.

Start-Up Expenses

The first money you will have to shell out will be for your business's start-up expenses. These include most of the costs of getting your business up and running, like advertising costs, attorney and accounting fees, and office supplies expenses. Start-up costs are not currently deductible—that is, you cannot deduct them all in the year in which you incur them. However, you can deduct up to $5,000 in start-up costs in the first year you are in business. You must deduct amounts that exceed the first-year threshold amount over the next 15 years. (See Chapter 10 for a detailed discussion of deducting start-up expenses.)

EXAMPLE: Cary recently obtained a real estate broker's license and decides to open his own real estate office. Before Cary's office opens for business in August 2012, he has to rent space, rent office furniture and equipment, and create a website. These start-up expenses cost Cary $10,000. Cary may deduct $5,000 of this amount the first year he's in business (2012). The remainder may be deducted over the first 180 months that he's in business—$417 per year for 15 years.

Operating Expenses

Operating expenses are the ongoing day-to-day costs a business incurs to stay in business. They include such things as rent, utilities, salaries, supplies, travel expenses, car expenses, and repairs and maintenance. These expenses (unlike start-up expenses) are currently deductible—that is, you can deduct them all in the same year in which you pay them.

EXAMPLE: After Cary's brokerage office opens, he begins paying $5,000 a month for rent and utilities. This is an operating expense that is currently deductible. When Cary does his taxes, he can deduct from his income the entire amount he paid for rent and utilities for the year.

Capital Expenses

Capital assets are things you buy for your business that have a useful life of more than one year, such as buildings, equipment, vehicles, books, and office furniture. These costs, called capital expenses, are considered to be part of your investment in your business, not day-to-day operating expenses.

Large businesses—those that buy at least several hundred thousand dollars of capital assets in a year—must deduct these costs by using depreciation. To depreciate an item, you deduct a portion of the cost in each year of the item's useful life. Depending on the asset, this could be anywhere from three to 39 years (the IRS decides the asset's useful life).

Small businesses can also use depreciation, but they have another option available for deducting many capital expenses. They can currently deduct a substantial amount of long-term asset purchases in a single year under a provision of the tax code called Section 179. Section 179 is discussed in detail in Chapter 9.

EXAMPLE: Cary spent $5,000 on a computer system for his office. Because the computers have a useful life of more than one year, they are capital assets that he will either have to depreciate over several years or deduct in one year under Section 179.

Certain capital assets, such as land and corporate stock, never wear out. Capital expenses related to these costs are not deductible; the owner must wait until the asset is sold to recover the cost. (See Chapter 9 for more on this topic.)

Real Estate Agents Who Lose Money

Unfortunately, real estate agents and brokers don't always earn a profit from their business. This is particularly common for part-time agents and brokers. If you're in this unfortunate situation, you may be able to obtain some tax relief. This could provide you with a refund of all or part of previous years' taxes in as little as 90 days—a quick infusion of cash that should be very helpful.

If, like most real estate agents and brokers, you're a sole proprietor, you may deduct any loss your business incurs from your other income for the year—for example, income from a job, investment income, or your spouse's income (if you file a joint return). If your business is operated as an LLC, S corporation, or partnership, your share of the business's losses are passed through the business to your individual return and deducted from your other personal income in the same way as a sole proprietor. However, if you operate your business through a C corporation, you can't deduct a business loss on your personal return. It belongs to your corporation.

If your losses exceed your income from all sources for the year, you have a "net operating loss" (NOL for short). While it's not pleasant to lose money, an NOL can provide important tax benefits: It may be used to reduce your tax liability for both past and future years.

Figuring a Net Operating Loss

Figuring the amount of an NOL is not as simple as deducting your losses from your annual income. First, you must determine your annual losses from your business (or businesses). If you're a sole proprietor who files IRS Schedule C, the expenses listed on the form will exceed your reported business income. If your business is a partnership, LLC, or S corporation shareholder, your share of the business's losses will pass through the entity to your personal tax return. Your business loss is added to all your other deductions and then subtracted from all your income for the year. The result is your adjusted gross income (AGI).

To determine if you have an NOL, you start with your AGI on your tax return for the year reduced by your itemized deductions or standard deduction (but not your personal exemption). This must be a negative number or you won't have an NOL for the year. Your adjusted gross income already includes all the deductions you have for your losses. You then add back to this amount any nonbusiness deductions you have that exceed your nonbusiness income. These include the standard deduction or itemized deductions, deduction for the personal exemption, nonbusiness capital losses, IRA contributions, and charitable contributions. If the result is still a negative number, you have an NOL for the year. You can use Schedule A of IRS Form 1045, *Application for Tentative Refund*, to calculate an NOL.

Carrying a Loss Back

You may apply an NOL to past tax years by filing an application for refund or amended return for those years. This is called carrying a loss back. (IRC Sec. 172.) As a general rule, it's advisable to carry a loss back, so you can get a quick refund from the IRS on your prior years' taxes. However, it may not be a good idea if you paid no income tax in prior years, or if you expect your income to rise substantially in future years and you want to use your NOL in the future when you'll be subject to a higher tax rate.

In addition, the carry-back period is increased to three years if the NOL is due to a casualty or theft, or if you have a qualified small business and the loss is in a presidentially declared disaster area. (A qualified small business is a sole proprietorship or partnership that has average annual gross receipts of $5 million or less during the three-year period ending with the tax year of the NOL.) The NOL is used to offset the taxable income for the earliest year first, and then applied to the next year or years. This will reduce the tax you had to pay for those years and result in a tax refund. Any part of your NOL left after using it for the carry-back years is carried forward for use for future years.

There are two ways to claim a refund for prior years' taxes: You can file IRS Form 1040-X, *Amended U.S. Individual Income Tax Return,* within three years, or you can seek a quicker refund by filing IRS Form 1045, *Application for Tentative Refund.* If you file Form 1045, the IRS is required to send your refund within 90 days. However, you must file Form 1045 within one year after the end of the year in which the NOL arose.

Carrying a Loss Forward

You have the option of applying your NOL only to future tax years. This is called carrying a loss forward. You can carry the NOL forward for up to 20 years and use it to reduce your taxable income in the future. You elect to carry a loss forward by attaching the following written statement to your tax return for the year you incur the NOL:

Tax Year: ____________ Taxpayer Name: ______________________________

Taxpayer Identification Number: ______________________________

Taxpayer elects to waive the carry-back period under IRC Section 173(b)(3).

Your signature ______________________________

Resource ______________________________

Need to know more about NOLs? Refer to IRS Publication 536, *Net Operating Losses*, for more information. You can download it from the IRS website at www.irs.gov.

CHAPTER

2

Choosing the Legal Form for Your Business

This chapter is about how your tax life is affected by the form of business entity you use to conduct your real estate business. If you're already in business, it will help you understand the pros and cons of the business form you have now, and decide whether you should consider converting to another type of entity or tax treatment. If you're just starting out, it will help you decide which business entity and tax treatment is best for you.

What Are Your Choices?

Most real estate agents are independent contractors—self-employed business owners who are affiliated with a licensed real estate broker in their state. As such, they are running independent businesses, even though they must work under a licensed broker's supervision. Of course, real estate brokers are also running businesses—they, usually own a real estate brokerage firm, either themselves or with other brokers, for which one or more agents work. Every business has a legal form. If you're working as a broker or agent right now, you are almost certainly involved in one of the following types of business entities:

- sole proprietorship
- partnership
- limited liability company (LLC), or
- corporation.

The sole proprietorship and partnership are the "default" entities—they come into existence automatically unless a business's owners take the steps necessary to form one of the other entities.

Sole Proprietorship

The great majority of real estate agents who work as independent contractors for a real estate brokerage are sole proprietors. Many one-owner brokerage firms are also sole proprietorships. Often, real estate professionals attain this legal status without even realizing it: Quite simply, if you start in business by yourself and do not incorporate or form an LLC, you are automatically a sole proprietor.

A sole proprietorship is a one-owner business. Unlike a corporation, LLC, or partnership, it is not a separate legal entity. The business owner (proprietor) personally owns all the assets of the business and is in sole charge of its operation. Most sole proprietors run small operations, but a sole proprietor can hire employees and nonemployees, too. Indeed, some sole proprietor brokers have large operations with many employees.

The sole proprietorship is by far the simplest and cheapest way to legally organize any business. You don't have to do anything special or file any papers to set up a sole proprietorship (other than the usual license, permit, and other regulatory requirements your state or locality imposes on any business). Of course, you also need to comply with your state's real estate licensing requirements.

For a real estate agent who works as an independent contractor for a real estate broker, the sole proprietorship form is a good choice due to its simplicity and inexpensiveness. As far as taxes are concerned, it's an excellent choice because it provides pass-through taxation, which most agents prefer. You also won't have to file a separate tax return for your business, which saves time and money.

However, sole proprietorships do have one big drawback: They offer no limited liability. Corporations and LLCs provide limited liability, which is the main reason why many small business owners use them. However, if, like most agents, you're running a one-person operation, the limited liability you'll obtain by forming a corporation or LLC is often more illusory than real. Thus, sticking with the unflashy, simple, and cheap sole proprietorship is a perfectly rational choice.

General Partnership

If two or more brokers decide to co-own a brokerage firm and split their income and expenses, they cannot be sole proprietors because they are not running a one-person business. Instead, they automatically become partners in a general partnership unless they incorporate or form a limited liability company. (From now on, general partnerships will be referred to simply as "partnerships.")

A partnership automatically comes into existence whenever two or more people enter into a venture together to earn a profit and don't choose to form some other business entity. As with sole proprietorships, it is not necessary to file any papers to form a general partnership. However, it's highly advisable to have a detailed written partnership agreement establishing how the partnership will be financed and governed.

A partnership is a form of shared ownership and management of a business. The partners contribute money, property, and/or services to the partnership and in return receive a share of the profits the partnership earns. Unlike a sole proprietorship, a partnership has a legal existence distinct from its owners—the partners. It can hold title to property, sue and be sued, have bank accounts, borrow money, hire employees, and do anything else in the business world that a human being can do. Indeed, in some states, a partnership can obtain a real estate brokerage license in its own name.

Because a partnership is a separate legal entity, property acquired by a partnership is property of the partnership and not of the partners individually. This differs from a sole proprietorship where the proprietor-owner individually owns all the sole proprietorship property.

As a general rule, all the partners in a partnership that operates a real estate brokerage must be licensed real estate brokers. Check your state's real estate broker licensing rules for details.

Limited Liability Company

The limited liability company, or LLC, is the newest type of business form in the United States. The LLC is a unique hybrid: a cross between a partnership and corporation. It provides the flexibility, informality, and tax attributes of a partnership and the limited liability of a corporation. For many, this is the best of both worlds, and LLCs have become very popular in recent years. Many real estate professionals have formed LLCs. However, some states—California, for example—bar most real estate brokers from using them.

To form an LLC, one or more people must file articles of organization with their state's business filing office. Although not required, it is highly desirable to adopt a written LLC operating agreement laying out how the LLC will be governed. If you don't prepare an operating agreement, the default provisions of the state's LLC Act will apply.

In most states, all the owners must be licensed to perform the professional services carried on by the LLC; and ownership cannot be transferred to unlicensed individuals. Thus, all owners of an LLC formed to operate a real estate brokerage must be licensed brokers, and no owner may transfer his or her ownership in the LLC to a non-broker.

Corporation

A corporation is a legal form in which you can organize and conduct a business and share in the profits or losses. The word "corporation" tends to conjure up images of huge business corporations like Wal-Mart or Microsoft that have thousands of shareholders and employees. In reality, most corporations are small operations with a small number of shareholders. Indeed, many corporations, especially those owned by real estate professionals, have just one shareholder.

A corporation has a legal existence completely separate from its owners—indeed, it is considered a "person" for legal purposes. It can hold title to property, sue and be sued, have bank accounts, borrow money, hire employees, and do anything else in the business world that a human being can do.

In theory, every corporation consists of three groups:

- those who direct the overall business, called directors
- those who run the business day-to-day, called officers, and
- those who just invest in the business, called shareholders.

However, in the case of a small corporation, these three groups can be (and often are) the same person; that is, a single person can direct and run the corporation and own all the corporate stock. So if you incorporate your one-person real estate business, you don't have to go out and recruit and pay a board of directors or officers.

If you incorporate your real estate business, it becomes the "owner" of the business—that is, it owns or leases all the necessary assets to run the business and hires employees and independent contractors to provide services to clients. It collects all the money clients pay, and pays all the bills including employee salaries and benefits. You own the corporation in the form of stock ownership. And you will ordinarily work as an employee of your corporation.

In many states, a corporation can obtain a real estate broker license in its own name. Most states require that some or all of the officers and/or directors of the corporation be licensed brokers.

You create a corporation by filing the necessary forms with, and paying the required fees to, your appropriate state agency—usually the office of the secretary of state or corporations commissioner. Each state specifies the forms to use and the filing cost.

You'll also need to choose a name for your corporation, adopt corporate bylaws, set up your corporate records, and "capitalize" your corporation—issue stock in return for money, property, and/or services provided to the corporation.

Professional Corporations

In some states, real estate brokers and agents must form a special type of corporation called a professional corporation. A professional corporation has the basic attributes of a regular corporation with certain restrictions about ownership and the type of work it can do. Typically, a professional corporation must be organized for the sole purpose of performing professional services, and all shareholders must be licensed to render that service. Thus, for example, in a real estate broker corporation, all the shareholders must be licensed brokers.

A professional corporation is a state law classification—it has nothing to do with the IRS or taxes. A professional corporation can be either a C or S corporation for tax purposes, as described below

The Four Ways Business Entities Are Taxed

There are four different ways businesses can be taxed—as a:

- sole proprietorship
- partnership
- S corporation, or
- C corporation.

Somewhat confusingly, your real estate business doesn't necessarily have to be legally organized as a partnership, S corporation, or C corporation to be taxed like one. Every type of entity automatically receives a default form of tax treatment when it is created. However, except for sole proprietorships, business entities have some leeway to change from their default treatment to another type of tax treatment.

For example, a multiowner LLC or partnership is automatically taxed as a partnership by default, but may choose to be taxed as a C corporation or S corporation. This is very easily accomplished by filing an election form with the IRS. Once this is done, as far as the IRS is concerned, the LLC or partnership is now the same as a corporation; it is required to file the tax forms for that type of entity. However, the great majority of LLCs and partnerships stick with their default partnership tax treatment.

Corporations are taxed as C corporations by default, but may change to S corporation tax treatment by filing an S corporation election. This is extremely common.

The table below shows the choices available for each type of entity.

Choices of How Businesses Are Taxed

Type of Entity	Tax Treatment Choices
Sole proprietorship	Sole proprietorship taxation
Partnership, multiowner LLC	Partnership taxation (default treatment); or C corporation taxation; or S corporation taxation
One-owner LLC	Sole proprietorship taxation (default treatment); or C corporation taxation; or S corporation taxation
Corporation	C corporation taxation (default treatment); or S corporation taxation

Sole Proprietorship Taxation

When you're a sole proprietor, you and your business are one and the same for tax purposes. Sole proprietorships don't pay taxes or file tax returns. Instead, you must report the income you earn or losses you incur on your own personal tax return, IRS Form 1040. If you earn a profit, the money is added to any other income you have (for example, interest income or your spouse's income if you're married and file a joint tax return) and that total is taxed.

Although you are taxed on your total income regardless of its source, the IRS does want to know about the profitability of your business. To show whether you have a profit or loss from your sole proprietorship, you must file IRS Schedule C, *Profit or Loss From Business*, with your tax return. On this form, you list all your business income and deductible expenses. If you have more than one business, you must file a separate Schedule C for each one.

> EXAMPLE: Irina is a real estate agent (salesperson) who works for a small brokerage firm as an independent contractor. This year, she had $100,000 in real estate commission income and $15,000 in expenses, leaving a $85,000 profit. She files Schedule C with her personal tax return (IRS Form 1040) listing the expenses and income from her practice. She reports her $85,000 profit on her Form 1040 and pays personal income tax on it, as well as Social Security and Medicare taxes. To figure her taxes, she adds her business income to any other taxable income she has for the year—for example, investment income—and pays taxes on it at personal tax rates.

Sole proprietors must use the sole proprietor form of taxation. Sole proprietors who want a different type of tax treatment must form a business entity such as a corporation or LLC.

In addition, LLCs with one owner are automatically treated like sole proprietorships for tax purposes. However, they have the option of switching to a C or S corporation taxation.

Partnership Taxation

The next basic form of business taxation is partnership taxation. This form of taxation applies not only to partnerships, but to multi-member LLCs as well. When they are first formed, these entities all automatically use partnership taxation; and, the great majority continue to use it throughout their existence. However, they have the option to switch to other forms of taxation as described below.

Under partnership tax treatment, the business entity is a "pass-through" entity for tax purposes—that is, it ordinarily pays no taxes itself. Instead, the profits, losses, deductions, and tax credits of the business are passed through the business to the owners' individual tax returns. If the business has a profit, the owners pay income tax on their share on their individual returns at individual income tax rates. If the business incurs a loss, it is likewise shared among the owners who may deduct it from other income on their individual returns, subject to certain limitations.

Unlike a sole proprietorship, a partnership is considered to be separate from the partners for the purposes of computing income and deductions. The partnership files its own tax return on IRS Form 1065. Form 1065 is not used to pay taxes; rather, it is an "information return" that informs the IRS of the partnership's income, deductions, profits, losses, and tax credits for the year. Form 1065 also includes a separate part called Schedule K-1 in which the partnership lists each partner's share of the items listed on Form 1065. A separate Schedule K-1 must be provided to each partner. Each partner reports on his or her individual tax return (Form 1040) his or her share of the partnership's net profit or loss as shown on Schedule K-1. Ordinary business income or loss is reported on Schedule E, *Supplemental Income or Loss*. However, certain items must be reported on other Schedules—for example, capital gains and losses must be reported on Schedule D and charitable contributions on Schedule A.

> **EXAMPLE:** Leo and Irina, both licensed brokers, decide to open their own real estate brokerage firm that they will co-own. They form an LLC to own and operate the firm and choose to use its default form of taxation—partnership taxation. The LLC earns $500,000 in income in one year and has $200,000 in deductible expenses. The $300,000 annual profit the LLC earned is passed through the company to Leo and Irina's individual tax returns—each gets 50% of the profit or $150,000. They each must pay personal income taxes on their share of the profits. Their profit is added to any other income they have and taxed at the individual tax rates listed in the chart above.

S Corporation Taxation

S corporations are taxed much like partnerships. Like a partnership, an S corporation is a pass-through entity—income and losses pass through the corporation to the owners' personal tax returns. However, the owners are shareholders in a corporation, not partners in a partnership. Because they are corporations owned by shareholders, S corporations are subject to some special tax rules described below.

S corporations report their income and deductions much like partnerships. Like a partnership, an S corporation files an information return (Form 1120S) reporting the corporation's income, deductions, profits, losses, and tax credits for the year. Like partners, shareholders must be provided a Schedule K-1 listing their shares of the items on the corporation's Form 1120S. The shareholders file Schedule E with their personal tax returns (Form 1040) showing their shares of corporation income or losses.

No business entity starts out with the S corporation form of taxation. There are two ways to obtain it. By far the most common way is to form a regular C corporation and then file an election to be taxed as an S corporation with the IRS. This simply involves filing IRS Form 2253 with the IRS. S corporation status is allowed, however, only if:

- the corporation has no more than 100 shareholders
- none of the corporation's shareholders are nonresident aliens—that is, noncitizens who don't live in the United States
- the corporation has only one class of stock—for example, there can't be preferred stock giving some shareholders special rights, and
- none of the corporation's shareholders are other corporations or partnerships.

These requirements pose no problems for the vast majority of real estate professionals.

Partnerships and LLCs can also obtain S corporation tax treatment by filing an S corporation election with the IRS.

C Corporation Taxation

Under the C corporation form of taxation, the business is treated as a separate taxpaying entity. Profits and losses do not pass through to the owners' individual tax returns as they do with the sole proprietorship, partnership, and S corporation forms of taxation. Instead, C corporations must pay income taxes on their net income and file their own tax returns with the IRS using Form 1120 or Form 1120-A.

In effect, when one or more real estate professionals form a C corporation, they create two or more separate taxpayers—the corporation and themselves, the shareholders. This separate tax identity has both advantages and disadvantages.

A C corporation pays income tax only on its net profit for the tax year, and it pays it at its own corporate tax rates, not the personal tax rates of its owners. It gets to deduct from its income all of its ordinary and necessary business expenses, including employee salaries, most fringe benefits, and bonuses, as well as operating expenses like office rent. However, dividends distributed to the shareholders are not deductible, which, in theory, can lead to double taxation.

C corporation shareholders don't pay personal income tax on income the incorporated business earns until it is distributed to them (as individual income) in the form of salary, bonuses, or dividends. They also don't get to deduct the corporation's business expenses on their personal returns. These belong to the corporation.

> EXAMPLE: Bill forms a C corporation, Bill, Inc., to own and operate his real estate brokerage firm. He owns all the stock in the corporation. The corporation takes in $500,000 in income. It pays out $300,000 in operating expenses and salaries for Bill's employees and independent contractor salespeople, and pays Bill a $100,000 salary. Bill, Inc., had a net profit for the year of $100,000 ($500,000 income – $400,000 expenses = $100,000 net profit.) It must pay taxes on its profit at the applicable corporate tax rate. Bill, Inc., files its own tax return and pays the tax from its own funds. Bill, the individual and employee of Bill, Inc., must file his own personal income tax return and pay income taxes on his salary at individual income tax rates.

All corporations are initially taxed as C corporations and stay that way unless they file an election to be taxed as an S corporation with the IRS. In addition, partnerships and LLCs can elect to be taxed like C corporations.

Comparing the Types of Tax Treatment

Your employment status will be affected by the type of business entity you choose for your real estate business and your tax treatment. If you are a sole proprietor, partnership, or LLC that has not elected corporate tax treatment, you will have business owner status, which means you'll be taxed as a self-employed person. If you have formed a C or S corporation or an LLC with corporate tax treatment, you will be treated as an employee of the corporation or LLC. The tax ramifications of being an employee versus a self-employed person are huge.

Sole Proprietor and Partnership Tax Treatment

If your real estate business is taxed as a sole proprietorship or partnership, you are not an employee of your business entity. Instead, you are a business owner; or self-employed person. The types of entities this encompasses include sole proprietorships, partnerships, and LLCs that haven't elected to change their partnership tax treatment. Your business doesn't have to pay payroll taxes on your income or withhold income tax from your pay. It need not file employment tax returns, or pay state or federal unemployment taxes. You don't have to be covered by workers' compensation insurance. All this can save hundreds of dollars per year.

However, you do have to pay self-employment taxes—that is, Social Security and Medicare taxes—on your business income, called self-employment income by the IRS. This consists of a 10.4% Social Security tax on the first $110,100 in income in 2012, and a 2.9% Medicare tax on all self-employment income, no matter how much. Thus, a total 13.3% tax must be paid up to the ceiling amount. (These rates reflect a 2% reduction in the Social Security tax which is in effect for 2011 and 2012. The Social Security tax is usually 12.4%, for a total self-employment tax of 15.3% up to the annual ceiling.) The Social Security tax ceiling is adjusted annually for inflation. These taxes must be paid four times a year, along with income taxes, in the form of estimated taxes. Self-employment taxes are equivalent to the total Social Security and Medicare tax (FICA tax) paid for an employee.

> EXAMPLE: Mel is a sole proprietor real estate agent (salesperson). In 2012, he earned $150,000 in profit from his business. He must pay a 13.3% self-employment tax on the first $110,100 of his self-employment income, and a 2.9% Medicare tax on the remaining $39,900. His total self-employment tax is ($13.3% × $110,100) + (2.9% × $39,900) = $15,800.

S Corporation Tax Treatment

As far as employment status goes, things work very differently for real estate professionals who choose S corporation status. Although an S corporation is taxed much like a partnership, it is still a corporation, a separate legal entity. An S corporation shareholder who performs more than minor services for the corporation will be its employee for tax purposes, as well as a shareholder. In effect, an active shareholder in a corporation wears at least two hats: as a shareholder (owner) of the corporation, and as an employee of that corporation. If the corporation is small, the shareholder/employee normally serves as an officer and director of the corporation as well. So there are four hats.

A shareholder/employee must be compensated for his or her services to the business with a reasonable salary and any other employee compensation the corporation wants to provide. The shareholder/employee must report any S corporation's earnings on his or her personal income tax return, and pay his or her share of Social Security and Medicare taxes on any employee salary received. The corporation must withhold federal income and employment tax from the shareholder/employee's pay, and pay state and federal unemployment taxes and Social Security and Medicare taxes on the employee's behalf.

The Social Security and Medicare tax rate for an employee is the same as for a self-employed business owner; however, it's paid differently. Half the total tax is deducted by the employer from the employee's pay, and half paid by the employer itself. When you own the business that is paying these taxes, it makes no practical difference that half is paid by the employer—you are the employer.

EXAMPLE: Assume that Mel from the above example has formed a corporation to run his real estate business and has chosen S corporation tax treatment. He is the sole shareholder of the corporation. Because he performs real estate sales services for the corporation, he is its employee for tax purposes. In one recent year, the corporation paid Mel a $150,000 employee salary. The corporation withholds half of Mel's Social Security and Medicare taxes from his wages and pays the other half itself. The total tax is $15,800, just like when Mel was a sole proprietor.

Being classified as an S corporation employee has one potential big advantage: S corporation tax treatment can provide a way to take some money out of your corporation without paying employment taxes. This is because you do not have to pay this tax on distributions (dividends) from your S corporation—that is, on earnings and profits that pass through the corporation to you as a shareholder, not as an employee in compensation for your services. The larger your distribution, the less employment tax you'll pay. The S corporation is the only business form that makes it possible for its owners to save on Social Security and Medicare taxes. This is the main reason S corporations have been, and remain, popular with real estate professionals.

EXAMPLE: Assume that Mel's S corporation pays him only a $90,000 salary. The remaining $60,000 of the corporation's profits are passed through the S corporation and reported as an S corporation distribution on Mel's personal income tax return, not as employee salary. Because it is not viewed as employee wages, neither Mel nor his corporation need to pay Social Security or Medicare tax on this amount. Mel and his corporation only pay a total of $11,970 in employment taxes (13.3% × $90,000 = $11,970) instead of $15,800—a tax savings of $3,830.

If you took no salary at all, you would not owe any Social Security and Medicare taxes. As you might expect, however, this is not allowed.

The IRS requires S corporation shareholder-employees to pay themselves a reasonable salary—at least what other businesses pay for similar services.

C Corporation Tax Treatment

When you form a C corporation (or choose that method of taxation for your LLC, or partnership) and actively work in the business, you become your corporation's employee, with the tax consequences described for an S corporation employee above. However, C corporation shareholder/employees can't avoid taxes by paying themselves corporate distributions instead of employee salaries. This is because a C corporation is a taxpaying entity and cannot deduct distributions made to shareholders. Thus, it must pay corporate income tax on the distributions.

> EXAMPLE: Assume that Mel from the above examples has a C corporation. It pays him $100,000 in employee wages and a $50,000 shareholder distribution. Mel and his corporation must pay $13,330 in employment taxes on Mel's wages (13.3% × $100,000 = $13,330), and the corporation must pay $7,500 in corporate income taxes on the distribution (15% × 50,000 = $7,500). The total tax is $20,830.

However, being a C corporation employee, instead of a self-employed business owner or S corporation employee, has tax advantages when it comes to fringe benefits.

Tax Deductions

Does your form of taxation change the type of tax deductions you may take for your business? Mostly, no. Tax deductions are largely the same no matter how a business is taxed. Any business may deduct the ordinary and necessary expenses it incurs, and take depreciation for long-term business assets. This covers almost all the deductions in this book.

However, some deductions differ for C and S corporations, as compared with sole proprietor and partnership taxation:

- C and S corporations need not pay tax on all or part of the dividends they receive from stock they own in other corporations
- there are major differences in the way capital gains and losses are taxed (see IRS Publication 544, *Sales and Other Dispositions of Assets,* for details).

In addition, C corporation employees need not pay tax on many types of fringe benefits, including health insurance and other medical benefits (see Chapter 11).

Tax Rates

When sole proprietorship, partnership, or S corporation tax treatment applies, all the business's profits are taxed at the owners' personal tax rates. The current rates are listed in the following chart.

2012 Federal Personal Income Tax Rates

Tax Bracket	Income If Single	Income If Married Filing Jointly
10%	Up to $8,700	Up to $17,400
15%	$8,701 to $35,350	$17,401 to $70,700
25%	$35,351 to $85,650	$70,701 to $142,700
28%	$85,651 to $178,650	$142,701 to $217,450
33%	$178,651 to $388,350	$217,451 to 388,350
35%	All over $388,350	All over $388,350

In contrast, C corporations have their own income tax rates as shown in the chart below. At certain income levels these rates are lower than those for individuals—for example, a single individual must pay a 28% tax on income from $85,651 to $100,000, while a C corporation only pays a 25% tax on this amount. C corporations have these lower rates to help them keep money in the business for expansion purposes. If you can use these lower corporate rates, it can be advantageous to keep profits in the corporation rather than paying them to yourself in the form of salary, bonus, or fringe benefits.

Regular C Corporation Income Tax Rates	
Taxable Income	**Tax Rate**
Up to $50,000	15%
$50,001 to $100,000	25%
$100,001 to $335,000	34%
$335,001 to $10,000,000	39%
$10,000,001 to $15,000,000	35%
$15,000,001 to $18,333,333	38%
All over $18,333,333	35%

Potential for Double Taxation

If you're the owner of a C corporation (or choose that method of taxation for your LLC or partnership), any direct payment of your corporation's profits to you will be considered a dividend by the IRS and taxed twice. First, the corporation will pay corporate income tax on the profit at corporate rates on its own return, and then you'll pay personal income tax on what you receive from the corporation. This is called "double taxation."

In real life, however, double taxation is rarely a problem for real estate professionals who have C corporations (or LLCs, or partnerships taxed that way). Ordinarily, you'll be an employee of your corporation and the salary, benefits, and bonuses you receive will be deductible expenses for corporate income tax purposes. If you handle things right, your employee compensation will eat up all the corporate profits so there's no taxable income left on which your corporation will have to pay income tax. In accounting parlance, the corporation's income is "zeroed out." You'll only pay income tax once—personal income tax on your employee compensation.

When you own your own C corporation, whether alone or with one or more co-owners, you get to decide how much to pay yourself, and what form your payments will take. Obviously, you'll want to make sure you avoid double taxation by paying yourself as much compensation as necessary to "zero out" your corporation's income. However, your decision about how much to pay yourself is subject to review by the IRS in the event of an audit. The IRS only allows corporate owner-employees to pay themselves a reasonable salary for work they actually perform. Any amounts that are deemed unreasonable are treated as disguised dividends by the IRS and are subject to double taxation.

Personal Deductions for Business Losses

In the current difficult business environment, it is not uncommon for real estate professionals to lose money. If this occurs, the business owners want to be able to deduct the losses from any personal income they have. There are big differences among the various forms of taxation when it comes to deducting losses.

Sole Proprietorship and Partnership Tax Treatment

Just as income passes through a sole proprietorship or partnership to the owners' personal tax returns, so do losses. Thus, subject to some important limitations, losses from an entity taxed as a sole proprietorship (either a sole proprietorship or an LLC) or an entity taxed as a partnership (either an LLC or a partnership) can be deducted from any other income the owners have. They can even be deducted from income earned in prior years that has already been taxed, or saved up and used in future years. This makes sole proprietorship or partnership tax treatment ideal for a business that expects to lose money.

> **EXAMPLE:** Lisa starts work as a part-time sales associate for a real estate broker. She operates as a sole proprietor. During her first year as a sole proprietor, she incurs $11,000 in expenses and earns $5,000 in commissions, giving her a $6,000 loss from her business. She reports this loss on IRS Schedule C, which she files with her personal income tax return (Form 1040). Because Lisa is a sole proprietor, she can deduct this $6,000 loss from any other income she has.

However, there are some limitations on how much in losses an owner of an entity taxed as a partnership can deduct on his or her personal tax return. The most important limit is that the deduction for losses cannot exceed the owner's basis in a partnership or LLC taxed like a partnership. "Basis" means your total investment in the business for tax purposes. In general, a business owner cannot deduct a loss that exceeds his or her cash contribution to the entity, plus income previously recognized from the entity, reduced by any losses or deductions that were previously deducted. Importantly, owners of entities taxed as partnerships may also add to their basis their share of all the entity's liabilities—loans and other debts—which can greatly increase their basis and allow them to deduct more losses.

> EXAMPLE: Ralph and Norton, both real estate brokers, decide they want to merge their businesses. They form the R & C Realty Company, an LLC taxed like a partnership. They each own a 50% interest in the LLC and equally share all profits and losses. They each contribute $10,000 to the LLC. The LLC also obtained a $50,000 bank loan to cover its first-year operating expenses. Ralph and Norton each have a $35,000 basis in the LLC ($10,000 cash contribution + 50% of the $50,000 loan = $35,000). The LLC loses $50,000 the first year. Ralph and Norton may each deduct $25,000 of the loss on their personal returns. This leaves them each with a $10,000 basis. If the LLC loses $50,000 the next year, they will each only be able to deduct $10,000 of the loss, and will end up with a zero basis.

S Corporation Tax Treatment

S corporation shareholders (or owners of LLCs or partnerships taxed that way) may also deduct their share business losses from their personal incomes. However, unlike owners of partnership tax entities, S corporation shareholders may not add S corporation liabilities to their basis. The only liabilities that may be added to an S corporation shareholder's basis are shareholder loans to the corporation. Thus, if Ralph and Norton from the above example had formed an S corporation, they each would have only a $10,000 starting basis and could only deduct that amount of their first-year loss. As a result, partnership taxation has a big advantage over S corporation taxation when it comes to deducting losses.

C Corporation Tax Treatment

If a C corporation has a loss for the tax year, it is "trapped" in the corporation—it stays in the corporation and can only be deducted on the corporation's tax return. Losses do not pass through to the shareholders' personal returns as is the case with pass-through entities. Thus, the shareholders don't get to deduct the losses from their personal income from other sources. This makes the C corporation form of taxation the worst possible for a money-losing business.

Special Allocations of Profits and Losses

Partnerships and LLCs taxed like partnerships (as most are) have another tax advantage: They have great flexibility on how to allocate profits and losses among the owners—for example, one owner can get 75% of the profits and the other 25%, even though they are each equal owners of the LLC or partnership. Real estate professionals who co-own their business with others find this flexibility very attractive because it allows them to be creative in fashioning their compensation. For example, partnership or LLC profits can be distributed according to each owner's sales, shared equally, shared according to each owner's percentage of ownership, based on complex formulas involving points or units, or based on a combination of methods—for example, distributions can be based partly on ownership percentages and partly on commissions. A less rational approach can also be used: Partners or LLC members can simply get together at the end of the year and decide on how much each person should get; by the end of the day, the firm's net profits are divided up.

However, there are limits on how creative LLCs and partnerships can get. Complex IRS rules ("substantial economic effect rules") permit the IRS to disregard a partnership allocation of profits or losses if it's done only to avoid taxes

You don't have this flexibility with an S corporation. The owners of an S corporation must split their profits in proportion to their stock ownership. For example, if there are two shareholders and each owns 50% of the stock, they must each pay tax on 50% of the corporation's profits. Likewise, C corporation shareholders must split profits in proportion to their share ownership; but small C corporations usually have no profits to split—all the business's profits are paid to the shareholders in the form of salary or other compensation. S and C corporation shareholders may be paid more employee compensation to increase their earnings beyond the amount justified by their stock ownership. But there is a limit on how much employee compensation a C corporation shareholder/employee may reasonably be paid. And, it's preferable to pay S corporation shareholders as little employee compensation as possible to avoid employment taxes.

Fringe Benefits

Fringe benefits are things like health, disability, and life insurance; paid vacations; a company car; and reimbursement of medical expenses not covered by insurance. This is the one major tax arena where C corporation tax treatment is far superior to the other tax regimes.

C Corporation Tax Treatment

As noted above, when you form a C corporation (or elect to have your LLC or partnership taxed as a C corporation) and actively work in the business, you become your corporation's employee. Being a corporate employee, instead of a self-employed business owner, has significant tax advantages when it comes to fringe benefits. The tax law allows a C corporation to provide its employees with many types of fringe benefits which it can deduct from the corporation's income as a business expense. But the employees need not include the value of the fringe benefits in their taxable income, effectively making them tax-free. This can save many thousands of dollars in taxes. No other business entity can do this.

Possible tax-free employee fringe benefits include:

- health, accident, and dental insurance for you and your family
- disability insurance
- reimbursement of medical expenses not covered by insurance
- deferred compensation plans
- working condition fringe benefits such as company-owned cars
- group term life insurance, and
- death benefit payments up to $5,000.

EXAMPLE: Real estate broker Marilyn incorporates her real estate business, of which she is the only employee. Marilyn's corporation provides her with health insurance and a medical reimbursement plan for uninsured medical expenses for her and her family at a cost of $10,000 per year. The entire cost can be deducted from the corporation's income for corporate income tax purposes, but is not included as income on Marilyn's personal tax return. In effect, no tax need be paid on the $10,000.

Sole Proprietorship, Partnership, and S Corporation Tax Treatment

Real estate professionals taxed as sole proprietors, S corporation owners, and partners, may deduct 100% of their health insurance premiums from their personal income tax, including their own health insurance premiums and those for their spouses and dependents. But this is a special personal deduction, not a business deduction. Thus, it doesn't reduce their income for Social Security and Medicare tax purposes.

Such professionals get no other tax advantaged fringe benefits. If the entity provides the owner with such a fringe benefit, its value must be included in the owner's personal tax return and income tax paid on it. For example, if an entity taxed as a partnership provides an owner with disability insurance, the owner must include the value of the insurance in his or her taxable income for the year. But there is one way around this: the business owner can hire his or her spouse as an employee and provide the spouse with benefits. Of course, the spouse must be a legitimate employee and be paid a reasonable amount.

State Taxes

Depending on where you practice, state taxes might be an important factor in your choice of business entity. Some states impose higher taxes on businesses than others.

All states (except Nebraska and South Dakota) impose corporate income based on the amount of taxable income earned in the state by the corporation. The rates vary from state to state. But some states also charge franchise taxes—for example, California exacts a hefty $800 "minimum franchise tax" per year after the first year a corporation is in business.

Most states tax sole proprietorships, partnerships, and LLCs the same way the IRS does: The owners pay taxes to the state on their personal returns; and the entity itself does not pay a state tax. But some states impose special taxes on pass-through entities. For instance, California levies a tax on LLCs that make over $250,000 per year; the tax ranges from about $900 to $11,000. A similar tax is imposed on California S corporations. Illinois, Massachusetts, and Pennsylvania charge LLCs annual report filing fees.

In addition, some states (including California, Delaware, Illinois, Massachusetts, New Hampshire, Pennsylvania, and Wyoming) impose an annual LLC fee that is not income-related. This may be called a "franchise tax," an "annual registration fee," or a "renewal fee." In most states, the fee is about $100; but California exacts an $800 "minimum franchise tax" per year from LLCs as well. Before forming any business entity, find what taxes or fees your state charges. You can find this at the website of your state's secretary of state, department of corporations, or department of revenue or tax.

What About Limiting Your Liability?

Although this is a tax book, tax considerations alone don't govern the choice of business entity. Indeed, most often they are not the most important consideration. What is? Liability—that is, the extent a business's owners are personally responsible for paying for their business's debts and business-related lawsuits. Indeed, this issue is seen as so important that the corporation, limited partnership, and limited liability company were created for the express purpose of limiting their owners' liability.

It's likely that you're as concerned about your liability as anybody else. For this reason, you might think that you should form a corporation or limited liability company. After all, these business forms are supposed to provide "limited liability"—protection from debts and lawsuits. Indeed, many people seem to believe that forming a corporation or LLC is like having a magic shield against liability. However, the sad truth is that there are many holes in the limited liability shield offered by the corporation or LLC.

What Is Liability?

"Liability" means being legally responsible for a debt or for doing something that injures someone, such as committing professional malpractice or injuring someone in a traffic accident. If you are personally liable for a debt or wrong and a person sues you and obtains a judgment against you, you'll have to pay the judgment yourself. If you don't pay, the person who obtained the judgment can take your personal property to pay it (subject to certain limits). Thus, you could end up losing your personal bank accounts, personal property like cars, and even your house.

On the other hand, if only your business is liable for a debt or wrongdoing, you have no legal obligation to pay from your personal funds a person who obtains a judgment against your business. But, of course, you business assets can by taken to satisfy a judgment against your business.

Obviously, business owners, including real estate professionals, don't want to put their personal assets at risk if they get sued for malpractice or other alleged wrongdoing, or their business incurs debts. It was to help avoid personal liability and encourage people to invest in businesses that the corporation was created. Much later, the limited liability company was established to provide the same degree of limited liability without the expense and bother of forming and running a corporation. Corporations and LLCs are all "limited liability entities."

The "default" business entities—the sole proprietorship and partnership—provide no limited liability at all—you are personally liable for your business's debts and wrongdoing by you or anyone else who works in your business. If you want limited liability, you must take the necessary steps to form a corporation or LLC under your state law.

Liability has nothing to do with taxation or the way a business entity is taxed. For example, the owners of a partnership will have unlimited liability even if they choose to have their partnership taxed as a corporation. You must actually form a limited liability business entity under the applicable state law to benefit from its limited liability attributes.

Liability for Professional Malpractice

The single greatest liability exposure most real estate agents and brokers face is for malpractice—lawsuits by dissatisfied buyers or sellers alleging things like fraud, misrepresentations, negligence, failure to disclose, and other violations of the agent's or broker's legal and fiduciary duties. Even if you're innocent, defending a malpractice lawsuit can cost hundreds of thousands of dollars. Can a limited liability entity help you avoid personal liability for malpractice? Yes, but probably not as much as you might think.

Your Own Malpractice

No limited liability entity—whether a corporation or LLC—protects you against personal liability for your own malpractice or other personal wrongdoing. If your business doesn't have enough assets to pay a judgment obtained against you, your personal assets can be taken. Thus, your personal assets will always be on the line if you are sued for malpractice. This is why real estate sales professionals should always have errors and omissions insurance.

> EXAMPLE: Janet, a real estate broker, forms a corporation of which she is the sole shareholder. She represents a client in the sale of a home. Shortly after the sale closes, the buyer discovers severe building defects that were not disclosed. The buyer sues Janet and her client, the seller, for fraud. Even though Janet is incorporated, she could be held personally liable (along with her corporation) for any damages caused by her alleged fraud in failing to disclose the defects. Both Janet's personal assets and those of her corporation are at risk.

Malpractice by Others

As a rule, a real estate broker is legally responsible for the actions of the real estate agents (salespeople) who work in his or her office. Forming a corporation or limited liability company may help limit the extent the broker can be held personally liable for malpractice committed by independent contractor agents or employees as long as the broker wasn't personally involved in the alleged wrongdoing. Many states require that real estate brokers have malpractice insurance to obtain this limited liability. Other states limit the amount of limited liability incorporating can provide a broker. The rules vary from state to state—you should learn yours to determine if incorporating or forming an LLC makes sense to limit your personal liability for others' malpractice.

Other Types of Liability

Malpractice isn't the only type of liability you need to be worried about. Other forms of liability include:

- Premises liability: Responsibility for injuries or damages that occur at your office or other place of business.
- Infringement liability: When someone claims that you have infringed on a patent, copyright, trademark, or trade secret.
- Employer liability: Liability for injuries or damages caused by an employee while he or she was working for you.

If you're a sole proprietor or partner in a partnership, you'll be personally liable for these types of lawsuits. Theoretically, you're not personally liable if you form a corporation or LLC.

However, remember that you're always personally liable for your own negligence or intentional wrongdoing. You can be personally liable under a negligence theory for all the different types of lawsuits outlined above. Here are some examples of how you could be sued personally even though you've formed a corporation or LLC:

- An employee accidentally injures someone while running an errand for you. The injured person sues you personally for damages claiming you negligently hired, trained, and/or supervised the employee.
- Someone sues you, claiming you've infringed upon a copyright. Even if you've formed a corporation or LLC, you can be personally liable for such claims.
- The person in charge of your payroll fails to properly withhold and pay income and Social Security taxes for your employees. You can be personally liable even if you weren't personally involved.

In all these cases, forming a corporation or LLC will prove useless to protect you from personal liability.

Liability for Business Debts

In addition to liability for malpractice and other wrongs, you could be personally liable for debts incurred by your business.

Sole Proprietors and Partnerships

When you're a sole proprietor, you are personally liable for all the debts of your business. This means that a business creditor—a person or company to whom you owe money for items you use in your inventing business—can go after all your assets, both business and personal. This may include, for example, your personal bank accounts, stocks, your car, and even your house. Similarly, a personal creditor—a person or company to whom you owe money for personal items—can go after your business assets, such as business bank accounts and equipment.

Partners are personally liable for all partnership debts and lawsuits, the same as sole proprietors. However, partnership creditors are required to proceed first against the partnership property. If there isn't enough to satisfy the debts, they can then go after the partners' personal property.

In addition, each partner is deemed to be the agent of the partnership when conducting partnership business in the usual way. This means you'll be personally liable for partnership debts your partners incur while carrying on partnership business, whether you knew about them or not.

Limited Liability Entities

Corporations and LLCs were created to enable people to invest in businesses without risking all their personal assets if the business failed or became unable to pay its debts. Limited liability for debts really exists where large corporations or LLCs are concerned. If you buy stock in Microsoft, for example, you don't have to worry about Microsoft's creditors suing you. But it usually doesn't work that way for small corporations and LLCs—especially newly established ones without a track record of profits and good credit history.

Piercing the Corporate Veil

Another way you can be personally liable even though you've formed a corporation is through a legal doctrine called "piercing the corporate veil." Under this legal rule, courts disregard the corporate entity and hold its owners personally liable for any harm done by the corporation *and* for corporate debts.

Corporate owners are in danger of having their corporation pierced if they treat the corporation as their "alter ego," rather than as a separate legal entity—for example, they fail to contribute money to the corporation or issue stock, they take corporate funds or assets for personal use, they commingle corporate and personal funds, or they fail to observe corporate formalities such as keeping minutes and holding board meetings. The same type of piercing can probably be used against LLC owners.

Major creditors such as banks don't want to be left holding the bag if your business goes under. To help ensure payment, they will want to be able to go after your personal assets as well as your business assets. As a result, if you've formed a corporation or LLC, they will demand that you personally guarantee business loans, credit cards, or other extensions of credit—that is, sign a legally enforceable document pledging your personal assets to pay the debt if your business assets fall short. This means that you will be personally liable for the debt, just as if you were a sole proprietor or partner.

Not only do banks and other lenders universally require personal guarantees, other creditors do as well. For example, you may be required to personally guarantee payment of your office lease and even leases for expensive equipment. Standard forms used by suppliers often contain personal guarantee provisions making you personally liable when your company buys equipment and similar items.

You can avoid having to pledge a personal guarantee for some business debts. These will most likely be routine and small debts. But, of course, once a creditor gets wise to the fact that your business is not paying its bills, it won't extend you any more credit. If you don't pay your bills and obtain a bad credit rating, no one may be willing to let you buy things for your business on credit. Other creditors might be careless and not require a personal guarantee.

The Role of Insurance

If incorporating or forming an LLC won't relieve you of all your personal liability, what are you supposed to do to protect yourself from business-related lawsuits? There's a very simple answer: get insurance. Your insurer will defend you in such lawsuits and pay any settlements or damage awards up to your policy limits. This is what all wise business owners do, whether they are sole proprietors, partners, LLC members, or corporation owners. Liability and many other forms of business insurance are available to protect you from the types of lawsuits described above. Liability insurance premiums are deductible as a business expense.

Note carefully, however, that insurance won't protect you from liability for business debts—for example, if you fail to pay back a loan or default on a lease. This is where bankruptcy comes in.

CHAPTER

3

Are You Really in Business?

This chapter is primarily for the many real estate agents who work only part time, or who work at real estate for a while and then leave the field. If you're in this situation and you don't earn a profit from your real estate activity, the IRS could claim that you are not really in business. If this happens, you're not entitled to take any business deductions. That's why—if you want to take business deductions—it's crucial that you be able to show the IRS that you are running a real business.

How to Prove You Are in Business

For tax purposes, a business is an activity you regularly and continuously engage in primarily to earn a profit. You can't get a real estate license, sit back and do nothing, and then claim you had a profit motive. This won't pass the "smell" test. You need to be able to show that you were actively working to make money by trying to obtain listings or close sales or something else.

It's also not necessary to show a profit every year to qualify as a business. You just need to be able to prove that your primary purpose is to make money. Many businesses have losses in their first year—and some may continue to have losses on and off for years afterwards. That's okay as long as you can establish that your intent was to earn a profit.

Your real estate business can be conducted from home, full time or part time, as long as you work at it regularly and continuously. And you can have more than one business at the same time—many real estate agents work part time and have other businesses or jobs. However, if your primary purpose for being a real estate agent is something other than making a profit—for example, to incur deductible expenses—the IRS may find that your activity is a hobby and not a business. If this happens, you'll face some potentially disastrous tax consequences.

> EXAMPLE: J. Thomas Orr, a Los Angeles schoolteacher, obtained a real estate broker's license, apparently with the goal of working part time at the activity. Unfortunately, he was not successful. For two years, he obtained no listings and sold no real estate. His only income from real estate was $150 for doing an appraisal. Nevertheless, he claimed he had over $5,600 in deductible business

expenses from his real estate activity. The IRS and tax court concluded that Orr's real estate activity was not a business because there was no evidence he engaged in it in an organized, businesslike manner to earn a profit. All his business expense deductions were disallowed. (*Orr v. Comm'r*, 64 TCM 882 (1992).)

For a detailed discussion of what will happen to your deductions if the IRS concludes your real estate activity is a hobby, see "What If Your Business Is a Hobby?" below.

The IRS has established two tests to determine whether someone has a profit motive. One is a simple mechanical test that looks at whether you have earned a profit in three of the last five years. The other is a more complex test designed to determine whether you act like you want to earn a profit.

CAUTION

Having a real estate license doesn't mean you're in business. You must be able to show the IRS that you're trying to earn a profit from real estate sales, as described below.

Show Your Profits

If your real estate sales venture earns a profit in three of five consecutive years, the IRS will presume that you have a profit motive. The IRS and courts look at your tax returns for each year you claim to be in business to see whether you turned a profit. Any legitimate profit qualifies; you don't have to earn a particular amount or percentage. However, if your annual profits are very small, while your annual losses are very large, the IRS may claim you can't pass the test.

Careful year-end planning can help your business show a profit for the year. For example, you can reduce your expenditures (and increase your profit) by putting off paying some expenses or buying new equipment until the following tax year.

Even if you meet the three-of-five test, the IRS can still try to claim that your activity is a hobby, but it will have to prove that you don't have a profit motive. In practice, the IRS usually doesn't attack ventures that pass the profit test unless the numbers have clearly been manipulated just to meet the standard.

The presumption that you are in business applies to your third profitable year and extends to all later years within the five-year period beginning with your first profitable year.

EXAMPLE: Tom began work as an independent contractor real estate agent in 2007. Due to economic conditions and the difficulty of establishing a new real estate business, his income varied dramatically from year to year. However, as the chart below shows, he managed to earn a profit in three of the first five years that he was in business.

Year	Losses	Profits
2007	$3,000	
2008		$5,500
2009		$9,000
2010	$6,000	
2011		$18,000
2012		$30,000

If the IRS audits Tom's taxes for 2011, it must presume that he was in business during that year because he earned a profit during three of the five consecutive years ending with 2011. The presumption extends through 2013, five years after his first profitable year. In 2014, he'll qualify for a new presumption if he earned a profit during three of the five consecutive years ending with 2014, and so on.

The IRS doesn't have to wait for five years after you start your activity to decide whether it is a business—it can audit you and classify your venture as a business or hobby at any time. However, you can give yourself some breathing room by filing IRS Form 5213, *Election to Postpone Determination as to Whether the Presumption Applies That an Activity Is Engaged in for Profit*, which requires the IRS to postpone its determination until you've been in business for at least five years.

Although this may sound like a good idea, it can backfire. Filing the election alerts the IRS to the fact that you might be a good candidate to audit on the hobby loss issue after five years. It also adds two years to the statute of limitations—the period in which the IRS can audit you and assess a tax deficiency. For this reason, almost no one ever files Form 5213. Also, you can't wait five years and then file the election once you know that you will pass the profit test. You must make the election within three years after the due date for the tax return for the first year you were in business—that is, within three years after the first April 15th following your first business year. So if you started doing business in 2011, you would have to make the election by April 15, 2015 (three years after the April 15, 2012 due date for your 2011 tax return).

There is one situation in which it might make sense to file Form 5213. If the IRS has already told you that you will be audited, you may want to file the election to postpone the audit for two years. However, you can do this only if the IRS audit notice is sent to you within three years after the due date for your first business tax return. If you're notified after this time, it's too late to file the election. In addition, you must file your election within 60 days after you receive an IRS audit notice, whenever it is given, or you'll lose the right to make the election.

Act Like a Business

If you can't satisfy the three-out-of-five-year profit test, don't panic. Many real estate agents are in the same boat. This has been particularly true during the last few years when real estate sales have been in a terrible slump. The sad fact is that many agents don't earn profits every year or even for years in a row, especially when they're first starting out; yet the IRS does not categorize all of these agents as hobbyists.

You can continue to treat your real estate activity as a business and fully deduct your losses, even if you have yet to earn a profit. However, you must take steps to demonstrate that your business isn't a hobby, in case you ever face an audit. You must be able to convince the IRS that earning a profit—not accumulating tax deductions—is your primary motive for doing what you do. This will require some time and effort on your part.

How does the IRS figure out whether you really want to earn a profit? IRS auditors can't read your mind to establish your motives, and they certainly aren't going to take your word for it. Instead, they look at whether you behave as though you want to make money.

What the IRS Considers

The IRS looks at the following "objective" factors to determine whether you are behaving like a person who wants to earn a profit (and therefore, should be classified as a business). You don't have to satisfy all of these factors to pass the test—the first three listed below (acting like a business, expertise, and time and effort expended) are the most important by far. Studies demonstrate that taxpayers who meet these three factors are always found to be in business, regardless of how they do on the rest of the criteria.

- **Whether you act like a business.** Among other things, acting like a business means you keep good books and other records and carry on your activities in a professional manner.
- **Your expertise.** People who are trying to make money usually have some knowledge and skill in the field of their endeavor.
- **The time and effort you spend.** People who want to make profits work regularly and continuously. You don't have to work full time, but you must work regularly.
- **Your track record.** Having a track record of success in other businesses—whether or not they are related to your current business—helps show that you are trying to make money in your most recent venture.
- **Your history of profit and losses.** Even if you can't satisfy the profit test described above, earning a profit in at least some years helps show that you have a profit motive. This is especially true for real estate sales, which tend to be cyclical.
- **Your profits.** Earning a substantial profit, even after years of losses, can help show that you are trying to make a go of it. On the other hand, earning only small or occasional yearly profits when you have years of large losses in the activity tends to show that you aren't in it for the money.

- **Your personal wealth.** The IRS figures that you probably have a profit motive if you don't have substantial income from other sources. After all, you'll need to earn money from your real estate activity to survive. On the other hand, the IRS may be suspicious if you have substantial income from other sources (particularly if the losses from your real estate activity generate substantial tax deductions).
- **The nature of your activity.** Activities that are inherently fun or recreational are particularly likely to be found to be hobbies by the IRS. Obviously, this doesn't pose a problem for a real estate agent. No one would claim that selling real estate is a "fun" activity—in the same category as art, photography, writing, antique or stamp collecting, or training and showing dogs or horses (for example).

How to Pass the Behavior Test

Any real estate agent can pass the behavior test, but it takes time, effort, and careful planning. Focus your efforts on the first three factors listed above. As noted earlier, a venture that can meet these three criteria will always be classified as a business. Here are some tips that will help you satisfy these crucial factors—and ultimately ace the behavior test.

Act Like a Businessperson

First and foremost, you must show that you carry on your real estate activity in a businesslike manner. Doing the things outlined below will not only help you with the IRS, but will also help you actually earn a profit someday (or at least help you figure out that your business will not be profitable).

- **Keep good business records.** Keeping good records of your expenses and income from your real estate activity is the single most important thing you can do to show that you want to earn a profit. Without good records, you'll never have an accurate idea of where you stand financially. Lack of records shows that you don't really care whether you make money or not—and it is almost always fatal in an IRS audit. You don't necessarily need an elaborate set of books; a simple record of your expenses and income will usually suffice.

- **Keep a separate checking account.** Open up a separate checking account for your real estate business. This will help you keep your personal and business expenses separate—another factor that shows you want to make money.
- **Create a business plan.** Draw up a business plan with a realistic profit and loss forecast—a projection of how much money your business will bring in, your expenses, and how much profit you expect to make. The forecast should cover the next five or ten years. It should show you earning a profit some time in the future (although it doesn't have to be within five years). Both the IRS and courts are usually impressed by good business plans.

RESOURCE

Need help drawing up a business plan? A business plan is useful not only to show the IRS that you are running a business, but also to convince others—such as lenders and investors—that they should support your venture financially. For detailed guidance on putting together a business plan, see *How to Write a Business Plan*, by Mike McKeever (Nolo).

- **Market yourself.** Real estate agents who are trying to earn a profit ordinarily take steps to market themselves and their services. At a minimum, you should have a business card and letterhead. Having your own real estate sales website or blog also shows you are serious about earning a profit. Engaging in advertising also shows you're trying hard to get business.
- **Obtain all necessary business licenses and permits.** Getting the required licenses and permits for your activities will show that you are acting like a business. Obviously, you must have a real estate license. You should also have any other license or permits required to operate a business in your locality, such as a city business license.
- **Join professional organizations and associations.** Taking part in professional groups and organizations will help you make valuable contacts and obtain useful advice and expertise. This helps to show that you're motivated to earn a profit. There are many professional organizations real estate agents can join, such as the National Association of Realtors.

Show Expertise

If you're already a real estate expert, you're a step ahead of the game. But if you lack the necessary expertise, you can develop it by attending educational seminars and similar activities and consulting with other experts. Keep records of your efforts (for example, a certificate for completing a real estate sales training course or your notes documenting your attendance at a seminar or convention).

Work Steadily

You don't have to work full time to show that you want to earn a profit. It's fine to hold a full-time job and work part time at real estate sales. However, you must work regularly and continuously rather than sporadically. You may establish any schedule you want, as long as you work regularly.

Although there is no minimum amount of time you must work, you'll have a hard time convincing the IRS that you want to make money if you work less than five or ten hours a week. Keep a log showing how much time you spend working. Your log doesn't have to be fancy—you can just mark down your hours and a summary of your activities each day on your calendar or appointment book.

What If Your "Business" Is a Hobby?

A hobby is something you do primarily for a purpose other than to make a profit—for example, to have fun, learn something, help your community, or impress your neighbors. Almost anything can be a hobby; common examples include creating artwork or crafts, photography, writing, or collecting coins, stamps, or other objects.

You do not want what you consider real estate activity to be deemed a hobby by the IRS. Because hobbies are not businesses, hobbyists cannot take the tax deductions to which businesspeople are entitled. Instead, hobbyists can deduct only their hobby-related expenses from the income the hobby generates. If you have no income from the hobby, you get no deduction. And you can't carry over the deductions to use in future years when you earn income—you lose them forever.

EXAMPLE: Charles is a part-time real estate agent. This year, he spent $1,000 on expenses, but earned no income from the activity. The IRS determines that this activity is a hobby. As a result, his $1,000 in expenses can be deducted only from any income he earned from his hobby. Because he earned no money from real estate during the year, he can't deduct any of these expenses this year—and he can't carry over the deduction to any future years.

Even if you have income from your hobby, you must deduct your expenses in a way that is less advantageous (and more complicated) than regular business deductions. Hobby expenses are deductible only as a Miscellaneous Itemized Deduction on IRS Schedule A, *Itemized Deductions* (the form that you file with your Form 1040 to itemize your deductions). This means that you can deduct your hobby expenses only if you itemize your deductions instead of taking the standard deduction. You should itemize deductions only if your total deductions are greater than the standard deduction. If you do itemize, your hobby expenses can be used to offset your hobby income—but only to the extent that your expenses plus your other miscellaneous itemized deductions exceed 2% of your adjusted gross income (your total income minus business expenses and a few other deductions).

You don't need to understand all of this in great detail. Just be aware that an IRS finding that your real estate activity is a hobby will probably result in tax disaster if you claimed business deductions for your expenses.

Real Estate Investing

Many people who have real estate licenses invest in real estate in addition to, or instead of, selling property. In some cases, real estate investing is classified as a business for tax purposes. In many others, it is classified as an income-producing activity with generally less favorable tax treatment.

Real Estate Dealers—A Business in the Eyes of the IRS

People who are classified as real estate dealers by the IRS are considered to be in business. A real estate dealer is someone who is in the business of owning property primarily for sale to customers. A dealer buys property and resells it, usually at a price higher than the purchase price, and normally after only a short holding period.

A real estate dealer resembles a merchant or retailer of goods, except that the product being bought and sold is real estate. For example, a merchant in the business of selling computers typically purchases numerous computers each year—not for his or her own use or to rent out to users—but to resell as quickly as possible to customers at a profit. Likewise, a real estate dealer buys real property to resell at a profit to customers. A real estate dealer's holdings are inventory for sale to customers, the same as any merchant's inventory.

Real estate dealers typically include (but are not limited to):

- real estate speculators who buy and sell many properties each year
- subdividers who buy large tracts of vacant land, divide them into smaller lots, and then resell the lots piecemeal
- real estate developers and home builders who construct new houses and resell them soon after completion, and
- people in the business of converting apartment buildings into condominiums for resale.

A person can be real estate broker or agent and a dealer in real estate at the same time.

> EXAMPLE: Dean Morley a Virginia real estate broker, purchased a 180-acre farm with the intention of quickly reselling it. Unfortunately, the real estate market collapsed and he was unable to find a buyer, despite many attempts to do so. The tax court found that Morley was a real estate dealer as to the farm, and that the purchase of the farm was not merely an extension of his real estate brokerage business. (*Morley v. Comm'r.*, 87 TC 1206 (1986).)

Being classified as a dealer is often a tax disadvantage because gains from sales of real property by a dealer are usually subject to ordinary income tax rates. In contrast, gains realized by an investor are usually taxed at capital gains rates, which are lower. However, dealers are better off if real estate proves to be a money-losing proposition: A dealer is typically permitted to deduct the full amount of a loss, while an investor's deductions for losses may be strictly limited.

In addition, since they sell real estate as a business, real estate dealers must pay self-employment taxes on their earnings. Real estate investors who are not dealers do not have to pay such taxes.

Managing Rental Property—Sometimes a Business

You don't have to be a big-shot developer to be in the business of real estate. You can also run a business actively managing rental real estate. But the key word here is active. You can't just sit back and collect rent checks while someone else does all the work of being a landlord. You must be actively involved on a regular, systematic, and continuous basis.

Even if managing real estate is a business, you ordinarily don't file Schedule C, *Profit or Loss From Business*, to report your income and expenses. Instead, you file Schedule E, *Supplemental Income and Loss*. However, you must file Schedule C if you run a hotel, motel, or apartment building where you provide hotel-type services to the occupants (such as maid services).

RESOURCE

Need more help with rental property taxation? Taxation of activities relating to property is a complex subject that is beyond the scope of this book. For detailed guidance on these issues, refer to *Every Landlord's Tax Deduction Guide*, by Stephen Fishman (Nolo).

When Real Estate Investing Is an Income-Producing Activity

If you don't actively engage in your real estate investing activity, it will be classified as an income-producing activity, rather than a business. You are entitled to deduct the ordinary and necessary expenses you incur to produce income, or to manage property held for the production of income—for example, real estate rentals. (IRC § 212.) This includes many of the same expenses that businesspeople are allowed (many are covered in later chapters). For example, a person with a real estate rental can deduct maintenance and repair costs.

However, there are some crucial limitations on deductions for income-producing activities (these restrictions do not apply to businesses). For example, you can't claim the home office deduction, Section 179 expensing, or start-up expense deductions. But there is one good tax effect of having an income-producing activity: You don't have to pay any self-employment tax on your income from the activity. Only people in business have to pay self-employment taxes. This is a substantial savings because the self-employment tax is 15.3% of your self-employment income, up to an annual ceiling amount.

When you have an income-producing activity, you don't file an IRS Schedule C, *Profit or Loss From Business*, with your tax return. You don't have a business, so that schedule doesn't apply. Instead, you list your expenses on Schedule A, *Itemized Deductions*. However, if your income comes from real estate or royalties, you list it and your expenses on Schedule E, *Supplemental Income and Loss*. Investors who incur capital gains or losses must file Schedule D, *Capital Gains and Losses*.

RESOURCE

Need more information on investment deductions? For detailed guidance on tax deductions for investments, refer to IRS Publication 550, *Investment Income and Expenses*. Like all IRS publications, you can download it from the IRS website at www.irs.gov, or obtain it by calling the IRS at 800-829-3676.

CHAPTER

4

Getting Around Town: Deducting Local Travel Expenses

Most real estate agents and brokers spend a good deal of time behind the wheel of their car. Indeed, it's not uncommon for real estate agents to drive over 20,000 miles per year for business. Obviously, this is a big expense—fortunately, these expenses are fully deductible.

This chapter shows you how to deduct expenses for local transportation —that is, business trips that don't require you to stay away from home overnight. These rules apply to local business trips using any means of transportation, but this chapter focuses on car expenses, the most common type of deduction for local business travel by real estate agents.

Overnight trips, whether by car or other means, are covered in Chapter 5.

Deductible Local Transportation Expenses

Local transportation costs are deductible as business operating expenses if they are ordinary and necessary for your real estate business. Real estate agents and brokers usually do most of their work away from their office, so these expenses are ordinary and necessary. It makes no difference what type of transportation you use to make the local trips—car, SUV, limousine, motorcycle, taxi—or whether the vehicle you use is owned or leased. You can deduct these costs as long as they meet the requirements discussed below.

Travel Must Be for Business

You can only deduct local trips that are for your real estate business—that is, travel to a business location like a house you are showing a client. Personal trips—for example, to the supermarket or the gym—are not deductible as business travel expenses. A business location is any place where you perform business-related tasks. Common examples of deductible local travel by real estate agents include:

- driving to newly listed properties for brokers' tours
- driving clients to look at properties for sale
- driving to clients' properties to hold open houses
- driving to meet with buyers to prepare offers or meet with sellers to present offers

- driving to a local college or other place for real estate training programs
- driving to the bank where you do your business banking, or
- driving to the store where you buy business supplies.

Going to the Supermarket Is Not a Business Trip

Willie Moore, a Houston-based real estate broker, listed over $35,000 in car expenses on his tax return. He claimed he used two of his three cars solely for his real estate business. Moore admitted that he often used these cars to go to the supermarket or drive to church, but he said that these trips were business related because he would often hand out his business cards to people he met at these places. When the tax court asked Moore what part of the grocery store was best for conducting business, he replied "I would say the meat section, where they have the chips and all that good stuff." Needless to say, the tax court found that these trips were personal, not business trips. The court said that Moore could not transform "nondeductible personal expenses into deductible business expenses through kinesis." (*Moore v. Comm'r*, T.C. Summary Opinion 2010-102.)

Commuting Is Not Deductible

Most real estate agents and brokers have an outside office where they work on a regular basis. Unfortunately, you can't deduct the cost of traveling from your home to your regular place of business. These are commuting expenses, which are a nondeductible personal expense.

Commuting occurs when you go from home to a permanent work location—either your:

- office or other principal place of business, or
- another place where you have worked or expect to work for more than one year.

EXAMPLE: Kim, a real estate agent, works out of a brokerage office in a downtown office building. Every day, she drives 20 miles from her suburban home to her office and back. None of this commuting mileage is deductible. But she may deduct trips from her office to an open house or any other business-related trip that starts from her office.

Even if a trip from home has a business purpose—for example, to deliver important papers to your office—it is still considered commuting and is not deductible.

Nor can you deduct a commuting trip because you make business calls on your cell phone, listen to work-related tapes, or have a business discussion with an associate or employee during the commute. Also, placing an advertising display on your vehicle won't convert a commute to a business trip.

Because commuting is not deductible, where your office is located affects the amount you can deduct for local business trips. You will get the fewest deductions if you work solely from an outside office. You lose out on many potential business miles this way because you can't deduct any trips between your home and your office.

As explained below, you can get the most deductions for local business trips if you have a home office.

You Have a Home Office

If you have a home office that qualifies for the home office tax deduction, you can deduct the cost of any trips you make from your home to another business location. For example, you can deduct the cost of driving from home to your outside office, an open house, or to attend a work-related seminar. The commuting rule doesn't apply.

Your home office qualifies for the home office tax deduction if it is the place where you (1) earn most of your income, or (2) perform the administrative or management tasks for your business. (See Chapter 7 for more on the home office deduction.) If your home office qualifies for a deduction, you can vastly increase your deductions for business trips.

EXAMPLE: Kim works at an outside brokerage office and also maintains a home office where she does all the administrative work for her real estate business. She goes to her real estate brokerage office four days a week where she does other work, such as meeting with clients. She can deduct all her business trips from her home office, including the 20-mile daily trip to her outside office. Thanks to her home office, she can now deduct 80 miles per week as a business trip expense, all of which was a nondeductible commuting expense before she established her home office.

You Go to a Temporary Business Location

Travel between your home and a temporary work location is not considered commuting and is therefore deductible. A temporary work location is any place where you realistically expect to work less than one year.

EXAMPLE: Sally, an independent contractor real estate agent, works for a brokerage office in a downtown office building and does not have a home office. Her firm agrees to sell properties offered for sale at a new housing development that is 50 miles from Sally's home. For six months, Sally travels from her home to the development to help with the sales. Sally may deduct the cost of driving from home to the real estate development.

Temporary work locations are not limited to places where properties are offered for sale. Any place where you perform business-related tasks for less than one year is a temporary work location. This may include a bank, title company, office supply store, school, or similar place.

EXAMPLE: Jim is a real estate broker and has no home office. One day he travels from home to a local title company to drop off a buyer's initial deposit check. This is not commuting and is deductible.

However, a place will cease to be a temporary work location if you continue to go there for more than one year.

EXAMPLE: Jim goes from his house to the title company every month, year after year, to deliver checks and other paperwork. The title company is no longer a temporary work location and his trips there from home are nondeductible commuting expenses.

You can convert a nondeductible commute into a deductible local business trip by making a stop at a temporary work location on your way to your office. Stopping at a temporary work location converts the entire trip into a deductible travel expense.

> EXAMPLE: Eleanor's real estate office is in a downtown building. She has no home office. One morning, she leaves home, stops at a buyer's agent's office to drop off disclosure paperwork, and then goes to her office. The entire trip is deductible because she stopped at a temporary work location on her way to her office.

Keep in mind, though, that making such stops is necessary only if you don't have a home office. If Eleanor had a home office, the commuting rule wouldn't apply and the trip would be deductible with or without the stop.

The Standard Mileage Rate

If you drive a car, SUV, or van for business (as most real estate agents do), you have two options for deducting your vehicle expenses: You can use the standard mileage rate or you can deduct your actual expenses.

Let's start with the easy one: the standard mileage rate. This method works best for agents who don't want to bother with a lot of record keeping or calculations. But this ease comes at a price—it often results in a lower deduction than you might otherwise be entitled to using the actual expense method. However, this isn't always the case. The standard mileage rate may give you a larger deduction if you drive many business miles each year, especially if you drive an inexpensive car.

How the Standard Mileage Rate Works

Under the standard mileage rate, you deduct a specified number of cents for every business mile you drive. The IRS sets the standard mileage rate each year. For 2012, the rate was 55.5 cents per mile. To figure out your deduction, simply multiply your business miles by the applicable standard mileage rate.

EXAMPLE: Ed drove his car 10,000 miles for his real estate agent business during 2012. To determine his car expense deduction, he simply multiplies his business miles by the applicable standard mileage rate: 55.5 cents per mile. This gives him a total deduction for the year of $5,550.

The big advantage of the standard mileage rate is that it requires very little record keeping. You only need to keep track of how many business miles you drive, not the actual expenses for your car, such as gas, maintenance, or repairs.

If you choose the standard mileage rate, you cannot deduct actual car operating expenses—for example, maintenance and repairs, gasoline and its taxes, oil, insurance, and vehicle registration fees. All of these items are factored into the rate set by the IRS. And you can't deduct the cost of the car through depreciation or Section 179 expensing because the car's depreciation is also factored into the standard mileage rate (as are lease payments for a leased car).

The only expenses you can deduct (because these costs aren't included in the standard mileage rate) are:

- interest on a car loan
- parking fees and tolls for business trips (but you can't deduct parking ticket fines or the cost of parking your car at your place of work), and
- personal property tax that you paid when you bought the vehicle, based on its value—this is often included as part of your auto registration fee.

When to Use the Standard Mileage Rate

You must use the standard mileage rate in the first year you use a car for business or you are forever foreclosed from using that method for that car. If you use the standard mileage rate the first year, you can switch to the actual expense method in a later year, and then switch back and forth between the two methods after that, provided the requirements listed below are met. For this reason, if you're not sure which method you want to use, it's a good idea to use the standard mileage rate the first year you use a car for business. This leaves all your options open for later years. However, this rule does not apply to leased cars. If you lease your car, you must use the standard mileage rate for the entire lease period if you use it in the first year.

There are some restrictions on switching back to the standard mileage rate after you have used the actual expense method. You can't switch back to the standard mileage rate after using the actual expense method if you took accelerated depreciation, a Section 179 deduction, or bonus depreciation on the car. You can switch back to the standard mileage rate only if you used the straight line method of depreciation during the years you used the actual expense method. This depreciation method gives you equal depreciation deductions every year, rather than the larger deductions you get in the early years using accelerated depreciation methods. (See Chapter 9.)

The Actual Expense Method

Instead of using the standard mileage rate, you can deduct the actual cost of using your car for business. This requires much more record keeping, but it can result in a larger deduction. However, because there are low caps on the allowable depreciation deductions for automobiles, the increase in the amount of the deduction you get by using the actual expense method is often quite small. You may well conclude that it does not justify the additional record keeping required.

How the Actual Expense Method Works

As the name implies, under the actual expense method, you deduct the actual costs you incur each year to operate your car, plus depreciation. If you use this method, you must keep careful track of all your car-related costs during the year, including:

- gas and oil
- repairs and maintenance
- depreciation of your original vehicle and improvements
- car repair tools
- license fees
- parking fees for business trips

- registration fees
- tires
- insurance
- garage rent
- tolls for business trips
- car washing
- lease payments
- interest on car loans
- towing charges, and
- auto club dues.

Watch Those Tickets

You may not deduct the cost of driving violations or parking tickets, even if you were on business when you got the ticket. Government fines and penalties are never deductible as a matter of public policy.

When you do your taxes, add up the cost of all these items. For everything but parking fees and tolls, multiply the total cost of each item by the percentage of time you use your car for business. For parking fees and tolls that are business-related, include (and deduct) the full cost. The total is your deductible transportation expense for the year.

> EXAMPLE: In one recent year, Laura drove her car 10,000 miles for her real estate business and 10,000 miles for personal purposes. She can deduct 50% of the actual costs of operating her car, plus the full cost of any business-related tolls and parking fees. Her expenses amount to $10,000 for the year, so she gets a $5,000 deduction, plus $500 that she paid in tolls and parking for business.

Record-Keeping Requirements

When you deduct actual car expenses, you must keep records of all the costs of owning and operating your car. This includes not only the number of business miles and total miles you drive, but also gas, repairs, parking, insurance, tolls, and any other car expenses. Record keeping for car expenses is covered in Chapter 17.

Vehicle Depreciation Deductions

Using the actual expense method, you can deduct the cost of your vehicle. However, you can't deduct the entire cost in the year when you purchase your car. Instead, you must deduct the cost a portion at a time over several years, using a process called depreciation. Although the general concept of depreciation is the same for every type of property, special rules apply to depreciation deductions for cars. These rules give you a lower deduction for cars than you'd be entitled to using the normal depreciation rules. For a detailed discussion, see Chapter 9.

Auto Repairs and Improvements

Auto repairs and maintenance costs are fully deductible in the year they are incurred. You add these costs to your other annual expenses when you use the actual expense method. (You get no extra deduction for repairs when you use the standard mileage rate.) If you fix your car yourself, you may deduct the cost of parts and depreciate or deduct tools, but you get no deduction for your time or labor.

Unlike repairs, improvements to your car are capital expenses and must be depreciated over several years, not deducted all in the year when you pay for them. What's the difference between a repair and an improvement? Good question. Unlike a repair, an improvement:

- makes a long-term asset much better than it was before
- restores the asset to operating condition, or
- adapts the asset to a new use. (IRS Temp. Reg. § 1.263(a)-3T.)

Expenses you incur that don't result in a betterment, restoration, or adaptation are currently deductible repairs.

> EXAMPLE: The hard disk on Dora's business computer crashes. She takes it to Don, who repairs computers. He charges her $100 to fix the hard disk, which involved replacing a minor part. This expense simply keeps Dora's computer in good running order. It

does not make the computer substantially better, restore it, or adapt it to a new use. Thus, the expense is a repair that may be currently deducted in the year it was incurred.

Unfortunately, there are no "bright-line rules" that explain exactly how much an asset must be altered to constitute an improvement. Instead, you have to look at all the facts and circumstances and make a judgment call to determine whether an expense results in a betterment, restoration, or adaptation of a business asset.

> EXAMPLE: Dora decides to get a new hard disk for her computer after the old one crashes. She spends $250 for a brand new internal hard drive that has twice the capacity of the old hard drive. This is an improvement because it makes the computer much better than it was before. Dora may not deduct the expense in a single year. Instead, she must depreciate it over five years.

This rule can be difficult to apply because virtually all repairs increase the value of the property being repaired. Just remember that an improvement makes your vehicle more valuable than it was before it was worked on, while a repair simply restores the car's value to what it was worth before it broke down.

Leasing a Car

If you lease a car that you use in your real estate business, you can use the actual expense method to deduct the portion of each lease payment that reflects the business percentage use of the car. You cannot deduct any part of a lease payment that is for commuting or personal use of the car.

> EXAMPLE: John pays $400 a month to lease a Lexus. He uses it 50% for his real estate business and 50% for personal purposes. He may deduct half of his lease payments ($200 a month) as a local transportation expense for his business.

Leasing companies typically require you to make an advance or down payment to lease a car. You can deduct this cost, but you must spread the deduction out equally over the entire lease period.

TIP

You can't deduct lease payments if you use the standard mileage method. With the standard mileage method, the cost of your lease payments is included in the standard mileage rate set by the IRS. You don't get any separate deduction for them.

Is It Really a Lease?

Some transactions that are called auto leases are really not leases at all. Instead, they are installment purchases—that is, you pay for the car over time, and by the end of the lease term you own all or part of the car. You cannot deduct any payments you make to buy a car, even if the payments are called lease payments. Instead, you have to depreciate the cost of the car as described above.

Leasing Luxury Cars

If you lease what the IRS considers to be a luxury car for more than 30 days, you may have to reduce your lease deduction. The purpose of this rule is to prevent people from leasing very expensive cars to get around the limitations on depreciation deductions for cars that are purchased. (See "Vehicle Depreciation Deductions," above.) A luxury car is currently defined as one with a fair market value of more than $16,700.

The amount by which you must reduce your deduction (called an inclusion amount) is based on the fair market value of your car and the percentage of time that you use it for business. The IRS recalculates it each year. You can find the inclusion amount for the current year in the tables published in IRS Publication 463, *Travel, Entertainment, Gift, and Car Expenses*. For example, if you leased a $40,000 car in 2012 and used it solely for business that year, you would have to reduce your car expense deduction by $14 for the year. If you used the car only 50% for business, the reduction would be $7. The inclusion amount for the first year is prorated based on the month when you start using the car for business.

Should You Lease or Buy Your Car?

When you lease a car, you are paying rent for it—a set fee each month for the use of the car. At the end of the lease term, you give the car back to the leasing company and own nothing. As a general rule, leasing a car instead of buying it makes economic sense only if you absolutely must have a new car every two or three years and drive no more than 12,000 to 15,000 miles per year. If you drive more than 15,000 miles a year, leasing becomes an economic disaster because it penalizes you for higher mileage.

There are numerous financial calculators available on the Internet that can help you determine how much it will cost to lease a car compared to buying one. Be careful when you use these calculators—they are designed based on certain assumptions, and different calculators can give different answers. For a detailed consumer guide to auto leasing created by the Federal Reserve Board, go to the board's website at www.federalreserve.gov/pubs/leasing.

Other Local Transportation Expenses

You don't have to drive a car or other vehicle to get a tax deduction for local business trips. You can deduct the cost of travel by taxi, bus or other public transit, train, ferry, motorcycle, bicycle, or any other means. However, all the rules limiting deductions for travel by car discussed in "Commuting Is Not Deductible," above, also apply to other transportation methods. This means, for example, that you can't deduct the cost of commuting from your home to your office or other permanent work location. The same record-keeping requirements apply as well.

Reporting Transportation Expenses on Schedule C

If you're a sole proprietor, you will list your car expenses on Schedule C, *Profit or Loss From Business*. Schedule C asks more questions about this deduction than almost any other deduction (reflecting the IRS's general suspicion about auto deductions).

Part IV of Schedule C is reproduced below. If you answer "no" to question 46, you cannot claim to use your single car 100% for business (unless you are an unusual case—see "How the Actual Expense Method Works," above). If you answer "no" to questions 47a or 47b, you do not qualify for the deduction.

Part IV **Information on Your Vehicle.** Complete this part **only** if you are claiming car or truck expenses on line 9 and are not required to file Form 4562 for this business. See the instructions for line 13 to find out if you must file Form 4562.

43 When did you place your vehicle in service for business purposes? (month, day, year) ▶ ___ / ___ / ___

44 Of the total number of miles you drove your vehicle during 2010, enter the number of miles you used your vehicle for:

a Business ______ b Commuting (see instructions) ______ c Other ______

45 Was your vehicle available for personal use during off-duty hours? ☐ Yes ☐ No

46 Do you (or your spouse) have another vehicle available for personal use?. ☐ Yes ☐ No

47a Do you have evidence to support your deduction? ☐ Yes ☐ No

b If "Yes," is the evidence written? ☐ Yes ☐ No

Report Your Interest Expenses Separately

If you deduct the interest you pay on a car loan, you have the option of reporting the amount in two different places on your Schedule C: You can lump it in with all your other car expenses on line 9 of the schedule titled "Car and truck expenses," or you can list it separately on line 16b as an "other interest" cost. Reporting your interest expense separately from your other car expenses reduces the total car expense shown on your Schedule C. This can help avoid an IRS audit.

Real Estate Professionals With Business Entities

If your real estate business is legally organized as a corporation, LLC, or partnership there are special complications when it comes to deducting car expenses. Moreover, you have the option of having your business own (or lease) the car you use, instead of using your personal car for business driving.

TIP

This section doesn't apply to real estate professionals who are sole proprietors or owners of one-person LLCs taxed as sole proprietorships. There is no separate legal entity to get between them and their business expense deductions. Moreover, sole proprietors don't have company cars because they personally own all their business assets.

Using Your Own Car

If you use your own car for business driving, how you can deduct your expenses depends on whether your real estate business is a corporation, LLC, partnership, or LLP.

LLCs and Partnerships

If you have organized your real estate business as an LLC or partnership, it is probably taxed as a partnership (see Chapter 2). Usually, you'll seek reimbursement for your deductible car and other local travel expenses from your business entity. You can use either the standard mileage rate or actual expense method to calculate your expenses.

As long as you comply with the record-keeping rules for car expenses and your reimbursement is made under an accountable plan, any reimbursement you receive will not be taxable income. Basically, you must submit all your documentation to the business in a timely manner and return any excess payments. Accountable plans are covered in detail in Chapter 17.

The business can deduct the amount of the reimbursed car expenses on its tax return (IRS Form 1065) and reduce its taxable profit for the year.

> EXAMPLE: Rick, a co-owner of a real estate brokerage organized as an LLC, uses his personal car for local business driving. He uses the standard mileage rate and keeps careful track of all of his business mileage. He submits a request for reimbursement to the brokerage, along with his mileage records. He was entitled to a $4,050 reimbursement from his firm. This money is not taxable income to Rick, and the brokerage may list it on its tax return as a business expense.

Instead of seeking reimbursement, you can deduct car expenses on your personal tax return, provided either of the following is true:

- you have a written partnership agreement or LLC operating agreement which provides that the expense will not be reimbursed by the partnership or LLC, or
- your business has an established routine practice of not reimbursing the expense.

Absent such a written agreement or established practice, no personal deduction may be taken. You must seek reimbursement from the partnership, or LLC instead. If you take a personal deduction for your car expenses, your business does not list them on its tax return, and they do not reduce your business's profits. But they will reduce your taxable income. (See Chapter 2.)

You deduct your unreimbursed car expenses (and any other unreimbursed business expenses) on IRS Schedule E (Part II) and attach it to your personal tax return. You must attach a separate schedule to Schedule E listing the car and other business expenses you're deducting.

> EXAMPLE: Assume that Rick's brokerage has a written policy that all the broker-owners must personally pay for their own car expenses. Instead of seeking reimbursement, Rick lists his $4,050 car expense on his own tax return, Schedule E, reducing his taxable income by that amount. The firm does not list the expense on its return, thus it does not reduce the brokerage's income.

Corporations

If your real estate business is legally organized as a corporation (whether a C or S corporation), you are probably working as its employee. Special rules govern all business expense deductions by employees. Your best option is to have your corporation reimburse you for your car expenses. You get reimbursement in the same way as described above for LLCs and partnerships. You must comply with all the documentation rules for car expenses and the accountable plan requirements. If you do, your corporation gets to deduct the expense and you don't have to count the reimbursement as taxable income. If you fail to follow the rules, any reimbursements must be treated as employee income subject to tax (but you may deduct your expenses as described below). (See Chapter 17.)

Using a Company Car

If your business entity buys a car for you to use (that is, your business holds the title to the car, not you personally), the dollar value of your business driving is a tax-free working condition fringe benefit provided to you by your business. In addition, the business gets to deduct all of its actual car expenses on its tax return—for example, depreciation, interest on a car loan, maintenance, fuel it pays for, and insurance costs.

You get no personal deduction for these expenses; but, of course, if your business is a pass-through entity, the deduction on its return will reduce the amount of taxable profit passed on to your tax return. However, you can personally deduct the actual cost of fuel or maintenance you pay for yourself, and the cost of anything else you buy for the car. You can't use the standard mileage rate to figure your costs; you must keep track of your mileage using one of the methods described in this chapter. And, if you personally buy fuel or other items for the car, you must comply with all the documentation rules for car expenses covered above.

> EXAMPLE: Rosa, a real estate broker, is a one-third owner of a brokerage firm organized as an LLC. The LLC buys a $30,000 car in 2012 that Rosa uses 100% for business driving. She keeps careful track of her mileage. In 2012 , she drove the car 20,000 miles. The LLC may deduct on its tax return all the expenses it incurs from owning the car, which amount to $15,000. Rosa's LLC lists the $15,000 as a deduction on its tax return. As a result, instead of reporting a $300,000 annual profit, it has a $285,000 profit. Rosa pays income and self-employment tax on her distributive share of this amount, which is one-third. Rosa gets no personal deduction for these expenses, but she may personally deduct as a business expense the cost of fuel she paid for with her own money. This gives her a $400 deduction. Rosa need not pay any tax on the value of having the car because it is a tax-free working condition fringe benefit provided to her by the LLC.

Things get more complicated if, as is often the case, you use a company car for both business and personal driving. The dollar value of your personal use of the car is treated as a taxable fringe benefit. The amount must be added to your annual compensation and income, Social Security, and Medicare taxes must be paid on it.

> EXAMPLE: Assume that Rosa (from the above example) uses her company car 60% for business driving and 40% for personal driving. Her LLC still gets the $15,000 deduction for its car expenses. However, the dollar value of Rosa's personal driving is a taxable fringe benefit that must be added to her annual compensation. If the value of her personal driving was $5,000, she has to pay income and self-employment tax on this amount. She still gets to deduct the cost of fuel she paid for when she drove the car for business.

Here's the key question: How do you place a dollar value on your personal use of a company car? This determines how much money must be added to your income for such use. You can use three different methods to figure this out, and they may yield very different results. You can either determine the fair market value of your use of the car, use the standard mileage rate, or use an Annual Lease Value created by the IRS. For more information, refer to IRS Publication 15-B, *Employer's Tax Guide to Fringe Benefits.*

CHAPTER

5

Leaving Town: Deducting Travel Expenses

If you travel overnight for your real estate business, you can deduct your car expenses, airfare, hotel bills, meals, and other expenses. If you plan your trip right, you can even mix business with pleasure and still get a deduction. Be forewarned, IRS auditors closely scrutinize these deductions. Many taxpayers claim them without complying with the stringent rules the IRS imposes. To avoid unwanted attention, you need to understand the limitations on this deduction and keep proper records.

What Is Business Travel?

For tax purposes, business travel occurs when you travel away from your tax home for your business on a temporary basis. You don't have to travel any set distance to get a travel expense deduction. However, you can't take this deduction if you just spend the night in a motel across town. You must travel outside your city limits. If you don't live in a city, you must go outside the general area where your business is located.

You must stay away overnight or at least long enough to require a stop for sleep or rest. You cannot satisfy the rest requirement by merely napping in your car.

> EXAMPLE: Phyllis, a commercial real estate broker based in Los Angeles, flies to San Francisco to look at a property for a client. She spends the night in a hotel and returns home the following day. Her trip is a deductible travel expense.

If you don't stay overnight (or long enough to require sleep or rest), your trip will not qualify as business travel. This does not necessarily mean that you can't take a tax deduction. Local business trips, other than commuting, are deductible. However, you may only deduct your transportation expenses—the cost of driving or using some other means of transportation. You may not deduct meals or other expenses the way you can when you travel for business and stay overnight.

> EXAMPLE: Philip drives from his brokerage office in Los Angeles to a meeting with a client in San Diego and returns the same day. His 200-mile round trip is a deductible local business trip. He may

deduct his expenses for the 200 business miles he drove, but he can't deduct the breakfast he bought on the way to San Diego.

Where Is Your Tax Home?

Your tax home is the entire city or general area where your principal place of business is located. This is not necessarily the place where you live.

The IRS doesn't care how far you travel for business. You'll get a deduction as long as you travel outside your tax home's city limits and stay overnight. Thus, even if you're just traveling across town, you'll qualify for a deduction if you manage to stay outside your city limits.

EXAMPLE: Pete works from a brokerage office in San Francisco. He travels to Oakland to host an open house. At the end of the meeting, he decides to spend the night in an Oakland hotel rather than brave the traffic back to San Francisco. Pete's stay qualifies as a business trip even though the distance between his San Francisco office and the Oakland open house is only eight miles. Pete can deduct his hotel and meal expenses.

If you don't live in a city, your tax home covers the general area where it is located. This general area is anywhere within about 40 miles of your tax home.

Multiple Work Locations

If you work in more than one location, your tax home is your main place of business. To determine this, consider:

- the total time you spend in each place
- the level of your business activity in each place, and
- the amount of income you earn from each place.

EXAMPLE: Lee, a real estate broker, has two offices: one in Houston and another in Dallas. He spends three weeks a month in Houston and one week in Dallas. He makes three quarters of his annual income from sales out of his Houston office. Houston—where he spends more time and makes more money—is his tax home.

Temporary Work Locations

You may regularly work at your tax home and also work at other locations away from your tax home. It may not always be practical to return from this other location to your tax home at the end of each workday. Your overnight stays at these temporary work locations qualify as business travel as long as your work there is truly temporary—that is, it is reasonably expected to last no more than one year. If that is the case, your tax home does not change and you are considered to be away from home for the entire period you spend at the temporary work location.

> EXAMPLE: Julie, a real estate broker with an office in Miami, has a client who commissions her to sell an office building in Orlando. The building is expected to sell in less than one year. Thus, Julie's sales work in Orlando is temporary and Miami remains her tax home. She may deduct the expenses she incurs traveling to and staying in Orlando to sell the property.

Even if the job ends up lasting more than one year, the job location will be treated as temporary and you can still take your travel deductions if you reasonably expected the job to last less than one year when you took it. However, if at some later point the job is expected to last more than one year, the job location will be treated as temporary only until the earlier of when your expectations changed, or 12 months.

On the other hand, if you reasonably expect your work at the other location to last more than one year, that location becomes your new tax home and you cannot deduct your expenses while there as travel expenses.

> EXAMPLE: Carlos, a real estate broker, is co-owner of a real estate brokerage with several offices throughout Washington State. He ordinarily works from the firm's Seattle office and lives in Seattle. However, the firm's Yakima office is short-staffed, so Carlos goes there to help mange the office. He expects he'll have to work out of the Yakima office for at least 12 months. He lives in a Yakima hotel. Yakima is now Carlos's tax home and he may not deduct his expenses while staying there as travel expenses, even though he lives in Seattle. Thus, he may not deduct his hotel or food expenses.

However, he may deduct his travel expenses if he travels back and forth between Yakima and Seattle for a business purpose.

If you go back to your tax home from a temporary work location on your days off, you are not considered away from home while you are in your hometown. You cannot deduct the cost of meals and lodging there. However, you can deduct your expenses, including meals and lodging, while traveling between your temporary work location and your tax home. You can claim these expenses up to the amount it would have cost you to stay at your temporary work location. In addition, if you keep your hotel room during your visit home, you can deduct that cost.

Your Trip Must Be for Business

Your trip must be primarily for business to be deductible, and you must have a business intent and purpose before leaving on the trip. You have a business purpose if the trip benefits your business in some way. Examples of business purposes include:

- finding new clients
- dealing with existing clients
- learning new skills to help in your business
- finding new markets for your services
- contacting people who could help your business, such as potential investors, or
- checking out what the competition is doing.

It's not sufficient merely to claim that you had a business purpose for your trip. You must be able to prove this by showing that you spent at least part of the time engaged in business activities while at your destination. Acceptable business activities include:

- visiting or working with existing or potential clients, and
- attending professional seminars or conventions where the agenda is clearly connected to your real estate business.

On the other hand, business activities do not include:

- sightseeing
- recreational activities that you attend by yourself or with family or friends, or
- attending personal investment seminars or political events.

Use common sense when deciding whether to claim that a trip is for business. If you're audited, the IRS will likely question any trip that doesn't have some logical connection to your existing real estate business.

Agent's San Francisco Trip Not for Business

Carolyn Reece, a Houston real estate broker, flew to San Francisco and stayed there for three days. She claimed that the trip was for business because while there she met with a client to discuss selling a property he owned in Houston. Reece got the listing, but never did sell the property. She told the IRS that she met with the client every day for five or six hours. Unfortunately for her, neither the IRS nor tax court believed her story. It didn't seem plausible that Reece would spend that much time discussing the sale of a single property. The IRS and court concluded that Reece's San Francisco trip was primarily for pleasure and therefore not deductible. (*Reece v. Comm'r*, T.C. Summ. Op. 2009-59 (2009).)

Travel for a New Business or Location

You must actually be in business to have deductible business trips. Trips you make to investigate a potential new business or to actually start or acquire a new business are not currently deductible business travel expenses. However, they may be deductible as business start-up expenses, which means you can deduct up to $5,000 of these expenses the first year you're in business if your total start-up expenses are less than $50,000. (See Chapter 10 for more on start-up expenses.)

Travel as an Education Expense

You may deduct the cost of traveling to an educational activity directly related to your business.

EXAMPLE: Louis, a real estate agent, travels from his home in Philadelphia to a real estate continuing education course held in Pittsburgh. The cost is a deductible travel expense.

Visiting Professional Colleagues

Visiting professional colleagues or competitors may be a legitimate business purpose for a trip. But you can't just socialize with them. You must use your visit to learn new skills, check out what your competitors are doing, seek investors, or attempt to get new clients.

What Travel Expenses Are Deductible

Subject to the limits discussed in "How Much You Can Deduct," below, virtually all of your business travel expenses are deductible. These fall into two broad categories: your transportation expenses and the expenses you incur at your destination.

Transportation expenses are the costs of getting to and from your destination—for example:

- fares for airplanes, trains, or buses
- driving expenses, including car rentals
- shipping costs for your personal luggage, equipment, or other things you need for your business, and
- 50% of meals and beverages, and 100% lodging expenses you incur while en route to your final destination.

If you drive your personal car to your destination, you may deduct your costs by using the standard mileage rate or your actual expenses. You may also deduct your mileage while at your destination. (See Chapter 4 for more on deducting car expenses.) You may also deduct the expenses you incur to stay alive (food and lodging) and do business while at your destination. Destination expenses include:

- hotel or other lodging expenses for business days
- 50% of meal and beverage expenses (see "How Much You Can Deduct," below)
- taxi, public transportation, and car rental expenses at your destination

- telephone, Internet, and fax expenses
- computer rental fees
- laundry and dry cleaning expenses, and
- tips you pay on any of the other costs.

You may deduct 50% of entertainment expenses if you incur them for business purposes. You can't deduct entertainment expenses for activities that you attend alone because this solo entertainment obviously wouldn't be for business purposes. If you want to deduct the cost of a nightclub or ball game while on the road, be sure to take a business associate along. (See Chapter 6 for a detailed discussion of the special rules that apply to deductions for entertainment expenses.)

Traveling First Class or Steerage

To be deductible, business travel expenses must be ordinary and necessary. This means that the trip and the expenses you incur must be helpful and appropriate for your business, not necessarily indispensable. You may not deduct lavish or extravagant expenses, but the IRS gives you a great deal of leeway here. You may, if you wish, travel first class, stay at four-star hotels, and eat at expensive restaurants. On the other hand, you're also entitled to be a cheapskate—for example, you could stay with a friend or relative at your destination to save on hotel expenses and still deduct meals and other expenses.

Taking People With You

You may deduct the expenses you pay for a person who travels with you only if he or she:

- is your employee
- has a genuine business reason for going on the trip with you, and
- would otherwise be allowed to deduct the travel expenses.

These rules apply to your family as well as to nonfamily members. This means you can deduct the expense of taking your spouse, child, or other relative only if the person is your employee and has a genuine business reason for going on a trip with you. Typing notes or assisting in entertaining clients is not enough to warrant a deduction; the work must be essential to your real estate business.

However, this doesn't mean that you can't take any deductions at all when you travel with your family. You may still deduct your business expenses as if you were traveling alone—and you don't have to reduce your deductions, even if others get a free ride with you. For example, if you drive to your destination, you can deduct the entire cost of the drive, even if your family rides along with you. Similarly, you can deduct the full cost of a single hotel room even if you obtain a larger, more expensive room for your whole family.

> EXAMPLE: Yamiko, a real estate broker, travels from Chicago to New Orleans to attend a national sales and education conference held by her brokerage firm. She takes her husband and young son with her. The total airfare expense for her and her family is $1,000. She may deduct the cost of a single ticket: $350. She spends $400 per night for a two-bedroom hotel suite in New Orleans. She may deduct the cost of a single room for one person: $150 per night.

How Much You Can Deduct

If you spend all of your time at your destination on business, you may deduct 100% of your expenses (except meal expenses, which are only 50% deductible). However, things are more complicated if you mix business and pleasure. Different rules apply to your transportation expenses and the expenses you incur while at your destination ("destination expenses").

Travel Within the United States

Business travel within the United States is subject to an all or nothing rule: You may deduct 100% of your transportation expenses only if you spend more than half of your time on business activities while at your destination. If you spend more time on personal activities than on business, you get no transportation deduction. In other words, your business days must outnumber your personal days. You may also deduct the destination expenses you incur on the days you do business. Expenses incurred on personal days at your destination are nondeductible personal expenses. (See "Calculating Time Spent on Business," below, for the rules used to determine what constitutes a business day.)

> EXAMPLE: Howell is a real estate agent based in Atlanta. He takes the train for a business trip to Houston. He spends six days in Houston, where he spends all his time on business and spends $400 for his hotel, meals, and other living expenses. On the way home, he stops in Mobile for three days to visit his parents and spends $100 for lodging and meals there. His round-trip train fare is $250. Howell's trip consisted of six business days and three personal days, so he spent more than half of the trip on business. He can deduct 100% of his train fare and the entire $400 he spent while on business in Houston. He may not, however, deduct the $100 he spent while visiting his parents. His total deduction for the trip is $650.

Three Business Days on 17-Day Trip Not Enough

Derk O. Pehrson, a Salt Lake City real estate broker, rented a car and took a 17-day trip with his wife and two children. First, he drove to Orlando, Florida, where the family visited Walt Disney World and Pehrson's wife attended a seminar. Then they drove north to Harrisburg, Pennsylvania, where Pehrson conducted real estate business. Pehrson admitted that only three days of the trip were attributable to his real estate business activity in Harrisburg. Since the trip was primarily personal, not business related, the IRS and tax court found that it was not deductible as a business expense. (*Pehrson v. Comm'r*, 74 TCM 226 (1997).)

If your trip is primarily a vacation—that is, you spend over half of your time on personal activities—the entire cost of the trip is a nondeductible personal expense. However, you may deduct any expenses you have while at your destination which are directly related to your business. This includes such things as phone calls or faxes to your office, or the cost of renting a computer for business work. It doesn't include transportation, lodging, or food.

> EXAMPLE: Howell (from the above example) spends two days in Houston on business and seven days visiting his parents in Mobile. His entire trip is a nondeductible personal expense. However, while in Houston he spends $50 on long distance phone calls to his office. This expense is deductible.

As long as your trip is primarily for business, you can add a vacation to the end of the trip, make a side trip purely for fun, or go to the theater and still deduct your entire airfare. What you spend while having fun is not deductible, but you can deduct all of your business and transportation expenses.

> EXAMPLE: Victor, a real estate broker, flies to Miami for a three-day realtor convention. He spends two extra days in Miami swimming and enjoying the sights. Because he spent over half his time on business—three days out of five—the cost of his flight is entirely deductible, as are his hotel and meal costs during the convention. He may not deduct his hotel, meal, or other expenses during his vacation days.

Travel Outside the United States

Although most real estate brokers and agents don't do much travelling outside the United States on business, some agents are engaged in international real estate sales transactions and travel internationally for their business. The rules for deducting transportation expenses for international travel depend on how long the person stays at his or her destination.

Trips of Up to Seven Days

If you travel outside the United States for no more than seven days, you can deduct 100% of your airfare or other transportation expenses, as long as you spend part of the time on business. You can spend a majority of your time on personal activities, as long as you spend at least some time on business. Seven days means seven consecutive days, not counting the day you leave but counting the day you return to the United States. You may also deduct the destination expenses you incur on the days you do business. (See "Calculating Time Spent on Business," below, for the rules used to determine what constitutes a business day.)

Trips for More Than Seven Days

The IRS does not want to subsidize foreign vacations, so more stringent rules apply if your foreign trip lasts more than one week. For these longer trips, the magic number is 75%: If you spend more than 75% of your time on business at your foreign destination, you can deduct 100% of your airfare or other transportation expense, plus your living expenses while you are on business and any other business-related expenses.

If you spend more than 50%—but less than 75%—of your time on business, you can deduct only the business percentage of your transportation and other costs. For example, if you spend 60% of your time on business, you can deduct 60% of your costs.

If you spend less than 51% of your time on business on foreign travel that lasts more than seven days, you cannot deduct any of your costs.

Conventions

Your travel to, and stay at, a convention in North America is deductible if your attendance benefits your real estate business. You may not, however, deduct any expenses for your family.

How do you know if a convention benefits your business? Look at the convention agenda or program (and be sure to save a copy). The agenda does not have to specifically address what you do in your business, but it must be sufficiently related to show that your attendance was for business purposes. Examples of conventions that don't benefit your business include those for investment, political, or social purposes.

Calculating Time Spent on Business

To calculate how much time you spend on business while on a business trip, you must compare the number of days you spend on business with the days you spend on personal activities. All of the following are considered business days:

- any day in which you work for more than four hours
- any day in which you must be at a particular place for your business—for example, to meet with a client—even if you spend most of the day on personal activities
- any day in which you spend more than four hours on business travel; travel time begins when you leave home and ends when you reach your hotel, or vice versa
- any day in which you drive 300 miles for business (you can average your mileage); for example, if you drive 1,500 miles to your destination in five days, you may claim five 300-mile days, even if you drove 500 miles on one of the days and 100 miles on another
- any day in which your travel and work time together exceeds four hours
- any day in which you are prevented from working because of circumstances beyond your control; for example, a transit strike or terrorist act, and
- any day sandwiched between two work days if it would have cost more to go home than to stay where you are; this rule can let you count weekends as business days. (See "Maximizing Your Business Travel Deductions," below.)

Be sure to keep track of your time while you're away. You can do this by making simple notes on your calendar or travel diary. (See Chapter 17 for a detailed discussion of record keeping while traveling.)

50% Limit on Meal Expenses

The IRS figures that whether you're at home or away on a business trip, you have to eat. Because home meals ordinarily aren't deductible, the IRS won't let you deduct all of your food expenses while traveling. Instead, you can deduct only 50% of your meal expenses while on a business trip. There are two ways to calculate your meal expense deduction: You can keep track of your actual expenses or use a daily rate set by the federal government.

Deducting Actual Meal Expenses

If you use the actual expense method, you must keep track of what you spend on meals (including tips and tax) en route to and at your business destination. When you do your taxes, you add these amounts together and deduct half of the total.

> EXAMPLE: Frank drives from Santa Fe, New Mexico, to Reno, Nevada, to inspect a property for a client. On the way, he spends $200 for meals. While in Reno, he spends another $200. His total meal expense for the trip is $400. He may deduct half of this amount, or $200.

If you combine a business trip with a vacation, you may deduct only those meals you eat while on business; for example, meals you eat while attending client meetings or doing other business-related work. Meals that are part of business entertainment are subject to the rules on entertainment expenses covered in Chapter 6.

You do not necessarily have to keep all your receipts for your business meals, but you need to keep careful track of what you spend, and you should be able to prove that the meal was for business. See Chapter 6 for a detailed discussion of record keeping for meal expenses.

Using the Standard Meal Allowance

When you use the actual expense method, you must keep track of what you spend for each meal, which can be a lot of work. So the IRS provides an alternative method of deducting meals: Instead of deducting your actual expenses, you can deduct a set amount for each day of your business trip. This amount is called the standard meal allowance. It covers your expenses for business meals, beverages, tax, and tips. The amount of the allowance varies depending on where and when you travel.

The good thing about the standard meal allowance is that you don't need to keep track of how much you spend for meals and tips. You only need to keep records to prove the time, place, and business purpose of your travel. (See Chapter 6 for more on meal and entertainment expenses.)

The bad thing about the standard meal allowance is that it is based on what federal workers are allowed to charge for meals while traveling, and is therefore relatively modest. In 2012, the daily rates for domestic travel ranged from $46 per day for travel in the least expensive areas to up to $71 for high-cost areas, which includes most major cities. While it is possible to eat on $71 per day in places like New York City or San Francisco, you won't have a very good time. If you use the standard meal allowance and spend more than the allowance, you get no deduction for the overage.

Not Everyone Can Use the Standard Meal Allowance

The standard meal allowance may not be used by an employer to reimburse an employee for travel expenses if the employee:

- owns more than 10% of the stock in an incorporated real estate business, or
- is a close relative of a 10% or more owner—a brother, sister, parent, spouse, grandparent, or other lineal ancestor or descendent.

In these instances, the employee must deduct actual meal expenses for business-related travel to be reimbursed by the employer. Thus, if you've incorporated your real estate business and work as its employee, you must keep track of what you spend on meals when you travel for business and are reimbursed for your expenses by your corporation.

The standard meal allowance includes $3 per day for incidental expenses—tips you pay to porters, bellhops, maids, and transportation workers. If you wish, you can use the actual expense method for your meal costs and the $3 incidental expense rate for your tips. However, you'd have to be a pretty stingy tipper for this amount to be adequate.

The standard meal allowance is revised each year. You can find the current rates for travel within the United States at www.gsa.gov (look for the link to "Per Diem Rates") or in IRS Publication 1542. The rates for foreign travel are set by the U.S. State Department and can be found at www.state.gov. When you look at these rate listings, you'll see several categories of numbers. You want the "M & IE Rate"—short for meals and incidental expenses. Rates are also provided for lodging, but these don't apply to nongovernmental travelers.

You can claim only the standard meal allowance for business days. If you travel to more than one location in one day, use the rate in effect for the area where you spend the night. You are allowed to deduct 50% of the standard meal allowance as a business expense.

> EXAMPLE: Art travels from San Diego to San Francisco for a five-day real estate continuing education and sales conference. San Francisco is a high-cost locality, so the daily meal and incidental expense rate (M&IE) is $71. Art figures his deduction by multiplying the daily rate by five and multiplying this by 50%: 5 days × $71 = $355; $355 × 50% = $177.50.

If you use the standard meal allowance, you must use it for all of the business trips you take during the year. You can't use it for some trips and then use the actual expense method for others. For example, you can't use the standard allowance when you go to an inexpensive destination and the actual expense method when you go to a pricey one.

Because the standard meal allowance is so small, it's better to use it only if you travel exclusively to low-cost areas or if you are simply unable or unwilling to keep track of what you actually spend for meals.

Maximizing Your Business Travel Deductions

Here are some simple strategies you can use to maximize your business travel deductions.

Plan Ahead

Plan your itinerary carefully before you leave to make sure you spend over half of your time on business. This way, your trip qualifies as a deductible business trip. For example, if you know you're going to spend three days on business at your destination, arrange to spend no more than two days on personal activities.

Make a Paper Trail

If you are audited by the IRS, there is a good chance you will be questioned about business travel deductions. Of course, you'll need to have records showing what you spent for your trips. However, you'll also need documents proving that your trip was for your existing business. You can do this by:

- making a note in your calendar or daily planner of all business-related work you do; be sure to note the time you spend on each business activity
- obtaining and saving business cards from anyone you meet while on business
- noting in your calendar or daily planner the names of all the people you meet for business on your trip
- keeping the program or agenda from a convention or training seminar you attend, as well as any notes you made
- after you return, sending thank-you notes to the business contacts you met on your trips; be sure to keep copies, and
- keeping copies of business-related correspondence or emails you sent or received before the trip.

Maximize Your Business Days

You don't have to work all day for that day to count as a business day: Any day in which you work at least four hours is a business day, even if you goof off the rest of the time. The day will count as a business day for purposes of determining whether your transportation expenses are deductible, and you can deduct your lodging, meal, and other expenses during the day, even though you only worked four hours.

You can easily maximize your business days by taking advantage of this rule. For example, you can:

- spread your business over several days; if you need to be present at three meetings, try to spread them over two or three days instead of one, and
- avoid using the fastest form of transportation to your business destination—travel days count as business days, so you'll add business days to your trip if you drive instead of fly; remember,

there's no law that says you have to take the quickest means of transportation to your destination.

Take Advantage of the Sandwich Day Rule

IRS rules provide that days when you do no business-related work count as business days when they are sandwiched between workdays, as long as it was cheaper to spend that day away than to go back home for the off days. If you work on Friday and Monday, this rule allows you to count the weekend as business days, even though you did no work.

Converting a Vacation Into a Business Trip

Here are three strategies you can use to legally convert a nondeductible personal vacation into a deductible business trip:

Combine your vacation with a continuing professional education program. Travel to take continuing education courses required for your profession is deductible. Sign up for a program in a desirable location and take the family along with you.

Visit a colleague. Travel to attend meetings with professional colleagues for business purposes—not to socialize—is tax deductible. Document your visit with letters and email.

Hold a board meeting. If your business is incorporated, you can hold your annual board meeting in a desirable location and deduct your travel expenses. You must really hold a board meeting and have documentation to prove it—corporate minutes and a written agenda.

CHAPTER

6

Romancing the Client: Deducting Meal and Entertainment Expenses

Selling real estate isn't done only in an office. Some of your most important sales meetings, client contacts, and marketing efforts may take place at restaurants, golf courses, or sporting events. The tax law recognizes this and permits you to deduct part of the cost of business-related entertainment. However, because many taxpayers have abused this deduction in the past, the IRS has imposed strict rules limiting the types of entertainment expenses you can deduct and the size of the deduction.

What Is Business Entertainment?

You are only allowed to deduct half of the total amount you spend on business entertainment activities. Ordinary and necessary business activities, on the other hand, are usually fully deductible, so it's important to be able to distinguish between these two activities.

The basic rule is that entertainment involves something fun, such as:

- dining out
- going to a nightclub
- attending a sporting event
- going to a concert, a movie, or the theater
- visiting a vacation spot (a ski area or beach resort, for example), or
- taking a hunting, yachting, or fishing trip.

Although eating out might fall into other categories of business operating expenses depending on the circumstances, it is by far the number one business entertainment expense.

If It's All Business and No Fun—It's Not Entertainment

Entertainment does not include activities that are for business purposes only and don't involve any fun or amusement, such as:

- providing supper money to an employee working overtime
- paying for a hotel room used while traveling on business, or
- paying for automobile expenses incurred while conducting business.

In addition, meals or other entertainment expenses related to advertising or promotion are not considered entertainment. As a rule, an expense for a meal or other entertainment item will qualify as advertising if you make it available to the general public—for example, if you provide free food at an open house, the cost would not be considered entertainment expenses. These kinds of advertising and promotion costs are fully deductible business operating expenses. (See Chapter 13 for more about business expenses.)

Meals—It Depends on the Circumstance

A meal can be a travel expense or an entertainment expense, or both. The distinction won't affect how much you can deduct: Both travel (overnight) and entertainment expenses are only 50% deductible. But different rules apply to the two categories.

A meal is a travel expense if you eat out of necessity while away on a business trip. For example, any meal you eat alone while on the road for business is a travel expense. On the other hand, a meal is an entertainment expense if you treat a client or other business associate and the purpose of the meal is to benefit your business. A meal is both a travel and an entertainment expense if you treat a client or other business associate to a meal while on the road. However, you may only deduct this cost once—whether you choose to do it as an entertainment or a travel expense, only 50% of the cost is deductible.

Who You Can Entertain

You must be with one or more people who can benefit your business in some way to claim an entertainment expense. This could include current or potential:

- clients
- employees (see Chapter 14 for special tax rules for employees)
- independent contractors
- agents
- partners, or
- professional advisers.

This list includes almost anyone you're likely to meet for business reasons. Although you can invite family members or friends along, you can't deduct the costs of entertaining them, except in certain limited situations.

When Entertainment Expenses Are Deductible

Entertainment expenses, like all business operating expenses, are deductible only if they are ordinary and necessary. This means that the entertainment expense must be common, helpful, and appropriate for your business. Taxpayers used to have to show only that the entertainment wasn't purely for fun and that it benefited their business in some way. This standard was so easy to satisfy that the IRS imposed additional requirements for deducting these expenses.

Before the IRS made the standard tougher, you could deduct ordinary and necessary entertainment expenses even if business was never discussed. For example, you could deduct the cost of taking a client to a restaurant, even if you spent the whole time drinking martinis and talking about sports (the infamous "three-martini lunch"). This is no longer the case—now you must discuss business with one or more business associates either before, during, or after the entertainment if you want to claim an entertainment deduction (subject to one exception; see "Entertainment in Clear Business Settings," below).

CAUTION

Who's going to know? The IRS doesn't have spies lurking about in restaurants, theaters, or other places of entertainment, so it has no way of knowing whether you really discuss business with clients or other business associates. You're pretty much on the honor system here. However, be aware that if you're audited, the IRS closely scrutinizes this deduction, because many taxpayers cheat when they take it. You'll also have to comply with stringent record keeping requirements. (See Chapter 17 for more on record keeping.)

Business Discussions Before or After Entertainment

The easiest way to get a deduction for entertainment is to discuss business before or after the activity. To meet this requirement, the discussion must be "associated" with your business—that is, it must have a clear business purpose, such as developing new business or encouraging existing business relationships. You don't, however, have to expect to get a specific business benefit from the discussion. Your business discussion can involve planning, advice, or simply exchanging useful information with a business associate.

You automatically satisfy the business discussion requirement if you attend a business-related convention or meeting to further your business. Business activities—not socializing—must be the main purpose for the convention. Save a copy of the program or agenda to prove this.

Generally, the entertainment should occur on the same day as the business discussion. However, if your business guests are from out of town, the entertainment can occur the day before or the day after the business talk.

> **EXAMPLE:** Mary is moving from Chicago to New York City. She travels to New York City to meet with Kim, a real estate agent, to look at condos for sale in Manhattan. Mary arrives on Tuesday evening and Kim treats her to dinner at a nice restaurant that night. The following morning, Mary and Kim look at several listings. Kim can deduct the dinner they had the night before as an entertainment expense.

You can get a deduction even if the entertainment occurs in a place like a nightclub, theater, or loud sports arena where it's difficult or impossible to talk business. This is because your business discussions occur before or after the entertainment, so the IRS won't be scrutinizing whether or not you actually could have talked business during your entertainment activity.

> **EXAMPLE:** John, a commercial real estate broker, engages in lengthy negotiations at a client's office. Afterwards he takes the client to a baseball game to unwind. The cost of the tickets is a deductible business expense.

The entertainment can last longer than your business discussions, as long as you don't spend just a small fraction of your total time on business. Thus, it's not sufficient simply to ask an associate, "How's business?" You must have a substantial discussion. Also, your business-related discussions don't have to be face to face—they can occur over the telephone or even by email.

Business Discussions During Meals

Another way you can deduct entertainment expenses is to discuss business during a meal at a restaurant. To get the deduction, you must show all of the following:

- The main purpose of the combined business discussion and meal was the active conduct of business—you don't have to spend the entire time talking business, but the main character of the meal must be business.
- You did in fact have a business meeting, negotiation, discussion, or other bona fide business transaction with your guest or guests during the meal.
- You expect to get income or some other specific business benefit in the future from your discussions during the meal—thus, for example, a casual conversation where the subject of business comes up won't do; you have to have a specific business goal in mind.

EXAMPLE: Ivan, a real estate broker, has had ongoing email discussions with a prospective client who is interested in listing his house for sale with Ivan's brokerage firm. Ivan thinks he'll be able to close the deal and get the listing in a face-to-face meeting. He chooses a lunch meeting because it's more informal and the prospective client will like getting a free lunch. He treats the client to a $40 lunch at a nice restaurant. During the lunch, they finalize the terms of a listing agreement and shake hands on it. This meal clearly led to a specific business benefit for Ivan, so he can deduct half of the cost as an entertainment expense.

You don't necessarily have to close a sale, sign a contract, or otherwise obtain a specific business benefit to get a deduction. But you do have to have a reasonable expectation that you can get some specific business benefit through your discussions at the meal—for example, to make progress toward obtaining new business.

Business Discussions During Other Kinds of Entertainment

As a general rule, you can't get a business entertainment deduction by claiming that you discussed business during an entertainment activity other than a meal. In the IRS's view, it's usually not possible to engage in serious business discussions at entertainment venues other than restaurants because of the distractions. Examples of places the IRS would probably find not conducive to serious talk include:

- nightclubs, theaters, or sporting events
- cocktail parties or other large social gatherings
- hunting or fishing trips
- yachting or other pleasure boat outings, or
- group gatherings at a cocktail lounge, golf club, athletic club, or vacation resort that include people who are not business associates.

This means, for example, that you usually can't claim that you discussed business during a golf game. In the IRS's view, golfers are unable to play and talk business at the same time. On the other hand, you could have a business discussion before or after a golf game—for example, in the clubhouse. If you did that, your golfing would be deductible as an entertainment expense. This might seem ridiculous, but it is the rule.

Entertaining at Home

The cost of entertaining at your home is deductible if it meets either of the above two tests. However, the IRS will be more likely to believe that you discussed business during home entertainment if only a small number of people are involved—for example, if you have a quiet dinner party. A larger gathering—a cocktail party, for example—will probably only qualify as an entertainment expense if you have business discussions before or after the event. You can't, however, deduct the costs of inviting nonbusiness guests to your house. (See "Who You Can Entertain," above.)

Entertainment in Clear Business Settings

An exception to the general rule that you must discuss business before, during, or after entertainment is when the entertainment occurs in a clear business setting. For example, you have a cocktail party at your office and invite local business and civic leaders in order to get publicity for your business. Because the party is in a clear business setting—your office—you can deduct the cost as an entertainment expense even if you don't actually discuss business before, during, or after the party.

Calculating Your Deduction—The 50% Rule

Most expenses you incur for business entertainment are deductible, including meals (with beverages, tax, and tips), your transportation expenses (including parking), tickets to entertainment or sporting events, catering costs of parties, cover charges for admission to night clubs, and rent paid for a room where you hold a dinner or cocktail party.

You are allowed to deduct only 50% of your entertainment expenses. If you spend $50 for a meal in a restaurant, you can deduct $25. You must, however, keep track of everything you spend and report the entire amount on your tax return. The only exception to the 50% rule is transportation expenses, which are 100% deductible.

If you have a single bill or receipt that includes some business entertainment as well as other expenses (such as lodging or transportation), you must allocate the expense between the cost of the entertainment and the cost of the other services. For example, if your hotel bill covers meals as well as lodging, you'll have to make a reasonable estimate of the portion that covers meals. It's best to try and avoid this hassle by getting a separate bill for your deductible entertainment.

Expenses Must Be Reasonable

Your entertainment expenses must be reasonable—the IRS won't let you deduct entertainment expenses that it considers lavish or extravagant. There is no dollar limit on what is reasonable; nor are you necessarily barred from entertaining at deluxe restaurants, hotels, nightclubs, or resorts. Whether your expenses will be considered reasonable depends on the particular facts and circumstances. Because there are no concrete guidelines, you have to use common sense.

Going "Dutch"

You can only deduct entertainment expenses if you pay for the activity. If a client picks up the tab, you obviously get no deduction. If you split the expense, you must subtract what it would have normally cost you for the meal from the amount you actually paid, and then deduct 50% of that total. For example, if you pay $20 for lunch and you usually pay only $5, you can deduct 50% of $15, or $7.50.

If you go Dutch a lot and are worried that the IRS might challenge your deductions, you can save your grocery bills or receipts from eating out for a month to show what you usually spend. You don't need to keep track of which grocery items you eat for each meal. Instead, the IRS assumes that 50% of your total grocery receipts are for dinner, 30% for lunch, and 20% for breakfast.

Expenses You Can't Deduct

There are certain expenses that you are prohibited from deducting as entertainment.

Entertainment Facilities

You may not deduct the cost of buying, leasing, or maintaining an entertainment facility such as a yacht, swimming pool, tennis court, hunting camp, fishing lodge, bowling alley, car, airplane, hotel suite, apartment, or home in a vacation resort. These entertainment facilities are not considered deductible business assets.

Expenses of Nonbusiness Guests

You may not deduct the cost of entertaining people who are not business associates. If you entertain business and nonbusiness guests at an event, you must divide your entertainment expenses between the two and deduct only the business part.

EXAMPLE: You take three business associates and six friends to dinner. Because there were ten people at dinner, including you, and only four were business-related, 40% of this expense qualifies as business entertainment. If you spend $200 for the dinner, only $80 would be business-related. And because entertainment expenses are only 50% deductible, your total deduction for the event is $40.

Ordinarily, you cannot deduct the cost of entertaining your spouse or the spouse of a business associate. However, there is an exception: You can deduct these costs if you can show that you had a clear business purpose (rather than a personal or social purpose) in having the spouse or spouses join in.

EXAMPLE: You take a client visiting from out of town to dinner with his wife. The client's wife joins you because it's impractical (not to mention impolite) to have dinner with the client and not include his wife. Your spouse joins the party because the client's spouse is present. You may deduct the cost of dinner for both spouses.

Club Dues and Membership Fees

In the good old days, you could deduct dues for belonging to a country club or other club where business associates gathered. This is no longer possible. The IRS says you cannot deduct dues (including initiation fees) for membership in any club if one of the principal purposes of the club is to:

- conduct entertainment activities for members, or
- provide entertainment facilities for members to use.

Thus, you cannot deduct dues paid to country clubs, golf and athletic clubs, airline clubs, hotel clubs, or clubs operated to provide members with meals. However, you can deduct other expenses you incur to entertain a business associate at a club.

EXAMPLE: Jack, a real estate broker, is a member of the Golden Bear Golf Club in Columbus, Ohio. His annual membership dues are $10,000. One night Jack invites a competitor to dinner at the club's dining room, where they discuss Jack buying him out. Jack pays

$100 for the dinner. Jack's $10,000 annual dues are not deductible, but his costs for the dinner are.

You can deduct dues to join business-related tax-exempt organizations or civic organizations as long as the organization's primary purpose isn't to provide entertainment. Examples include organizations like real estate boards, Kiwanis or Rotary Club, business leagues, chambers of commerce, trade associations, and professional associations such as the National Association of Realtors.

Entertainment Tickets

You can deduct only the face value of an entertainment ticket, even if you paid a higher price for it. For example, you cannot deduct service fees that you pay to ticket agencies or brokers or any amount over the face value of tickets that you buy from scalpers. However, you can deduct the entire amount you pay for a ticket if it's for an amateur sporting event run by volunteers to benefit a charity.

Ordinarily, you or an employee must be present at an entertainment activity to claim it as a business entertainment expense. This is not the case, however, with entertainment tickets. You can give tickets to clients or other business associates rather than attending the event yourself and still get a deduction. If you don't go to the event, you have the option of treating the tickets as a gift. You can get a bigger deduction this way sometimes. Gifts of up to $25 are 100% deductible, so with tickets that cost less than $50, you get a bigger deduction if you treat them as a gift. If they cost more, treat them as an entertainment expense.

EXAMPLE: You pay $40 to a scalper for a college basketball game ticket that has a face value of only $30. You give the ticket to a client but don't attend the game yourself. By treating the ticket as a gift, you may deduct $25 of the expense. If you treated it as an entertainment expense, your deduction would be limited to 50% of $30, or $15. However, if you paid $100 for a ticket with a $60 face value, you would be better off treating it as an entertainment expense. This way you would be able to deduct 50% of $60, or $30.

If you treated the ticket as a gift, your deduction would be limited to $25.

You may also deduct the cost of season tickets at a sports arena or theater. But, if you rent a skybox or other private luxury box, your deduction is limited to the cost of a regular nonluxury box seat. The cost of season tickets must be allocated to each separate event.

Meals for Employees

Ordinarily, meal and entertainment expenses for your employees are only 50% deductible, just like your own meal and entertainment expenses. However, you or your business may take a 100% deduction for employee meals:

- provided as part of a company recreational or social activity—for example, a dinner at a restaurant for your employees
- provided on business premises for your convenience—for example, you provide lunch because your employees must remain in the office to be available to work, or
- if the cost is included as part of the employee's compensation and reported as such on the employee's W-2.

Reporting Entertainment Expenses on Your Tax Return

How you report your entertainment expenses on your tax return depends on how your real estate business is organized and how you pay for the entertainment.

Sole Proprietors

If you're a sole proprietor, you must list your entertainment expenses on Schedule C, *Profit or Loss From Business*. The schedule contains a line just for this deduction. You list the total amount and then subtract from it the portion that is not deductible: 50%.

Partnerships, LLCs, and LLPs

If you've formed a partnership or LLC, entertainment expenses can be paid from your business's bank account or by using a business credit card, or they can be paid by you from your personal funds or by using your personal credit card.

Expenses paid with partnership or LLC funds are listed on the information return the entity files with the IRS. Your share of these and all other deductions for your entity pass through and are deducted on your individual tax return on Schedule E.

If you pay for entertainment expenses from your personal funds or credit card and you are reimbursed by your business entity, the expense is handled as if the entity paid it. You do not include the amount of the reimbursement in your income for the year.

If you personally pay for entertainment expenses and are not reimbursed by your business entity, you may directly deduct the expenses on your personal tax return by listing them on Schedule E. They are not included in your business entity's information return.

Corporations

If you've formed a C corporation and the corporation pays for your entertainment expenses, the corporation deducts the expenses on its own tax return. If you've formed an S corporation that pays your expenses, the tax reporting is the same as for a partnership or LLC.

Things are more complicated if you personally pay for entertainment expenses, because usually you will be your corporation's employee and special rules apply to expenses paid by employees. (See Chapter 14.)

Listing Meal and Entertainment Expenses on Tax Returns

Unlike Schedule C filed by sole proprietors, tax returns filed by partnerships, LLCs, and corporations do not contain a specific line to report the amount of deductible entertainment expenses. Instead, you list them as "meals and entertainment" on a separate "Other Expenses" schedule.

Be careful never to lump together expenses for meals and entertainment with other expenses, such as those for business travel, lodging, or continuing education. Some taxpayers put all these expenses into a single expense category called "travel and entertainment." This is a mistake because, while meal and entertainment expenses are only 50% deductible, expenses for business travel, lodging, and continuing education are 100% deductible. Both your financial statements and tax returns should use separate expense categories for "travel and lodging," "continuing education," "employee benefits," and "meals and entertainment."

CHAPTER

7

Deducting Your Home Office

Almost any real estate agent or broker can qualify for the home office deduction. This is true even if you work out of an outside sales office or spend most of your time on the road and at the properties you're trying to sell. However, if you plan on taking the deduction, you need to learn how to do it properly. There are strict requirements you must follow to claim the deduction, and some of it will be depend in part on what type of business entity you have.

Qualifying for the Home Office Deduction

To take the home office deduction, you must have a home office—that is, an office or other workplace in your home that you use regularly and exclusively for business. Your home may be a house, apartment, condominium, mobile home, or even a boat. You can also take the deduction for separate structures on your property that you use for your real estate business, such as an unattached studio. If you qualify, you can deduct your expenses for your home office.

EXAMPLE: Rich is an independent contractor real estate agent who works out of a real estate brokerage office in a downtown office building. However, he also regularly performs real estate-related work in the basement of his San Francisco rental home, which he has converted into a home office. If he meets the requirements discussed below, he can deduct his home office expenses, including a portion of his rent, from his real estate income. This saves him over $2,000 per year on his income and self-employment taxes.

TIP

It's easier now to claim the home office deduction. If you've heard stories about how difficult it is to qualify for the home office deduction, you can breathe more easily. Changes in the tax law that took effect in 1999 make it much easier for businesspeople to qualify for the deduction. So even if you haven't qualified for the deduction in the past, you may be entitled to take it now.

Threshold Requirements: Regular and Exclusive Business Use

There are two threshold requirements that everyone must meet to qualify for the home office deduction. You must:

- use your home office exclusively for business, and
- use your home office for your business on a regular basis.

If you get past this first hurdle, then you must also meet any one of the following requirements:

- your home office is your principal place of business
- you regularly and exclusively use your home office for administrative or management activities for your real estate business and have no other fixed location where you regularly perform such activities
- you meet clients at home, or
- you use a separate structure on your property exclusively for business purposes.

These rules apply whether you are a sole proprietor, partner in a partnership, limited liability company (LLC) owner, or if you have formed a C or S corporation. However, if you are an employee of a corporation that you own and operate, or have formed a multimember LLC, or partnership, there are some additional requirements (see "How to Deduct Home Office Expenses," below).

Exclusive Business Use

You can't take the home office deduction unless you use part of your home exclusively for your real estate business. In other words, you must use your home office only for your business. The more space you devote exclusively to your business, the more your home office deduction will be worth.

If you use part of your home—such as a room or garage—as your business office, but you also use that same space for personal purposes, you won't qualify for the home office deduction.

> **EXAMPLE 1:** Johnny, a real estate agent, has a den at home furnished with a desk, chair, bookshelf, filing cabinet, and a bed for visiting guests. He uses the desk and chair for both business and personal reasons. The bookshelf contains both personal and business books, the filing cabinet contains both personal and business files, and the bed is used only for personal reasons. Johnny can't claim a home office deduction for the den because he does not use it, or any part of it, exclusively for business purposes.

> **EXAMPLE 2:** Paula, a real estate agent, keeps her desk, chair, bookshelf, computer, and filing cabinet in one part of her den and uses them exclusively for her business. The remainder of the room—one-third of the space—is used to store a bed for houseguests. Paula can take a home office deduction for the two-thirds of the room that she uses exclusively as an office.

If you use the same room (or rooms) for your office and for other purposes, you'll have to arrange your furniture and belongings so that a portion of the room is devoted exclusively to your business. Place only your business furniture and other business items in the office portion of the room. Business furniture includes anything that you use for your business, such as standard office furniture like a desk and chair.

The IRS does not require you to physically separate the space you use for business from the rest of the room. However, doing so will help you satisfy the exclusive use test. For example, if you use part of your living room as an office, you could separate it from the rest of the room with folding screens or bookcases.

Although you must use your home office exclusively for business, you and other family members or visitors may walk through it to get to other rooms in your residence.

As a practical matter, the IRS doesn't have spies checking to see whether you're using your home office just for business. However, complying with the rules from the beginning means you won't have to worry if you are audited.

When the IRS Can Enter Your Home

IRS auditors may not enter your home unless you or another lawful occupant gives them permission. The only exception is if the IRS obtains a court order to enter your home, which is very rare. In the absence of such court order, an IRS auditor must ask permission to come to your home to verify your home office deduction. You don't have to grant permission for the visit—but if you don't, the auditor will probably disallow your deduction.

Regular Business Use

It's not enough to use a part of your home exclusively for business; you must also use it regularly. For example, you can't place a desk in a corner of a room and claim the home office deduction if you almost never use the desk for your real estate business.

Unfortunately, the IRS doesn't offer a clear definition of regular use. The agency has stated only that you must use a portion of your home for business on a continuing basis—not just for occasional or incidental business. One court has held that 12 hours of use a week is sufficient. (*Green v. Comm'r*, 79 T.C. 428 (1982).) You might be able to qualify with less use—for example, an hour a day—but no one knows for sure. It's a good idea to keep track of how much you use your home office. Your record doesn't have to be fancy—notes in an appointment book are sufficient.

One of Four Additional Requirements

Using a home office exclusively and regularly for business is not enough to qualify for the home office deduction: You also must satisfy any one of the additional four requirements described below. Moreover, if your real estate business is a corporation, you must meet the convenience-of-the-employer test covered in "Special Requirements for Employees," below.

Principal Place of Business

One way to satisfy the additional home office deduction requirement is to show that you use your home as your principal place of business. Your principal place of business is the place where you generate most of your income. If you work in more than one location, it is where you perform your most important business activities—those activities that most directly generate your income. For most real estate agents, the place where they generate most of their income is not their home office. Instead, it is their real estate brokerage office or at the houses or other properties they are trying to sell.

However, a broker or agent who does not have access to an outside office—such as a desk at a brokerage firm's office—can still satisfy this requirement, especially if he or she regularly meets with clients in the home office and conducts many sales efforts from there. But this is not the normal way agents and brokers qualify for the home office deduction.

Administrative Work

The vast majority of real estate agents and brokers qualify for the home office deduction by using it to perform administrative work. Under the rules, a home office qualifies for the home office deduction if:

- you use the office regularly and exclusively to perform administrative and/or management activities for your business, and
- there is no other fixed location where you conduct substantial administrative or management activities.

Administrative and management activities include, but are not limited to:

- keeping books and records
- setting up appointments
- paying bills
- maintaining client databases or contact lists,
- reviewing real estate publications, or
- engaging in real estate continuing education activities.

This means that you can qualify for the home office deduction even through your home office is not where you generate most of your income. It's sufficient that you regularly use it for the administrative and management activities you regularly perform for your real estate business. As long as you have no other fixed location where you regularly do these activities—for example, a desk you use at your brokerage office—you'll get the deduction.

You don't have to personally perform at home all the administrative or management activities your business requires to qualify for the home office deduction. Your home office can qualify for the deduction even if:

- you have others conduct your administrative or management activities at locations other than your home—for example, another company does your bookkeeping from its place of business
- you conduct administrative or management activities at places that are not fixed locations for your business, such as your car, or
- you occasionally conduct minimal administrative or management activities at a fixed location outside your home, such as an outside office provided by a brokerage firm.

Moreover, you can qualify for the deduction even if you could conduct administrative or management activities at an outside office but choose to use your home office for those activities instead.

EXAMPLE: Sally is an independent contractor real estate agent. She is affiliated with a national brokerage firm which provides her with a desk at its local office. She uses the desk primarily to meet with clients and to make and answer phone calls. Sally also has a home office she regularly uses to perform most of the administrative and management tasks for her real estate business, including bookkeeping, ordering supplies, setting up appointments, maintaining client databases, and engaging in continuing education. Sally also performs some of these tasks, such as making appointments, while in her car on the way to or from the properties she sells. She rarely uses the desk provided by her brokerage firm for these tasks, although she could if she wanted to. Sally's home office qualifies for purposes of the home office deduction. She conducts administrative or management activities for her business as a real estate agent there and has no other fixed location where she conducts substantial administrative or management activities for this business. The fact that she occasionally performs some administrative tasks in her car does not disqualify her for the deduction because it is not a fixed location for her real estate business. Likewise, she doesn't lose the deduction because she could perform these activities from the office provided by her brokerage firm, but she chooses not to do so.

Meeting Clients at Home

There is yet another way real estate agents and brokers can qualify for the home office deduction: by using a part of your home exclusively to meet with clients. You must physically meet with clients in this home location; phoning or emailing them from there is not sufficient. And the meetings must be a regular and integral part of your real estate business; occasional meetings don't qualify.

It's not entirely clear how often you must meet clients at home for those meetings to be considered regular. However, the IRS has indicated that meeting clients one or two days a week is sufficient. Exclusive use means you use the space where you meet clients only for business. You are free to use the space for business purposes other than meeting clients—for example, doing your business bookkeeping or other paperwork. But you cannot use the space for personal purposes, such as watching television.

EXAMPLE: June, a real estate broker with her own firm, works three days a week from her firm's office in the city and two days in her home office, which she uses only for business. Her home office does not qualify as her principal place of business under either of the tests discussed above—she does not generate most of her income from home, and she does not use her home office to perform most of the administrative and management tasks for her practice. However, she meets clients at her home office at least once a week. Because she regularly meets clients at her home office, she qualifies for the home office deduction even though her city office is her principal place of business.

Using a Separate Structure

You can also deduct expenses for a separate freestanding structure, such as a studio, garage, or barn, if you use it exclusively and regularly for your real estate business. The structure does not have to be your principal place of business or a place where you meet clients.

Exclusive use means that you use the structure only for business—for example, you can't use it to store gardening equipment or as a guesthouse. Regular use is not precisely defined, but it's probably sufficient to use the structure ten or 15 hours a week.

> EXAMPLE: Deborah is a real estate broker who spends 40 hours per week working at her outside brokerage office. This office is her principal place of business, and she does not meet with clients at home or perform most of her administrative and management work from home. Nevertheless, Deborah qualifies for the home office deduction: She has a pool house in her back yard that she has converted into a home office that she uses ten to 15 hours per week on her real estate business. Because she uses the separate pool house structure regularly and exclusively for her real estate business, she gets the home office deduction.

Special Requirement for Employees

If you have formed a corporation to own and operate your real estate business, you're probably working as its employee. (See Chapter 2.) To qualify for the home office deduction as an employee, you must satisfy all the requirements discussed above. In addition, you must be able to show that you maintain your home office for the convenience of your employer—that is, your corporation. An employee's home office is deemed to be for an employer's convenience if it is:

- a condition of employment
- necessary for the employer's business to properly function, or
- needed to allow the employee to properly perform his or her duties.

The convenience-of-employer test is not met if using a home office is for your convenience or because you can get more work done at home.

For example, you won't pass the test if you have an outside office but like to take work home with you.

When you own the business that employs you, you ordinarily won't be able to successfully claim that a home office is a condition of your employment—after all, as the owner of the business, you're the person who sets the conditions for employees, including yourself. Thus, you'll have to satisfy either the necessity or performance tests.

If there is no other office where you do your work, you should be able to successfully claim that your home office is necessary for your business to properly function and/or for you to perform your employee duties.

It will be more difficult to establish necessity if you have an outside office. Nevertheless, business owners in this situation have successfully argued that their home offices were necessary—for example, because their corporate offices were not open or not usable during evenings, weekends, or other nonbusiness hours, or were too far from home to use during off-hours.

Calculating the Home Office Deduction

This is the fun part—figuring out how much the home office deduction will save you in taxes.

How Much of Your Home Is Used for Business?

To calculate your home office deduction, you need to determine what percentage of your home you use for business. The law says you can use any reasonable method to do this. Obviously, you want to use the method that will give you the largest home office deduction. To do this, you want to maximize the percentage of your home that you claim as your office. There is no single way to do this for every home office. Try both methods described below and use the one that gives you the largest deduction.

Some tax experts advise not to claim more than 20% to 25% of your home as an office, unless you store inventory at home. However, home business owners have successfully claimed much more. In one case, for example, an interior decorator claimed 74% of his apartment (850 of

1,150 square feet) as a home office. He was audited, but the IRS did not object to the amount of space he claimed for his office. (*Visin v. Comm'r*, T.C. Memo 2003-246.) In another case, a professional violinist successfully claimed a home office deduction for her entire living room, which took up 40% of her one-bedroom apartment. She used the room solely for violin practice. (*Popov v. Comm'r*, 246 F.3d 1190 (9th Cir. 2002).) It is probably true, though, that the larger your home office deduction, the greater your chances of being audited.

Square-Footage Method

The most precise method of measuring your office space is to divide the square footage of your home office by the total square footage of your home. For example, if your home is 1,600 square feet and you use 400 square feet for your home office, 25% of the total area is used for business. You are allowed to subtract the square footage of common areas such as hallways, entries, stairs, and landings from the total area that you are measuring. You can also exclude attics and garages from your total space if you don't use them for business purposes. You aren't required to measure this way, but doing so will give you a larger deduction because your overall percentage of business use will be higher.

Room Method

Another way to measure is the room method. You can use this method only if all of the rooms in your home are about the same size. Using this method, you divide the number of rooms used for business by the total number of rooms in the home. Don't include bathrooms, closets, or other storage areas. You may also leave out garages and attics if you don't use them for business. For example, if you use one room in a five-room house for business, your office takes up 20% of your home.

TIP

The room method often yields a larger deduction. Even though IRS Form 8829, *Expenses for Business Use of Your Home,* (the form sole proprietors file to claim the home office deduction), seems to require you to use the square-footage method, this isn't the case. As long as all of the rooms in your home are about the same size, you can use the room method. Using the room method will often result in a larger deduction.

What Expenses Can You Deduct?

The home office deduction is not one deduction, but many. Most costs associated with maintaining and running your home office are deductible. However, because your office is in your home, some of the money you spend also benefits you personally. For example, your utility bill pays to heat your home office, but it also keeps the rest of your living space warm. The IRS deals with this issue by dividing home office expenses into two categories: direct expenses, which benefit only your home office; and indirect expenses, which benefit both your office and the rest of your home.

Direct Expenses

You have a direct home office expense when you pay for something just for the home office portion of your home. This includes, for example, the cost of painting your home office, carpeting it, or paying someone to clean it. The entire amount of a direct home office expense is deductible.

> EXAMPLE: Jean pays a housepainter $400 to paint her home office. She may deduct this entire amount as a home office deduction.

Virtually anything you buy for your office that becomes obsolete, wears out, or gets used up is deductible. However, you may have to depreciate permanent improvements to your home over 27.5 years, rather than deduct them in the year when you pay for them. Permanent improvements are changes that go beyond simple repairs, such as adding a new room to your home to serve as your office. (See Chapter 9.)

Indirect Expenses

An indirect expense is a payment for something that benefits your entire home, including both the home office portion and your personal space. You may deduct only a portion of this expense—the home office percentage of the total.

You Can Deduct Business Expenses Even If You Don't Qualify for the Home Office Deduction

Many real estate agents believe that they can't deduct any expenses they incur while working at home unless they qualify for the home office deduction. This is a myth that has cost many agents valuable deductions. Even if you don't qualify for, or take the home office deduction, you can still take tax deductions for expenses you incur while doing business at home. These are expenses that arise from the fact that you are doing business, not from the use of the home itself.

Telephone expenses. You can't deduct the basic cost of a single telephone line into your home, but you can deduct the cost of long-distance business calls and special phone services that you use for your business (such as call waiting or message center). You can also deduct the entire cost of a second phone line that you use just for business, including a cell phone.

Business equipment and furniture. The cost of office furniture, copiers, fax machines, and other personal property you use for your business and keep at home is deductible, whether or not you qualify for the home office deduction. If you purchase these items specifically for your real estate business, you can expense them (deduct them in one year) under Section 179 or depreciate them over several years. If you convert personal property you already own to business use, you may depreciate the fair market value. If you're a sole proprietor, you deduct these costs directly on Schedule C, *Profit or Loss From Business*. You don't have to list them on the special tax form used for the home office deduction. If you use the property for both business and personal reasons, the IRS requires you to keep records showing when the item was used for business or personal reasons—for example, a diary or log with the dates, times, and reasons the item was used.

Supplies. Supplies for your business are currently deductible as an operating expense if they have a useful life of less than one year. Otherwise, you must depreciate them or expense them under Section 179.

> **EXAMPLE:** Instead of just painting her home office, Jean decides to paint her entire home for $1,600. She uses 25% of her home as an office, so she may deduct 25% of the cost, or $400.

Most of your home office expenses will be indirect expenses, including:

Rent. If you rent your home or apartment, you can use the home office deduction to deduct part of your rent—a substantial expense that is ordinarily not deductible. Your tax savings will be particularly great if you live in a high-rent area.

> **EXAMPLE:** Sam uses 20% of his one-bedroom Manhattan apartment as a home office for his real estate business. He pays $2,000 per month in rent, and may therefore deduct $400 of his rent per month ($4,800 per year) as a home office expense. This saves him over $2,000 in federal, state, and self-employment taxes.

Mortgage interest and property taxes. Whether or not you have a home office, you can deduct your monthly mortgage interest and property tax payments as a personal itemized income tax deduction on your Schedule A (the tax form where you list your personal income tax deductions). But if you have a home office, you have the option of deducting the home office percentage of your mortgage interest and property tax payments as part of your home office deduction. If you do this, you may not deduct this amount on your Schedule A (you can't deduct the same item twice). The advantage of deducting the home office percentage of your monthly mortgage interest and real estate tax payments as part of your home office deduction is that it is a business deduction, not a personal deduction; as such, it reduces the amount of your business income subject to self-employment taxes, as well as reducing your income taxes. The self-employment tax is 15.3%, so you save $153 in self-employment taxes for every $1,000 in mortgage interest and property taxes you deduct as part of your home office deduction.

> **EXAMPLE:** Suzy, a real estate broker, uses 20% of her three-bedroom Tulsa home as a home office. She pays $10,000 per year in mortgage interest and property taxes. When she does her taxes for the year, she may deduct $2,000 of her interest and taxes as part of her home office deduction (20% × $10,000). She adds this amount

to her other home office expenses and decreases her business income for both income tax and self-employment tax purposes. The extra $2,000 business deduction saves her $306 in self-employment tax (15.3% × $2,000). She may deduct the remaining $8,000 of mortgage interest and property tax as a personal deduction on her Schedule A.

Depreciation. If you own your home, you're also entitled to a depreciation deduction for the office portion of your home. See Chapter 9 for a detailed discussion of depreciation.

Utilities. You may deduct your home office percentage of your utility bills for your entire home. These include electricity, gas, water, heating oil, and trash removal. If you use a disproportionately large amount of electricity for your home office, you may be able to deduct more.

Insurance. Both homeowner's and renter's insurance are partly deductible as indirect home office expenses. However, special insurance coverage you buy just for your home office—for example, insurance for your computer or other business equipment—is fully deductible as a direct expense.

Home maintenance. You can deduct the home office percentage of home maintenance expenses that benefit your entire home, such as housecleaning of your entire house, roof and furnace repairs, and exterior painting. These costs are deductible whether you hire someone or do them yourself. If you do the work yourself, however, you can deduct only the cost of materials, not the cost of your own labor. Termite inspection, pest extermination fees, and snow removal costs are also deductible. However, the IRS won't let you deduct lawn care unless you regularly use your home to meet clients or customers. Home maintenance costs that don't benefit your home office—for example, painting your kitchen—are not deductible at all.

Casualty losses. Casualty losses are damage to your home caused by such events as fire, floods, or theft. Casualty losses that affect your entire house—for example, a leak that floods your entire home—are deductible in the amount of your home office percentage. Casualty losses that affect only your home office—for example, a leak that floods only the home office area of the house—are fully deductible direct expenses. Casualty losses that don't affect your home office—for example, if only your kitchen floods—are not deductible as business expenses. However, they may be deductible as itemized personal deductions.

Condominium association fees. These fees (often substantial) are partly deductible as an indirect expense if you have a home office.

Security system costs. Security system costs are partly deductible as an indirect expense if your security system protects your entire home. If you have a security system that protects only your home office, the cost is a fully deductible direct expense.

Computer equipment. Computers and peripheral equipment (such as printers) are deductible whether or not you qualify for the home office deduction. However, if you don't qualify for the home office deduction, you must prove that you use your computer more than half of the time for business by keeping a log of your usage. If you qualify for the home office deduction, you don't need to keep track of how much time you spend using your computer for business.

Supplies and materials. Office supplies and materials you use for your home business are not part of the home office deduction. They are deductible whether or not you qualify for the home office deduction.

Profit Limit on Deductions

You cannot deduct more than the net profit you earn from your home office. If you run a successful business out of your home office, this won't pose a problem. But if your business earns very little or loses money, the limitation could prevent you from deducting part or even all of your home office expenses in the current year. If your deductions exceed your profits, you can deduct the excess in the following year and in each succeeding year until you deduct the entire amount. There is no limit on how far into the future you can deduct these expenses; you can claim them, even if you no longer live in the home where they were incurred. So, whether or not your real estate business is making money, you should keep track of your home office expenses and claim the deduction on your tax return.

> EXAMPLE: Gilbert works full time for a large accounting firm, but he starts to work part time as a real estate agent. He sets aside a portion of his home as an office he uses exclusively for administrative and management tasks for his real estate business.

Like many beginning agents (particularly those who work part time), he earns no commissions during his first year. His home office expenses for the year total $6,000. Although he has a legitimate home office, Gilbert is not entitled to a home office deduction this year because he earned no money from his real estate business. However, he can start deducting these expenses if he earns a profit the following year, or any other succeeding year.

The profit limitation applies only to the home office deduction. It does not apply to business expenses that you can deduct under other provisions of the tax code.

If you're a sole proprietor, your profit (for these purposes) is the gross income you earn from your real estate business minus your business deductions other than your home office deduction. You must also subtract the home office portion of your mortgage interest, real estate taxes, and casualty losses.

If your business is organized as a partnership, LLC, or corporation, the income limit still applies to your home office deduction. Your income when computing your allowable deduction is based on the gross income from your business allocable to your home office, minus all other deductions of the LLC, partnership, or corporation. IRS Publication 587, *Business Use of Your Home*, contains a worksheet you can use to figure this amount.

Special Concerns for Homeowners

Until relatively recently, homeowners who took the home office deduction were subject to a special tax trap: If they took a home office deduction for more than three of the five years before they sold their house, they had to pay capital gains taxes on the profit from the home office portion of their home. For example, if you made a $50,000 profit on the sale of your house, and your home office took up 20% of the space, you would have had to pay a tax on $10,000 of your profit (20% × $50,000 = $10,000).

Fortunately, IRS rules no longer require this. As long as you live in your home for at least two out of the five years before you sell it, the profit you make on the sale—up to $250,000 for single taxpayers and

$500,000 for married taxpayers filing jointly—is not taxable. (See IRS Publication 523, *Selling Your Home.*)

However, you will have to pay a capital gains tax on the depreciation deductions you took after May 6, 1997 for your home office. This is the deduction you are allowed for the yearly decline in value due to wear and tear of the portion of the building that contains your home office. (See Chapter 9 for more information on depreciation deductions.) These "recaptured" deductions are taxed at a 25% rate (unless your income tax bracket is lower than 25%).

> EXAMPLE: Sally bought a $200,000 home in the year 2007 and used one of her bedrooms as her home office. She sold her home in 2011 for $300,000, realizing a $100,000 gain (profit). Her depreciation deductions for her home office from 2007 through 2011 totaled $2,000. She must pay a tax of 25% of $2,000, or $500.

Having to pay a 25% tax on the depreciation deductions you took in the years before you sold your house is actually not a bad deal. This is probably no more—and is often less—tax than you would have had to pay if you didn't take the deductions in the first place and instead paid tax on your additional taxable income at ordinary income tax rates.

How to Deduct Home Office Expenses

How you deduct home office expenses depends on how you've legally organized your practice.

Sole Proprietors

If you are a sole proprietor or have a one-owner LLC taxed as a sole proprietorship (as most are), you deduct your business operating expenses by listing them on IRS Schedule C, *Profit or Loss From Business*. You also list your home office deduction on Schedule C. But, unlike any other operating expense deduction, you must file a special tax form to show how you calculated the home office deduction. This form, Form 8829, *Expenses for Business Use of Your Home*, tells the IRS that you're taking the deduction and shows how you calculated it. You should file this form even if you can't currently deduct your home office expenses because your business has no profits. By filing, you can apply the deduction to a future year in which you earn a profit. For detailed guidance on how to fill out Form 8829, see IRS Publication 587, *Business Use of Your Home.*

LLCs and Partnerships

If your real estate business is organized as a multimember LLC or partnership and receives partnership tax treatment, there are two ways you can claim a home office deduction:

- you can deduct your home office expenses on your personal tax return, or
- the LLC or partnership can reimburse you for your expenses and list them on its tax return (and the deduction is then passed through to, and shared by, all the business owners).

Personal Deduction

The preferred way for most LLC members or partners in partnerships to deduct home office expenses is to claim them on their personal tax returns. In order to do this, however, you must be able to show that:

- you satisfy all the requirements for the home office deduction covered in "Qualifying for the Home Office Deduction," above, and
- your partnership agreement or LLC operating agreement provides that the expense will not be reimbursed by the entity, or there must be an established routine practice of not reimbursing the expense.

If there is no written statement or practice prohibiting reimbursement for home office expenses, the IRS will assume that you have the right to be reimbursed for them by the entity. This means you get no personal deduction. Instead, you will have to seek reimbursement of the expenses from the partnership or LLC.

If you meet the requirements for claiming the deduction, you can deduct your home office expenses on Part II of IRS Schedule E. They are not miscellaneous itemized deductions (and, therefore, are not subject to a 2% of AGI reduction). You don't have to file Form 8829.

Reimbursement

Instead of taking a personal deduction, an LLC member or partner in a partnership can seek reimbursement for home office expenses from the business entity. In this event, the member or partner gets no separate deduction for the expenses on his or her personal return. The LLC or partnership lists the expenses on its return (IRS Form 1065, *U.S. Partnership Return of Income*), combines these expenses with all its other deductible expenses, and then subtracts all its expenses from its income to determine if the practice had a profit or loss for the year. The business's profits or losses then pass through the entity to the owners' individual tax returns. The owners pay individual tax on any profits. Thus, all reimbursed expenses are shared by all the LLC members or partners in a partnership.

To obtain reimbursement, you must:

- meet all the requirements for the home office deduction covered in "Qualifying for the Home Office Deduction," above
- document your expenses with receipts and other necessary records, and
- be reimbursed under an accountable plan, an agreement in which the LLC or partnership promises to reimburse you only if you provide proper timely substantiation for your expenses. (See Chapter 17 for more on accountable plans.)

If reimbursement is not made under an accountable plan, the money the LLC member or partner receives is treated as a distribution from the LLC, LLP, or partnership and is subject to both income and self-employment taxes.

Corporations

If you have formed a corporation to own and operate your practice and work as its employee, there are two ways you can claim a home office deduction: You can take a personal deduction, or your corporation can reimburse you and take the deduction.

Reimbursement

Your corporation can reimburse you directly for your home office expenses and then deduct this amount as an ordinary business expense on its tax return (Form 1120 or 1120S). You get no personal deduction, but you don't need one because your corporation has paid you directly for your home office expenses. Because of the limitations on employees' using the home office personal deduction (see below), this is often the best choice.

To do this, you must meet all the requirements for a home office deduction described in "Qualifying for the Home Office Deduction," above. Any reimbursement you receive will not be taxable to you personally if:

- you keep careful track of your home office expenses and can prove them with receipts or other records, and
- you have an accountable plan, an agreement in which the corporation promises to reimburse you only if you provide proper timely substantiation for your expenses. (See Chapter 17 for more on accountable plans.)

If you qualify for the deduction but fail to comply with the accountable plan rules, your reimbursement will be treated by the IRS as additional employee compensation and will be subject to income and employment taxes. In this event, you can deduct your home office expenses, but only as a miscellaneous itemized deduction as described below.

Personal Deduction

Corporate employees, including real estate professionals, who qualify for the home office deduction may deduct their home office expenses on their personal tax returns as an employee business expense. However, this is not a good choice because employees must take the home office deduction as a miscellaneous itemized personal deduction on Schedule A of their personal tax returns. This means you may deduct home office expenses only if you itemize your deductions and only to the extent that your home office expenses, along with your other unreimbursed employee business expenses and other miscellaneous itemized deductions (if any), exceed 2% of your adjusted gross income (AGI).

If your corporation reimburses you for some, but not all, of your home office expenses, you must file Form 2106, *Employee Business Expenses*, to deduct the unreimbursed amount.

Audit-Proofing Your Home Office Deduction

Some people believe that taking the home office deduction invites an IRS audit. The IRS denies this. But even if taking the deduction increases your audit chances, the risk of an audit is still low. Moreover, you have nothing to fear from an audit if you're entitled to take the deduction and you keep good records to prove it.

If you are audited by the IRS and your home office deduction is questioned, you want to be able to prove that you:

- qualify for the deduction, and
- have correctly reported the amount of your home office expenses.

If you can do both those things, you should be home free.

Prove That You Are Following the Rules

Here are some ways to convince the IRS that you qualify for the home office deduction:

- Take a picture of your home office and draw up a diagram showing your home office as a portion of your home. Do not send the photo or diagram to the IRS. Just keep it in your files in case you're audited. The picture should have a date on it—this can be done with a digital camera, or you can have your film date-stamped by a developer.
- Have all of your business mail sent to your home office.
- Use your home office address on all of your business cards, stationery, and advertising.
- Obtain a separate phone line for your business and keep that phone in your home office.
- Encourage clients to regularly visit your home office, and keep a log of their visits.
- To make the most of the time you spend in your home office, communicate with clients by phone, fax, or electronic mail instead

of going to their offices. Use a mail or messenger service to deliver your work to customers.

- Keep a log of the time you spend working in your home office. This doesn't have to be fancy; notes on your calendar will do.

Keep Good Expense Records

Be sure to keep copies of your bills and receipts for home office expenses, including:

- IRS Form 1098, *Mortgage Interest Statement* (sent by whoever holds your mortgage), showing the interest you paid on your mortgage for the year
- property tax bills and your canceled checks as proof of payment
- utility bills, insurance bills, and receipts for payments for repairs to your office area, along with your canceled checks paying for these items, and
- a copy of your lease and your canceled rent checks, if you're a renter.

CHAPTER

8

Deducting Your Sales Office

This chapter is for real estate brokers who have an outside sales office. Although some brokers work from a home office, those who have agents (salespeople) working with them usually have an outside sales office. Some brokers rent their outside office, while others own their office space. Either way, an outside office presents many opportunities for tax deductions.

Real estate agents, who work under a broker's supervision, typically have their office space provided by the broker. They are often required to pay a fee for use of the broker's sales office, which is deductible as an operating expense. (See Chapter 13.) However, agents ordinarily do not have their own offices, and therefore don't have the expenses and deductions covered in this chapter.

If You Rent Your Office

Virtually all the expenses you incur for an outside office that you rent for your real estate business are deductible, including:

- rent
- utilities
- insurance
- repairs
- improvements
- real estate broker fees and commissions to obtain the lease
- fees for option rights, such as an option to renew the lease
- burglar alarm expenses
- trash and waste removal
- security expenses
- parking expenses
- maintenance and janitorial expenses
- lease cancellation fees, and
- attorneys' fees to draft a lease.

If you sign a net lease, you'll have to pay part (or all) of the landlord's maintenance expenses, property taxes, insurance, and maybe even mortgage payments. These payments are treated the same as rent.

A rental deposit is not deductible in the year it is made if it is to be returned at the end of the lease. However, if the landlord applies the deposit to pay rent you owe, make repairs, or because you've breached the lease, you may deduct the amount in that year.

None of the rules applicable to the home office deduction covered in Chapter 7 apply to outside offices. Thus, unlike the home office deduction, there is no profit limit on deductions for outside rental expenses—you get your entire deduction even if it exceeds the profits from your business. You report rental expenses for an outside office just like any other business expense. You don't have to file IRS Form 8829, which is required when sole proprietors take the home office deduction.

Timing of Deductions

Because you will ordinarily be in your office for more than one year, some of the expenses you pay may benefit your business for more than a single tax year. In this event, you may have to deduct the expense over more than one year instead of currently deducting it all in a single year. (This discussion assumes that you, like most real estate professionals, are a cash basis taxpayer and use the calendar year as your tax year.)

Current Versus Multiyear Deductions

You may currently deduct any expense you pay for the use of your office during the current tax year.

> EXAMPLE: Leona pays $800 rent each month for the office she uses for her brokerage business. In one year, she paid a total of $9,600 in rent. Leona can deduct that total amount ($9,600) on her taxes for that year because the rental payments were a current expense that benefited her for that single tax year.

But if an expense you pay applies beyond the current tax year, the general rule is that you can deduct only the portion that applies to your use of the rented property during the current tax year. You can deduct the rest of your payment only during the future tax year to which it applies.

> EXAMPLE: Steve leased an outside office for three years for $6,000 a year. He paid the entire three-year $18,000 lease amount up

front. Each year, Steve can deduct only $6,000—the part of the rent that applies to that tax year.

Subject to the exceptions noted below, these rules apply to office expenses as well, not just rent you pay in advance. For example, they apply to all expenses you pay to get a lease.

12-Month Rule

There is an important exception to the general rule about deducting in the current year. Under the 12-month rule, cash basis taxpayers may currently deduct any expense in the current year as long as it is for a right or benefit that extends no longer than the earlier of:

- 12 months, or
- until the end of the tax year after the tax year in which you made the payment.

EXAMPLE: Stephanie leased an office for five years beginning July 1, 2012. Her rent is $12,000 per year. She paid the first year's rent ($12,000) on June 30. Under the current year rule, Stephanie may deduct in 2012 only the part of her rent payment that applies to that year. Her lease started on July 1 (which is half-way through the year), so she may deduct 50% of the $12,000, or $6,000. However, if Stephanie uses the 12-month rule, her entire $12,000 payment is deductible in 2012. The fact that 50% of her payment was for the following year doesn't matter because the benefit she obtained—the use of her office—lasted for only 12 months.

To use the 12-month rule, you must apply it when you first start using the cash method for your business. You must get IRS approval if you haven't been using the rule and want to start doing so. Such IRS approval is granted automatically. (See Chapter 9.)

Improvements and Repairs

It's common to make permanent improvements to an office—for example, you may install new carpeting or new walls. Landlords often give commercial tenants an allowance to make improvements before they move in. You get no deduction in this event. The landlord gets to depreciate improvements it paid for, not you.

However, if you pay for improvements with your own money, you may deduct the cost as a business expense. You have several options:

- you can depreciate the improvements
- you can treat the money you spent for the improvements as rent, or
- the improvements may qualify for the Disabled Access Tax Credit or tax deduction for removal of barriers to the disabled (see "Tax Incentives for Improving Access for the Disabled," below).

Improvements may be depreciated over several years as described in "If You Own Your Office," below. They are depreciated over their recovery periods assigned by the IRS, not over the whole term of the lease. For example, the cost of installing new carpeting would be depreciated over five years, even if the lease term is ten years. However, improvements placed in service in 2012 may qualify for Section 179 expensing or 100% bonus depreciation, with the entire cost deducted in one year (see Chapter 9).

If you treat your expenses for improvements as rent, you deduct the cost the same as any other rent. Rent is deductible in a single year unless it is prepaid in advance (see "Timing of Deductions," above). This means you'll get your deduction much more quickly than if you depreciated the improvements over several years. However, if the cost of the improvement is substantial, part of the cost may have to be treated as prepaid rent and deducted over the whole lease term as described above.

Whether an improvement must be depreciated or treated as rent depends on what you and your landlord intended. Your intent should be written into your lease agreement.

In contrast to improvements, repairs may always be currently deducted. How to tell the difference between improvements and repairs is discussed in "If You Own Your Office," below.

Depreciation of Qualified Leasehold Improvements

There are special rules for depreciating "qualified leasehold improvements." These are improvements to leased commercial property—whether paid for by the landlord or tenant—that meet the following criteria:

- The building was in use for more than three years when the improvements were made.
- The improvements were made under a lease, a sublease, or commitment to enter into a lease by people who are not related.
- The improved portion of the building is used exclusively by the tenant or subtenant.
- The improvement was not a building enlargement, an elevator or escalator installation, or improvement to the building's common areas or internal structural framework.

If the improvements were made during 2010 through 2012, they may qualify for Section 179 expensing and/or bonus depreciation, both of which provide a substantial deduction the first year you own the property. You can deduct up to $139,000 in 2012 using Section 179 expensing (however, the deduction is limited to the profit from your business). You can deduct 50% of the cost of the improvement, with no limit, using bonus depreciation if the improvements were made in 2012. From September 9, 2010 through December 31, 2011, bonus depreciation is limited to 50% of the cost of the improvement. (See Chapter 9 for a detailed discussion of Section 179 expensing and bonus depreciation.)

Cost of Modifying a Lease

You may have to pay an additional rent amount over part of the lease period to change certain provisions in your lease. You must ordinarily deduct these payments over the remaining lease period. You cannot deduct the payments as additional rent, even if they are described as rent in the agreement.

The only exception to this is if the 12-month rule can be used. The lease will have to have a short term for this rule to apply.

Cost of Canceling a Lease

Unlike the cost of modifying a lease, you can ordinarily deduct as rent the amount you pay to cancel a business lease.

If You Own Your Office

If you own your outside office, you'll be entitled to most of the same deductions as a renter discussed above. You'll also get to depreciate the cost of your real estate.

Operating Expenses

Operating expenses are the day-to-day expenses you incur as result of owning your office. They are currently deductible unless you prepay them for more than one year. These expenses include:

- utilities
- insurance
- repairs
- burglar alarm expenses
- trash and waste removal
- security expenses
- parking garage expenses, and
- maintenance and janitorial expenses.

Improvements and Repairs

Provided that they are ordinary, necessary, and reasonable in amount, repairs to your real property are operating expenses that are fully deductible in the year in which they are incurred.

> EXAMPLE: Sally owns a small office building in which she houses her real estate brokerage firm. She discovers a leak in the building's foundation. She has John, a contractor, examine the 20-year-old foundation. He tells her he can fix the leak for $1,000. She agrees and pays John the money. Sally has paid for a repair. She's out $1,000, but at least she gets a tax deduction. The repair is a currently deductible operating expense that she may deduct in full from her taxes for the year.

However, not all upkeep constitutes a repair for tax purposes. Some changes made to real property are capital improvements. Unlike repairs, improvements cannot be deducted in a single year. Instead, their cost must be depreciated over several years. Improvements to nonresidential real property must be depreciated over an especially long period—39 years.

EXAMPLE: Assume that John, the contractor, told Sally she had two options with her foundation: She could have the leak patched for $1,000, or she could have an entirely new foundation put in at a cost of $10,000. Sally elects to have a new foundation installed and pays $10,000. This expense is an improvement that she will have to depreciate over 39 years. Assuming the work was done in January, she'd get to deduct $234 from her taxes that year, and $257 for the next 38 years.

Section 179 Expensing

Section 179 expensing allows you to deduct, in a single year, a substantial amount of tangible personal property you buy for your business. It may be used for personal property you purchase for your office, except for:

- buildings
- building components, or
- air conditioning and heating units.

EXAMPLE: Sally from the examples above spends $5,000 for new office carpeting and $5,000 for new landscaping. A carpet is tangible personal property and is not a building component as long as it is not glued to the floor. She may deduct the entire $5,000 in one year using Section 179. Landscaping is not personal property, thus Sally may not deduct any of her landscaping costs using Section 179. She must depreciate the cost as described below.

Section 179 is covered in detail in Chapter 9.

Depreciation Deductions

You may deduct the cost of buying your outside office, and improving it, through depreciation. Depreciation is covered in detail in Chapter 9.

The following discussion just covers the unique aspects of depreciation for nonresidential real property.

What You Depreciate

Typically, you don't have a single depreciation deduction. Instead, you have many separate depreciation deductions over time.

When your real property is first placed into service, you get to depreciate its tax basis (value for tax purposes). This includes the value of:

- the building and building components
- land improvements, such as landscaping, and
- any personal property items that are not physically part of the building but were included in the purchase price—for example, office furniture.

These items can all be depreciated together. However, you have the option of separately depreciating personal property inside your building, and certain land improvements. This is more complicated, but yields a larger total deduction the first years you own the property.

How Much You Depreciate

You depreciate your property's tax basis—its value for tax purposes. If you've purchased your real property, your starting point in determining its basis is what you paid for the property. Logically enough, this is called cost basis. Your cost basis is the purchase price plus certain other expenses, less the cost of your land.

The following expenses are added to your property's basis:

- abstract fees
- charges for installing utility services
- legal fees
- mortgage commissions
- recording fees
- surveys
- transfer taxes
- title insurance, and
- any amounts the seller owes that you agree to pay, such as back taxes or interest, recording or mortgage fees, charges for improvements or repairs, and sales commissions.

Ordinarily, when you purchase a building with a structure or structures on it, you pay a single lump sum to the seller that includes both the cost of the building (along with its contents) and the land on which it sits. Because you can't depreciate land, you must deduct the value of the land from the purchase price to determine the basis for depreciation of the building. There are several ways to calculate how much your land is worth. Obviously, the less it's worth, the more depreciation you will have to deduct. Land valuation is the single most important factor within your control affecting the amount of your depreciation deductions.

If you construct your building yourself, your basis is the cost of construction. The cost includes the cost of materials and labor, as well as the cost of equipment (including rented equipment). However, you may not add the cost of your own labor to the property's basis. Interest you pay during the construction period must be added to the basis; but interest paid before and after construction may be deducted as an operating expense.

Depreciation Period and Method

Nonresidential real property has the longest depreciation period of any business property—39 years. But, in practice, it takes 40 years to fully depreciate a nonresidential building. You don't get a full year's worth of depreciation the first year, so you get some extra depreciation during the 40th year (if you own the building that long).

Older properties have a shorter depreciation period: 31.5 years for property placed in service before May 13, 1993 (or before January 1, 1994, if the purchase or its construction was under a binding contract in effect before May 13, 1993, or if construction began before May 13, 1993).

In addition to having the longest depreciation period, nonresidential real property must be depreciated using the slowest depreciation method: the straight-line method in which you receive equal deductions each year, except the first and last year. You may not use accelerated depreciation, which provides larger deductions in the first few years you own the property, and smaller deductions later on.

The following chart shows how much depreciation you get each year for a nonresidential building. From the second through the 39th year, you may deduct 2.564% of your property's tax basis—for example, if your basis is $200,000, you may deduct $5,128 each year (2.564% × $200,000 = $5,128). As the chart shows, the depreciation deductions for the first and 40th years differ depending on what month the property was placed in service.

Nonresidential Real Property Midmonth Convention Straight Line—39 Years

Month property placed in service	Year		
	1	2–39	40
1	2.461%	2.564%	0.107%
2	2.247%	2.564%	0.321%
3	2.033%	2.564%	0.535%
4	1.819%	2.564%	0.749%
5	1.605%	2.564%	0.963%
6	1.391%	2.564%	1.177%
7	1.177%	2.564%	1.391%
8	0.963%	2.564%	1.605%
9	0.749%	2.564%	1.819%
10	0.535%	2.564%	2.033%
11	0.321%	2.564%	2.247%
12	0.107%	2.564%	2.461%

Depreciating Improvements

Typically, you'll make additions and improvements to your property after it has been placed into service. These include:

- improvements to the building itself, or to building components—for example, upgrading the heating or air conditioning system
- land improvements, such as planting new trees or shrubbery, and
- adding new personal property to the building—for example, new office furniture.

Such later additions and improvements are depreciated separately from the original property itself.

Recovery period. The general rule is that building improvements are depreciated over 39 years. However, some building improvements made by a landlord or tenant may be depreciated over 15 years. (See "Depreciation of Qualified Leasehold Improvements," above.)

Depreciation method. Building improvements are depreciated using the straight-line method—the same method as used for the original building (described above). Land improvements are depreciated over 15 years using the 150% declining balance method.

Personal property. Personal property inside your building is depreciated in the same way as any other personal business property. If such property was placed in service during 2010 through 2012, it may qualify for Section 179 expensing and/or bonus depreciation, both of which provide a substantial deduction the first year you own the property. You can deduct up to $139,000 in 2012 using Section 179 expensing (however, the deduction is limited to the profit from your business). You can deduct 50% of the cost of the improvement, with no limit, using bonus depreciation if the improvements were made in 2012. From September 9, 2010 through December 31, 2011, bonus depreciation is limited to 50% of the cost of the improvement. (See Chapter 9 for a detailed discussion of Section 179 expensing and bonus depreciation.)

Interest Deductions

Most people borrow money from banks or other financial institutions to purchase real property. Mortgage interest you pay for your outside office is deductible as it is paid each year.

You deduct only the interest you pay on a loan to purchase or improve real property. You may not deduct payments of principal—that is, your repayments of the amount you borrowed. The principal is ordinarily added to the basis of your property and depreciated over 39 years.

In contrast, if you borrow money to repair your rental property, you may deduct the principle amount the year it is incurred as an operating expense.

Expenses you pay to obtain a mortgage on your real property cannot be deducted as interest. Instead, they are added to your basis in the property and depreciated along with the property itself.

Property Taxes

Regular property taxes you pay for your outside office are a deductible business expense. However, real estate taxes imposed to fund specific local benefits such as streets, sewer lines, and water mains, are not deductible as business expenses. Because these benefits increase the value of your property, you should add what you pay for them to the tax basis (cost for tax purposes) of your property. Water bills, sewer charges, and other service charges assessed against your business property are not real estate taxes, but they are deductible as business expenses.

Tax Incentives for Improving Access for the Disabled

Two tax incentives are available to businesses to help cover the cost of making their offices more accessible to the disabled—for example, installing wheelchair ramps. Ordinarily, real property improvements such as these would have to be depreciated over as much as 39 years. These tax breaks permit small businesses to currently deduct, up to certain limits, their expenses for such improvements.

The first tax incentive is a tax *credit*. The second is a tax *deduction*. Both can be used at the same time, and they can be claimed each year you meet the requirements. These deductions may be used by real estate pros who own or lease their office.

Disabled Access Tax Credit

The Americans with Disabilities Act (ADA) prohibits private employers with 15 or more employees from discriminating against people with disabilities in the full and equal enjoyment of goods, services, and facilities offered by any "place of public accommodation." Real estate offices are included in the definition of public accommodation.

The disabled access tax credit is designed to help small businesses defray the costs of complying with the ADA. The credit may be used by any business with either:

- $1 million or less in gross receipts for the preceding tax year, or
- 30 or fewer full-time employees during the preceding tax year.

The credit can be used to cover a variety of expenses, including the cost to remove barriers that prevent a business from being accessible to disabled people. However, the credit may be used only for buildings constructed before November 5, 1990. The credit may also be used for equipment acquisitions, and services such as sign language interpreters.

The disabled tax credit is a tax credit, not a tax deduction. Tax credits are better than tax deductions because, instead of just reducing your taxable income, they reduce the actual amount of tax you have to pay dollar for dollar.

The amount of the tax credit is equal to 50% of your disabled access expenses in a year that exceed $250 but are not more than $10,250. Thus, the maximum credit is $5,000. To claim the credit, you must file IRS Form 8826, *Disabled Access Credit.*

Disabled Access Tax Deduction

Businesses may deduct in a single year up to $15,000 of the cost of making their buildings or other facilities—such as roads, walks, and parking lots—accessible to the elderly or disabled.

The most you can deduct as a cost of removing barriers to the disabled and the elderly for any tax year is $15,000. However, you can add any costs over this limit to the basis of the property and depreciate them. The $15,000 deduction limit applies to a partnership as a whole and also to each individual partner in the partnership. This rule also applies to LLCs taxed as partnerships (as most are).

Your renovations must comply with applicable accessibility standards. Detailed standards are set forth in the ADA Accessibility Guidelines, which can be found on the Internet at www.access-board.gov/adaag/html/adaag.htm. IRS Publication 535, *Business Expenses,* also contains a summary of these standards.

You may claim the deduction on your income tax return for the tax year you paid for the work, or the year you incurred the expenses. Identify the deduction as a separate item. The choice applies to all of the qualifying costs you have during the year, up to the $15,000 limit. You must maintain adequate records to support your deduction—keep your receipts.

EXAMPLE: Jason houses his brokerage firm in a building that is not wheelchair accessible. He installs four wheelchair ramps at a cost of $5,000. Ordinarily this would be an improvement that Jason would have to depreciate. But due to the disabled access tax deduction, he may deduct the entire $5,000 in one year.

Using Both the Credit and Deduction

The two incentives can be used in combination during the same year if the requirements for each are met. In this event, the maximum tax deduction you may take during the year is equal to the difference between your total disabled access expenses and the amount of the tax credit you claim. You should take the maximum tax credit you can first, because it reduces your taxes dollar for dollar. Then, claim as much of the tax deduction as you can.

EXAMPLE: The ABC Realty Co., a corporation, spent $25,000 in one year to make its 20-year-old building more accessible to the disabled. It should first claim the maximum $5,000 tax credit, then deduct from its taxable income another $15,000 using the disabled access tax deduction. It can add the remaining $5,000 it spent to its property's basis and depreciate it.

Energy Efficiency Deduction

The Energy Tax Incentives Act, enacted by Congress in 2005, created a new deduction for expenses to make commercial buildings more energy efficient. It's intended to encourage building owners to upgrade their existing buildings and to design more energy-efficient new structures. The deduction may be used for both existing and new buildings placed in service from January 1, 2006 through December 31, 2013.

In a nutshell, you may deduct in one year up to $1.80 per building square foot when, as part of a plan to reduce your total energy costs, you upgrade your:

- interior lighting system
- heating, cooling, ventilation, and hot water system, or

- building envelope.

For example, the owner of a 10,000-square-foot building who qualifies for the deduction can deduct $18,000 ($1.80 × 10,000 = $18,000).

To obtain the full deduction, the upgrade must reduce the power costs for the system involved by at least 50%. If the reduction is less than 50%, a partial tax deduction may be available. There is no dollar limit on the deduction.

To qualify for the deduction, the building upgrade must meet detailed certification requirements. See IRS Notice 2006-52 and Notice 2008-40 for more information. You can find this information at the IRS website (www.irs.gov).

If You Lease a Building to Your Real Estate Business

If your real estate business is organized as an LLC, partnership, or corporation, you can realize tax savings if you personally own an office building and lease it to the business. You'll be the landlord and your business your tenant. Your business will pay you rent for the lease. This rent is a deductible expense for the business as described above in "If You Rent Your Office." You'll have to pay income tax on the rent you receive. However, you won't have to pay Social Security or Medicare taxes because income from real estate rentals is not subject to these taxes (except in the unlikely event that you are a real estate dealer).

This is a great way to take money out of your business without paying these taxes. Additionally, if your business is a C corporation, this type of lease arrangement helps you avoid double taxation by reducing your corporation's profits. (See Chapter 2.)

This arrangement is perfectly legitimate as long as you have a real lease (it should be in writing) and charge your business a reasonable rent. Don't charge more than market rates to obtain greater Social Security and Medicare tax savings.

> EXAMPLE: Edna is a real estate broker whose business is organized as an LLC and taxed as a partnership. She personally buys a small building and leases it to her LLC for $5,000 per month, which

is the going rate in the area. Edna must pay income tax on the $60,000 in rent she receives each year from her LLC, but not self-employment taxes (Social Security and Medicare taxes). Her LLC deducts the rent as a business operating expense. This reduces by $60,000 the total profit that is passed through the LLC to Edna's personal return. Obviously, if the LLC, not Edna, owned the building, it wouldn't have to pay any rent to Edna and there would be an additional $60,000 to pass through the LLC to her personal return. But this money would be subject to both income and self-employment taxes.

Instead of personally owning the building, you can form another business entity, such as an LLC, to own it and in turn own the entity. This gives you a degree of limited liability if something goes wrong on the property. (See Chapter 2.) You still won't have to pay self-employment tax on any income your entity receives from renting real estate.

Moreover, you can have a family member or members own the building instead of you. This will result in a lower income tax burden if the family member is in a lower tax bracket than you. Family members can also own all or part of an LLC or other entity that owns the building.

CHAPTER

9

Deducting Cars, Computers, and Other Long-Term Assets

This chapter explains how you can deduct long-term property you buy for your real estate business. You will need to be aware of, and follow, some tax rules that at times may seem complicated. But it's worth the effort. After all, by allowing these deductions, the government is effectively offering to help pay for your equipment and other business assets. All you have to do is take advantage of the offer.

What Are Long-Term Assets?

A long-term asset is business property that can reasonably be expected to last for more than one year. Long-term assets are also called capital expenses; the terms are used interchangeably in this book. Whether an item is a long-term asset (a capital expense) or not depends on its useful life. The useful life of an asset is not its physical life, but rather the period during which it may reasonably be expected to be useful in your business—and the IRS, not you, makes this call. For real estate professionals, long-term assets typically include items such as office furniture, computer equipment, cameras, buildings, automobiles and other vehicles, telephones, cell phones, and copiers. Anything you purchase that will benefit your business for less than one year is an operating expense, not a long-term asset. For example, your monthly phone bill is an operating expense, not a capital expense; but the telephones you purchase for your office are capital expenses.

The difference between operating and capital expenses is important for tax purposes because operating expenses can always be deducted in the year you pay for them (assuming you're a cash basis taxpayer). In contrast, the cost of long-term assets may have to be deducted over several years.

Are Paper Clips Long-Term Assets?
They Don't Qualify for the Home Office Deduction

Are paper clips and other inexpensive items that you buy for your business long-term assets for tax purposes? No. Although things like paper clips might be expected to last more than one year, you can treat these and other similar items as a current expense for tax purposes. Most businesses establish a minimum an asset must cost before they will treat it as a long-term asset. New IRS regulations provide that a business may currently deduct materials and supplies that cost less than $100. (IRS Reg. Sec. 1.162-3T(c)(1)(iv).) For example, you could treat a $50 bookcase you buy for your business as a currently deductible operating expense, but a $500 bookcase would be a long-term asset.

Methods for Deducting Property

How you are allowed to deduct a long-term asset depends, first of all, on whether it is personal property or real property. There are currently three methods for deducting personal property, while there is only one way to deduct real property.

Personal Property

Personal property consists of any tangible property other than:

- land and land improvements
- buildings and other inherently permanent structures, such as pools and parking lots, and
- structural components of buildings and other permanent structures.

Thus, virtually anything tangible you buy for your real estate business other than land, buildings, or building components is personal property. This includes, for example:

- automobiles and other vehicles
- computer equipment
- telephones and cell phones

- office furniture
- fax machines
- pagers
- cameras
- recorders
- briefcases
- map books
- lock boxes and keys, and
- real estate books.

There are two basic methods for deducting long-term personal property. You can depreciate it, deducting a portion of the cost each year over the asset's useful life. Or, if the property qualifies, you can use Section 179 of the Internal Revenue Code (IRC) to deduct all or most of the cost in one year—a process called expensing. In recent years (2008 through 2012), there has been a third way to deduct the cost of long-term business property: a special first-year bonus depreciation for new personal property. For qualified property placed in service during 2012, you can use this first-year bonus depreciation to deduct 50% of the cost in the first year the property is purchased.

So, at least through the end of 2012, there are three different ways to deduct the cost of long-term personal property:

- Section 179 expensing
- first-year bonus depreciation (50%), and
- regular depreciation.

You get to decide which depreciation method you use. You don't have to use the same method for all your property. (However, as discussed below, bonus depreciation must be used for all property in the same asset class.) Many small business owners choose to use Section 179 and/or bonus depreciation whenever they can because it gives the largest deduction possible in the first year they buy the asset. Regular depreciation, on the other hand, forces you to spread your deduction over several years. Because of inflation and the time value of money, it is often better to get the largest possible deduction the first year you own an asset. There are some circumstances, however, when it may be more advantageous to use regular depreciation instead. (See "When to Use Regular Depreciation," below.)

Often, but not always, the same asset will qualify for Section 179 expensing and bonus depreciation. In this event, you decide what method to use or you may choose to combine depreciation methods. If you decide to claim Section 179 expensing and bonus depreciation for the same asset, you must use Section 179 first, then bonus depreciation, and then regular depreciation (if needed). The biggest difference between the two is that Section 179 can be used for both new and used property and bonus depreciation is limited to new property. For this reason, many taxpayers claim Section 179 expensing for their used property and bonus depreciation for their new property.

Section 179 Versus 100% Bonus Depreciation

Section 179	Bonus Depreciation
Limited to annual business profit	No profit limitation
Can use for new and used property	Can use only for new property
Cannot create NOL to be carried back to prior years	Can create a net operating loss to be carried back to prior years and result in an immediate tax refund
$139,000 annual limit for 2012	No annual limit: 50% of cost of qualified property placed in service during 2012 can be deducted in one year
Must use property for business more than 50% of the time	No minimum percentage business use of property required (except for listed property)
Recapture of deduction if business use falls below 50%	No recapture
Does not apply class wide	Applies class wide
Optional	Optional, but must opt out not to take

Real Property

Real property consists of buildings and other structures, including their components, and land and land improvements. There is only one way to deduct the cost of real property you use in your real estate business—using regular depreciation to deduct a portion of the cost each year over many years. These rules are discussed below in "Regular Depreciation."

Rules for Deducting Any Long-Term Asset

The following rules apply to all methods for deducting long-term assets.

What You Can Deduct

You can only depreciate or expense the cost of purchasing long-term business property that wears out, deteriorates, or gets used up over time. You cannot deduct:

- property that doesn't wear out, including land (whether undeveloped or with structures on it), stocks, securities, or gold
- property you use solely for personal purposes
- property purchased and disposed of in the same year
- inventory, or
- collectibles that appreciate in value over time, such as antiques and artwork.

If you use nondepreciable property in your business, you get no tax deduction while you own it. But if you sell it, you get to deduct its tax basis (see below) from the sales price to calculate your taxable profit. If the basis exceeds the sales price, you'll have a deductible loss on the property. If the price exceeds the basis, you'll have a taxable gain.

> EXAMPLE: A real estate brokerage purchased a digital camera in January for $1,000 and sold it in December of the same year for $600. It was purchased and disposed of in the same year so it can't be depreciated or expensed. Instead, the property's basis (its original cost) is deducted from the sale price. This results in a loss of $400, which is a deductible business loss.

You also may not depreciate or expense property that you do not own. For example, you get no depreciation or expensing deduction for property you lease. The person who owns the property—the lessor—gets to depreciate it. (However, you may deduct your lease payments as current business expenses.) Leasing may be preferable to buying and depreciating equipment that wears out or becomes obsolete quickly. (See "Deciding Between Leasing and Buying," below.)

Mixed-Use Property

In order to deduct a long-term asset, you must have used the property in your business. You can't deduct an asset you use solely for personal purposes.

> EXAMPLE: Jill, a real estate agent, bought a computer for $2,000. She used it to play games, manage her checkbook, and surf the Internet for fun. In other words, she used it only for personal purposes. The computer is not deductible.

However, you need not use an asset 100% of the time for business to claim a deduction. You can use it for personal purposes part of the time. In this event, your deduction is reduced by the percentage of your personal use. This will, of course, reduce the amount of your deduction.

> EXAMPLE: Miranda buys a $400 camera for her real estate business. She uses the camera 75% of the time for business and 25% for personal use. Her deduction is reduced by 25%, so Miranda can deduct only $300 of the camera's $400 cost.

You can take a regular or bonus depreciation deduction even if you use an asset only 1% of the time for business, as long as it's not listed property. This is one advantage of depreciation over the Section 179 deduction, which is available only for property you use more than 50% of the time for business.

If you use property for both business and personal purposes, you must keep a diary or log with the dates, times, and reasons the property was used to distinguish business from personal use. Moreover, special rules apply if you use cars and other types of listed property less than 50% of the time for business.

Listed Property

The IRS imposes special rules on certain personal property items that can easily be used for personal as well as business purposes. These items, called "listed property," include:

- cars and other passenger vehicles below 6,000 pounds
- motorcycles, boats, and airplanes
- computers, and
- any other property generally used for entertainment, recreation, or amusement—for example, VCRs, cameras, stereos, and camcorders.

Special Record Keeping Rules

The IRS fears that taxpayers might use listed property for personal reasons, but claim a business deduction. For this reason, you're required to document your business use of listed property, even if you use it 100% for business. You can satisfy this requirement by keeping a logbook showing when and how the property is used.

There is an exception to the record keeping rule for computers: If you use a computer or computer peripheral (such as a printer) only for business and keep it at your business location, you need not comply with the record keeping requirement for listed property. This includes computers that you keep at your home office if the office qualifies for the home office deduction. (See Chapter 7 for more on the home office deduction.) This exception does not apply to items other than computers and computer peripheral equipment—for example, it doesn't apply to calculators, copiers, or fax machines.

> EXAMPLE: John, a real estate broker, works out of his home office that he uses exclusively for his business. The office qualifies for the home office deduction. He buys a $4,000 computer for his office and uses it exclusively for his real estate business. He does not have to keep records showing how and when he uses the computer.

TIP

New rules for cell phones. Starting in 2010, cell phones and similar personal communications devices are no longer considered listed property. Thus, the strict record keeping requirements for listed property no longer apply to these devices. In addition, you don't have to include the fair market value of a cell phone provided to an employee for business purposes in the employee's gross income for tax purposes.

Deducting Listed Property

If you use listed property more than 50% of the time for business, you may deduct its cost just like any other long-term business property. For example, you may deduct all or part of the cost in one year using Section 179 or bonus depreciation, or depreciate it over several years using regular depreciation.

However, if you use listed property 50% or less of the time for business, you may not deduct the cost under Section 179 or use bonus depreciation or accelerated regular depreciation. Instead, you must use the slowest method of regular depreciation: straight-line depreciation. (See "How to Depreciate Listed Property," below, for more on deducting listed property.)

When Depreciation Starts and Ends

You begin to depreciate and/or expense your property when it is placed in service—that is, when it's ready and available for use in your real estate business. As long as it is available for use, you don't have to actually use the property for business during the year to take depreciation.

> EXAMPLE: Tom, a real estate broker, purchased a copy machine for his office. He had the device ready for use in his office on December 31, 2012, but he didn't actually use it until January 2, 2013. Tom may take a depreciation deduction for the copier for 2012 because it was available for use that year.

You stop depreciating property either when you have fully recovered your cost or other basis or when you retire it from service, whichever occurs first. Property is retired from service when you stop using it for business, sell it, destroy it, or otherwise dispose of it.

> EXAMPLE: Tom depreciates the $5,000 cost of his copier a portion at a time over seven years. At the end of that time, he has recovered his $5,000 basis and depreciation ends. He is free to continue using the machine, but he can't get any more depreciation deductions for it.

CAUTION

You must actually be in business to take depreciation or expensing deductions. In other words, you cannot depreciate or expense an asset until your real estate business is up and running. This is one important reason why it is a good idea to postpone large property purchases until your business has begun. (See Chapter 10 for a detailed discussion of tax deductions for business start-up expenses.)

> EXAMPLE: In 2012, Julia buys $10,000 worth of equipment for her real estate office. However, the office does not open its doors for business until 2013. Julia may not take a depreciation deduction for the equipment until 2013 and later years.

How Much You Can Deduct

You are allowed to deduct your total investment in a long-term asset you buy for your business, up to your business use percentage of the property. In tax lingo, your investment is called your basis or tax basis. Basis is a word you'll hear over and over again when the subject of depreciation comes up. Don't let it confuse you; it just means the amount of your total investment in the property.

Usually, your basis in long-term property is whatever you paid for it. This includes not only the purchase price, but also sales tax, delivery charges, installation, and testing fees, if any. You may deduct the entire cost, no matter how you paid for the property—in cash, with a credit card, or with a bank loan.

EXAMPLE: The ABC Brokerage buys ten computers for its office. They are used 100% for business. ABC pays $20,000 cash, $1,800 in sales tax, and $500 for delivery and installation. Its basis in the property is $22,300.

Whenever you use Section 179 expensing or bonus or regular depreciation, you must subtract the amount of your deduction from the property's basis—this is true regardless of whether you actually claimed any depreciation on your tax return. This new basis is called the adjusted basis, because it reflects adjustments from your starting basis. When your adjusted basis is reduced to zero, you can no longer deduct any of the property's cost.

EXAMPLE: The ABC Brokerage (from the above example) bought ten computers in 2012. Its starting basis was $22,300. It expenses the entire cost in 2012 using Section 179. The computers' adjusted basis is zero, and ABC gets no more deductions for the property.

If you sell long-term property, your gain or loss on the sale is determined by subtracting the property's adjusted basis from the sales price.

EXAMPLE: ABC sells its ten computers for $5,000 in 2013. Because its adjusted basis in the computers is zero, its taxable gain on the sale will be $5,000.

If you abandon long-term business property instead of selling it, you may deduct its adjusted basis as a business loss. Of course, if your adjusted basis in the property is zero, you get no deduction. You abandon property when you voluntarily and permanently give up possessing and using it with the intention of ending your ownership and without passing it on to anyone else. Loss from abandonment of business property is deductible as an ordinary loss, even if the property is a capital asset.

For more information on the tax implications of selling or otherwise disposing of business property, refer to IRS Publication 544, *Sales and Other Dispositions of Assets*.

Section 179 Expensing

If you learn only one section number in the tax code, it should be Section 179. This humble piece of the tax code is one of the greatest tax boons ever for small business owners, including real estate professionals. Section 179 doesn't increase the total amount you can deduct, but it allows you to get your entire deduction in one year, rather than taking it a little at a time over the term of an asset's useful life. This is called first-year expensing or Section 179 expensing. (Expensing is an accounting term that means currently deducting a long-term asset.)

EXAMPLE: In 2012, Ginger buys a $4,000 photocopy machine for her real estate business. Under the regular depreciation rules (using the straight-line depreciation method—see "Regular Depreciation," below), Ginger would have to deduct a portion of the cost each year over its five-year useful life as follows:

Year	Depreciation Deduction
2012	$400
2013	$800
2014	$800
2015	$800
2016	$800
2017	$400

By deducting the copier under Section 179 instead, Ginger can deduct the entire $4,000 expense from her income taxes in 2012. So she gets a $4,000 deduction under Section 179, instead of the $400 deduction she gets using depreciation.

Property You Can Expense

You qualify for the Section 179 deduction only if you buy long-term, tangible personal property that you use in your real estate business more than 50% of the time. Let's look at these requirements in more detail.

Tangible Personal Property

Under Section 179, you can deduct the cost of tangible personal property (new or used) that you buy for your real estate business, if the property will last more than one year. Examples of tangible personal property include computers, business equipment, and office furniture. Although it's not really tangible property, computer software can also be deducted under Section 179. (See "Computer Software," below, for more on deducting software.)

You can't use Section 179 to deduct the cost of:

- personal property used inside rental property—for example, kitchen appliances, carpets, drapes, or blinds
- land
- permanent structures attached to land, including buildings and their structural components, fences, or paved parking areas
- intangible property such as patents, copyrights, and trademarks
- property used outside the United States, or
- air conditioning and heating units.

However, nonpermanent property attached to a nonresidential, commercial building is deductible. For example, refrigerators and signs are all deductible under Section 179. Special rules apply to cars (see below).

Property Used Primarily (51%) for Business

To deduct the cost of property under Section 179, you must use the property primarily for your business—that is, to provide your professional services. You can take a Section 179 deduction for property you use for both personal and business purposes, as long as you use it for your practice more than half of the time. The amount of your deduction is reduced by the percentage of your personal use. (See "Calculating Your Deduction," below.) You'll need to keep records showing your business use of the property. If you use an item for business less than half the time, you will have to use bonus or regular depreciation instead.

There is another important limitation regarding the business use of property. You must use the property over half the time for business *in the year in which you buy it.* You can't convert property you previously used for personal use to business use and claim a Section 179 deduction for the cost.

> EXAMPLE: Kim, a real estate broker, bought a $2,000 digital camera in 2010 and used it to take family and other personal pictures. In 2012, Kim starts using her digital camera 75% of the time for her real estate business. She may not deduct the cost under Section 179 because she didn't use the camera for business until two years after she bought it.

Property That You Purchase

You can use Section 179 expensing only for property that you purchase —not for leased property or property you inherit or receive as a gift. You also can't use it for property that you buy from a relative or a corporation or an organization that you control.

Used or New Property

Section 179 may be used for both used and new personal property, as long as you purchase it. This differs from bonus depreciation which may only be used for new property.

Calculating Your Deduction

The total amount you can deduct under Section 179 annually will depend on:

- what you paid for the property
- how much you use the property for business
- how much Section 179 property you buy during the year, and
- your annual business income.

Cost of Property

The amount you can deduct for Section 179 property is initially based on the property's cost. The cost includes the amount you paid for the property, plus sales tax, delivery, and installation charges. It doesn't matter if you pay cash or finance the purchase with a credit card or bank loan. However, if you pay for property with both cash and a trade-in, the value of the trade-in is not deductible under Section 179. You must depreciate the amount of the trade-in using regular or bonus depreciation.

> EXAMPLE: Stuart, a real estate broker, buys a $2,000 digital camera. He pays $1,500 cash and is given a $500 trade-in for an older camera that he owns. He may deduct $1,500 of the $2,000 purchase under Section 179; he must depreciate the remaining $500.

Percentage of Business Use

If you use Section 179 property solely for business, you can deduct 100% of the cost (subject to the other limitations discussed below). However, if you use property for both business and personal purposes, you must reduce your deduction by the percentage of the time that you use the property for personal purposes.

> EXAMPLE: Max buys a $4,000 computer that he uses 75% for his real estate business and 25% for personal purposes. The year that he buys the computer, he may currently deduct 75% of its cost (or $3,000) under Section 179. The remaining $1,000 is not deductible as a business expense.

You must continue to use property that you deduct under Section 179 for business at least 50% of the time for as many years as it would take to depreciate the item under the normal depreciation rules. For example, computers have a five-year depreciation period. If you deduct a computer's cost under Section 179, you must use the computer at least 50% of the time for business for five years.

If you don't meet these rules, you'll have to report as income part of the deduction you took under Section 179 in the prior year. This is called recapture, and is discussed in more detail below.

Annual Deduction Limit

There is a limit on the total amount of business property expenses that you can deduct each year under Section 179. Historically, the limit was a fairly low $25,000. However, in an attempt to help businesses during tough economic years, Congress increased the amount that could be deducted under Section 179—from $128,000 in 2007 to a whopping $500,000 in 2010 and 2011. For 2012, the limit was reduced to $139,000 and is scheduled to go back down to $25,000 in 2013 and later. However, there is a good possibility that Congress will increase the limit again. Thus, if you're planning on buying more than $25,000 in tangible personal property for your business, and you want to deduct the entire amount in one year under Section 179, you should make your purchases before 2013.

The annual deduction limit applies to all of your businesses combined, not to each business you own and run.

> EXAMPLE: Britney is a real estate broker who also owns an antiques store. In 2012, she may expense up to a total of $139,000 in long-term personal property purchases for both businesses because the Section 179 limit applies to all the businesses she owns.

You don't have to claim the full amount—it's up to you to decide how much to deduct under Section 179. Whatever amount you don't claim under Section 179 must be depreciated instead. (See below—depreciation is not optional.)

There is also a limit on the total amount of Section 179 property you can purchase each year. You must reduce your Section 179 deduction by one dollar for every dollar your annual purchases exceed the applicable limit. For 2012, the limit is $560,000. In 2012 and later, the limit will be much lower.

> EXAMPLE: The ABC Realty, Inc., a national real estate brokerage, purchases $610,000 in office equipment in 2012—$50,000 over the $560,000 total limit. As a result, ABC's annual deduction limit is reduced by $50,000, which means that ABC can deduct only $89,000 (of $139,000 allowed) of its asset purchases under Section 179. It must depreciate the remaining $521,000.

Year	Section 179 Deduction Limit	Property Value Limit
2008 to 2009	$250,000	$800,000
2010 to 2011	$500,000	$2 million
2012	$139,000	$560,000
2013	$25,000	$200,000

Currently, the Section 179 limit is so high that the great majority of real estate professionals won't have to worry about ever reaching it. However, if you purchase enough personal business property in one year to exceed the limit, you can divide the deduction among the items you purchase in any way you want, as long as the total deduction is not more than the Section 179 limit. It's usually best to apply Section 179 to property that has the longest useful life and, therefore, the longest depreciation period. This reduces the total time you will have to wait to get your deductions, which usually works to your financial benefit.

Business Profit Limitation

There is a major limitation on using Section 179: You can't use it to deduct more in one year than your net taxable business income for the year. In determining this amount, you subtract your business deductions from your business income. However, don't subtract your Section 179 deduction, the deduction for 50% of self-employment tax, or any net operating losses you are carrying back or forward.

If you have a net loss for the year, you get no Section 179 deduction for that year. If your net taxable income is less than the cost of the property you wish to deduct under Section 179, your deduction for the year is limited to the amount of your income. Any amount you cannot deduct in the current year is carried forward to the next year to be deducted then (or any other year in the future).

> EXAMPLE: Rich, a real estate broker, had $10,000 in net income in 2012 from his business. However, he spent $15,000 buying a business auto and office equipment and furniture. Even though the Section 179 maximum limit is $560,000, Rich's deduction for the

year is limited to $10,000. He must carry forward the remaining $5,000 to the following year and deduct it then (provided he has sufficient income).

If you're a married sole proprietor (or owner of a one-person LLC taxed as a sole proprietorship) and file a joint tax return, you can include your spouse's salary and business income in the total business income as well. You can't count investment income (for example, interest you earn on your personal savings account) as business income. But you can include interest you earn on your business working capital—for example, interest you earn on your business bank account.

EXAMPLE: James purchased $10,000 of office equipment for his fledgling real estate brokerage, but earned only $5,000 in profit for the year. James's wife, however, earned $75,000 from her job as a college professor. Because James and his wife file a joint return, their Section 179 deduction limit is $80,000 ($5,000 + $75,000 = $80,000). Thus, James may deduct the entire $10,000 in equipment purchases for that year under Section 179.

If you're a partner in a partnership, member of a multiowner LLC, or shareholder in an S corporation, the Section 179 income limit applies both to the business entity and to each owner personally. The business determines its Section 179 deduction subject to the income limits. It then allocates the deduction among the partners or shareholders who each apply their own Section 179 income limit.

If your business is organized as a C corporation, nothing is allocated to the shareholders. The corporation takes the Section 179 deduction on its own return, based on its own taxable income. This puts real estate professionals who have C corporations in a bit of a quandary, because they ordinarily want their C corporations to have little or no taxable income for the year to avoid double taxation (see Chapter 2). If you have a C corporation and want to take a Section 179 deduction, you must make sure the corporation has sufficient taxable income at the end of the year to cover the amount of your desired deduction.

Date of Purchase

As long as you meet the requirements, you can deduct the cost of Section 179 property up to the limits discussed above, no matter when you place the property in service during the year (that is, when you buy the property and make it available for use in your ongoing business). This differs from regular depreciation rules, by which property bought later in the year may be subject to a smaller deduction for the first year. (See below for more on regular depreciation rules about placing property in service.) This is yet another advantage of the Section 179 deduction over regular depreciation.

> EXAMPLE: John buys and places in service a $5,000 copy machine for his real estate brokerage on January 1, 2012 and $5,000 of office furniture on December 31, 2012. Both purchases are fully deductible under Section 179 in 2012.

Recapture Under Section 179

Recapture is a nasty tax trap an unwary business owner can easily get caught in. It requires you to give back part of a tax deduction that you took in a previous year. You may have to recapture part of a Section 179 tax deduction if, during the property's recovery period:

- your business use of the property drops below 51%, or
- you sell the property.

The recovery period is the property's useful life as determined under IRS rules. The IRS has set the useful life of all types of property that can be depreciated. The useful life of an asset is the time period over which you must depreciate the asset. For personal property that can be expensed under Section 179, the useful life ranges from three years for computer software to seven years for office furniture and business equipment. If you deduct property under Section 179, you must continue to use it in your business at least 51% of the time for its entire useful life—this is the IRS recovery period. For example, if you buy office furniture, you must use it over half of the time for business for at least seven years.

If your business use falls below 51% or you sell the property before the recovery period ends, you become subject to recapture. This means that you have to give back to the IRS all of the accelerated deductions you took under Section 179. You get to keep the amount you would have been entitled to deduct under regular depreciation, but you must include the rest of your Section 179 deduction in your ordinary income for the year.

> **EXAMPLE:** In 2012, Paul purchases office equipment worth $10,000 and deducts the entire amount under Section 179. He uses the property 100% for business during 2012 and 2013, but in 2014 he uses it only 40% for business. The equipment has a seven-year recovery period, so Paul is subject to recapture. He figures the recapture amount as follows:

First, he figures all the annual depreciation he would have been entitled to had he depreciated the property under the regular depreciation rules:

2012	$1,666	
2013	2,222	
2014	296	($740.50 × 40% business use)
Total	$4,184	

He then deducts this amount from the $10,000 Section 179 deduction he claimed in 2012: $10,000 – $4,184 = $5,816. Paul's recapture amount is $5,816. He must add $5,816 to his income for 2014 and he can continue to depreciate the equipment for the next four years.

You eventually get back through depreciation any recapture amount you must pay. But recapture can spike your tax bill for the year, so it's best to avoid the problem by making sure that you use property you deduct under Section 179 at least 51% for business during its entire recovery period.

You can maximize your Section 179 deduction by keeping your percentage of business use of Section 179 property as high as possible during the year that you buy the property. After the first year, you can reduce your business use (as long as it stays above 50%) and avoid recapture.

> **EXAMPLE:** Paul buys $10,000 of office equipment and uses it 90% for business that year. He may currently deduct $9,000 of the cost under Section 179 (90% business use × $10,000 cost = $9,000 deduction). In the following two years, he uses the equipment for business only 60% of the time. Nevertheless, he need not recapture any of his Section 179 deduction because his business use is still above 50%.

Bonus Depreciation

In an ongoing effort to help jumpstart the faltering economy, business owners have been allowed to claim a first-year "bonus depreciation" for qualifying personal property. Using bonus depreciation, a business owner can deduct a specified percentage of a long-term asset's cost the first year it's placed in service. For 2012, the percentage you can claim is 50%; that is, you can deduct 50% of the cost of the asset in the first year, with the remaining cost deducted over several years using regular depreciation and/or Section 179 expensing.

The amount of the bonus depreciation deduction has varied over the past few years. As the chart below shows, the bonus depreciation deduction was even higher for assets placed in service during 2011 and much of 2010—an incredible 100%.

Year Qualified Property Placed in Service	Amount of Bonus Depreciation
2008 through 9/7/2010	50%
9/8/2010 to 12/31/2011	100%
2012	50%

> **EXAMPLE:** Barry is a successful real estate broker who owns the building housing his real estate office. During 2012, he spends $10,000 to purchase a fancy new sign for his building. He can't

deduct this expense in 2012 using Section 179 because it is an improvement to real property. However, he can deduct 50% of the cost in 2012 using 50% bonus depreciation, which may be used for any property with a useful life less than 20 years. For tax purposes, the sign has a useful life of 15 years. Barry may claim a $5,000 bonus depreciation deduction for the sign in 2012. He can deduct the remaining $5,000 of the sign's cost over 15 years using regular depreciation. Without bonus depreciation, he'd have to deduct the entire $10,000 over 15 years.

Bonus depreciation is optional—you don't have to take it if you don't want to. But if you want to get the largest depreciation deduction you can during the year that you buy long-term personal property for your business, you'll want to take advantage of it whenever you can.

CAUTION

Bonus depreciation is scheduled to end after 2012. Bonus depreciation was enacted as a temporary measure to help the ailing U.S. economy. It was originally scheduled to end on December 31, 2008. However, due to the continuing bad economy, it was extended through the end of 2012. This means that, unless Congress acts to extend it again, you won't be able to use bonus depreciation for long-term personal property that you place in service starting in 2013.

Property That Qualifies for Bonus Depreciation

Property qualifies for bonus depreciation only if:

- it is new (if the newly purchased property contains used parts, it is still treated as new if the cost of the used parts is less than 20% of the total cost of the property)
- it has a useful life of 20 years or less (this includes all types of tangible personal business property and software you buy, but not real property—see above), and
- you purchase it from someone who is unrelated to you (it can't be a gift or inheritance).

In addition, if the asset is listed property, it must be used over 50% of the time for business to qualify for bonus depreciation. (Listed property consists of automobiles and computers and certain other personal property—see "Listed Property," above.)

In contrast, you can use the Section 179 deduction and regular depreciation for both used and new personal property. And, you can use regular depreciation for any long-term business property, including listed property, without any restrictions on the percentage of business use.

Placed-in-Service Date

Bonus depreciation is available only for personal business use property purchased and placed in service during 2008 through 2012. In other words, you won't be able to take bonus depreciation for property purchased and placed in service during 2013 or later, or before 2008. Property is "placed in service" when it's ready and available for use in your business. As long as it is available for use, you don't have to actually use the property for business during the year to take depreciation.

> EXAMPLE: Tom, a real estate agent, purchased a digital camera to take photos of properties for sale. He had the device ready for use in his office on November 1, 2012. However, he had no properties to photograph until 2013. Tom may take a depreciation deduction for the camera for 2012, even though he didn't actually use it that year, because it was ready and available for use then.

There are certain exceptions to the time-period rules. For example, if the property is purchased to repair or replace business property damaged by a federally declared disaster that occurred during 2008 through 2009, then the time period is extended through December 31, 2012. There are other exceptions for airplanes and certain other property that costs more than $1 million and takes more than one year to produce.

Class-Wide Requirement

If you use bonus depreciation, you must use it for all assets that fall within the same class. Unlike Section 179 expensing, you may not pick and choose the assets you want to apply it to within a class. For example, if you buy a car and take bonus depreciation, you must take bonus depreciation for any other property you buy that year within the same class. Cars are five-year property, so you must take bonus depreciation that year for any other five-year property—for example, computers and office equipment. (See "IRS Depreciation Periods," below, for a list of the various classes of property.)

Calculating the Bonus Amount

You use bonus depreciation to figure out your depreciation deduction for the first year that you own an asset. You figure the deduction by multiplying the depreciable basis of the asset by the applicable bonus percentage. (See "Methods for Deducting Property," above, for how to figure an asset's depreciable basis.) For property placed in service in 2012, this calculation is easy because the bonus percentage is 50%.

> EXAMPLE: Stan, a real estate broker, purchased and placed into service $10,000 in computer equipment for his office during 2012. He claims 50% bonus depreciation, which allows him to deduct the $5,000 cost in 2012. (He couldn't use Section 179 to deduct the expense in 2012 because his business lost money that year and the Section 179 deduction is limited to a business owner's annual net income.) He may deduct the remaining $5,000 using regular depreciation. His regular depreciation for 2012 is $1,000 (20% x $5,000). Thus, his total deduction for 2012 is $6,000.

If you want to claim the Section 179 deduction and 50% bonus depreciation for the same asset, you first use Section 179, then 50% bonus depreciation, and then regular depreciation, in that order. This can give you an enormous deduction.

Opting Out of the Bonus

Bonus depreciation deduction is applied automatically to all taxpayers who qualify for it. However, the deduction is optional. You need not take it if you don't want to. You can elect not to take the deduction by attaching a note to your tax return. It may be advantageous to do this if you expect your income to go up substantially in future years, placing you in a higher tax bracket.

CAUTION

When you opt out, you do so for the entire class of assets. It's very important to understand that if you opt out of the bonus, you must do so for the entire class of assets, not just one asset within a class. This is the same rule that applies when you decide to take the bonus.

Regular Depreciation

The traditional method of getting back the money you spend on long-term business assets is to deduct the cost a little at a time over several years (exactly how long is determined by the IRS). This process is called depreciation. Depreciation is a complicated subject. The IRS instruction booklet on the subject (Publication 946, *How to Depreciate Property*) is over 100 pages long. For a comprehensive discussion of depreciation, read Publication 946. In this section, we cover the depreciation basics that all real estate pros should know.

CAUTION

Regular depreciation is not optional. Unlike the Section 179 deduction or bonus depreciation, regular depreciation is not optional. You must take a depreciation deduction if you qualify for it. If you fail to take it, the IRS will treat you as if you had taken it. This means that you could be subject to depreciation recapture when you sell the asset—even if you never took a depreciation deduction. This would increase your taxable income by the amount of the deduction you failed to take. (See "Depreciation Recapture," below.)
So if you don't expense a depreciable asset under Section 179 or claim bonus depreciation, be sure to take the proper regular depreciation deductions for it. If you realize later that you failed to take a depreciation deduction that you should have taken, you may file an amended tax return to claim any deductions that you should have taken in prior years.

When to Use Regular Depreciation

With the Section 179 deduction at $139,000 for 2012, and 50% first-year bonus depreciation for 2012, you might not need to use regular depreciation for the foreseeable future. However, you may need to use regular depreciation to write off the cost of long-term assets that don't qualify for Section 179 expensing or bonus depreciation. Also, under some circumstances, it may be better to use depreciation and draw out your deduction over several years instead of getting your deductions all at once under Section 179 and/or bonus depreciation.

When You Can't Use Section 179

There are many more limitations on using Section 179 than there are for regular depreciation. For example, you can't use Section 179 to deduct the cost of something that you use less than 50% of the time for business. There is no such minimum percentage business use for regular depreciation—you can use and deduct 1% of an item's cost if that's your business use. Other restrictions that apply to Section 179 that don't apply to regular depreciation include the following. Under Section 179, you can't deduct:

- personal property items that you convert to business use
- structures, such as a building or building component
- items financed with a trade-in (the value of the trade-in must be depreciated)
- intangible assets such a patent, copyright, trademark, or business goodwill
- items purchased from a relative
- property inherited or received it as a gift
- air conditioning or heating units, or
- personal property used inside rental property—for example, kitchen appliances, carpets, drapes, or blinds.

None of these limitations apply to regular depreciation.

In addition, your Section 179 deduction may not exceed your business income. If you're married and file a joint return, your spouse's income can be included. But if your real estate business is making little or no money and you have little or no income from wages or your spouse, you may not be able take a Section 179 deduction for the current year. In contrast, there is no income limitation on regular or bonus depreciation deductions. You can deduct regular or bonus depreciation from your business income; if this results in a net loss for a year, you can deduct the loss from income taxes you paid in prior years.

You will also have to use depreciation instead of Section 179 to the extent you exceed the Section 179 annual limit.

When You Can't Use Bonus Depreciation

There are also rules that limit the availability of bonus depreciation that don't apply to regular depreciation. With bonus depreciation, you can't deduct:

- used property, including property you convert to business use
- real property
- listed property used less than 51% of the time for business
- property received as a gift or inheritance, or
- intangible assets such patents, copyrights, trademarks, or business goodwill.

None of these limitations apply to regular depreciation, so there may be instances when you can't use bonus depreciation but the property is still eligible for regular depreciation.

Buying Property With a Trade-In Is Good Tax Strategy

Of course, not all business property is bought with cash. You may pay for it wholly or partly with a trade-in. In this event, you may only use regular depreciation to deduct the property's basis. Moreover, the property's basis is not determined according to its cost. If you buy property with a trade-in, your starting basis is equal to the adjusted basis in the trade-in property, plus any cash you pay for the property. Trading in old business property for new property can be a great tax strategy. When you sell business property, you have to pay taxes on any gain you receive. If you use old property for a trade-in, you defer any tax on the gain until you sell the newly acquired property.

Sometimes Regular Depreciation Is Better

Section 179 expensing and/or bonus depreciation let you deduct all or most of the cost of an asset up front and in one year, while regular depreciation requires you to deduct the cost of an asset a little at a time over several years. The slower depreciation method isn't always a bad thing. In some circumstances, you may be better off using depreciation instead of Section 179 or bonus depreciation.

Remember: The value of a deduction depends on your income tax bracket. If you're in the 15% bracket, a $1,000 deduction is worth only $150 of federal income tax savings. If you're in the 28% bracket, it's worth $280. (See Chapter 1 for more on the value of a tax deduction.) If you expect to earn more in future years, it may make sense to spread out your deductions so you save some for later years when you expect to be in a higher tax bracket.

IRS Depreciation Periods

The depreciation period (also called the recovery period) is the time over which you must take your depreciation deductions for an asset. The tax code has assigned depreciation periods to all types of business assets, ranging from three to 39 years. These periods are somewhat arbitrary. However, property that can be expected to last a long time generally gets a longer recovery period than property that has a short life. Nonresidential real property (an office building, for example) has a 39-year recovery period, while software has only a three-year period. Most of the property that you buy for your practice will probably have a five- or seven-year depreciation period.

The major depreciation periods are listed below. These periods are also called recovery classes, and all property that comes within a period is said to belong to that class. For example, computers have a five-year depreciation period and thus fall within the five-year class, along with automobiles and office equipment.

Depreciation Periods	
Depreciation Period	**Type of Property**
3 years	• Computer software • Tractor units for over-the-road use • Any race horse over 2 years old when placed in service • Any other horse over 12 years old when placed in service
5 years	• Automobiles, taxis, buses, and trucks • Computers and peripheral equipment • Office machinery (such as typewriters, calculators, and copiers) • Any property used in research and experimentation • Breeding cattle and dairy cattle • Appliances, carpets, furniture, and so on used in a residential rental real estate activity
7 years	• Office furniture and fixtures (such as desks, files, and safes) • Agricultural machinery and equipment • Any property that does not have a class life and has not been designated by law as being in any other class
10 years	• Vessels, barges, tugs, and similar water transportation equipment • Any single-purpose agricultural or horticultural structure • Any tree or vine bearing fruits or nuts
15 years	• Improvements made directly to land or added to it (such as shrubbery, fences, roads, and bridges) • Any retail motor fuels outlet, such as a convenience store at a gas station • Interior improvements to leased nonresidential property and certain restaurant property placed in service between October 22, 2004 and December 31, 2009
20 years	• Farm buildings (other than single-purpose agricultural or horticultural structures)
27.5 years	• Residential rental property—for example, an apartment building
39 years	• Nonresidential real property, such as a home office, office building, store, or warehouse

First-Year Depreciation

The IRS has established certain rules (called conventions) that govern how many months of regular depreciation you can take for the first year that you own an asset.

Half-Year Convention

The basic rule is that, no matter what month and day of the year an asset you purchase becomes available for use in your business, you treat it as being placed in service on July 1—the midpoint of the year. This means that you get one-half year of depreciation for the first year that you own an asset.

Midquarter Convention

You are not allowed to use the half-year convention if more than 40% of the long-term personal property that you buy during the year is placed in service during the last three months of the year. The 40% figure is determined by adding together the basis of all the depreciable property you bought during the year and comparing that with the basis of all of the property you bought during the fourth quarter only.

If you exceed the 40% ceiling, you must use the midquarter convention. You group all the property that you purchased during the year by the quarter it was bought and treat it as being placed in service at the midpoint of that quarter. (A quarter is a three-month period: The first quarter is January through March; the second quarter is April through June; the third quarter is July through September; and the fourth quarter is October through December.)

As a general rule, it's best to avoid having to use the midquarter convention. To do this, you need to buy more than 60% of your total depreciable assets before September 30 of the year. Assets you currently deduct using Section 179 do not count toward the 40% limitation, so you can avoid the midquarter convention by using Section 179 to deduct most or all of your purchases in the last three months of the year.

Depreciation Methods

There are several ways to calculate depreciation. However, most tangible property is depreciated using the Modified Accelerated Cost Recovery System, or MACRS. A slightly different system, called Alternative Depreciation System or ADS, applies to certain listed property (see below), property used outside the United States, and certain farm property and imported property.

You can ordinarily use three different methods to calculate the depreciation deduction under MACRS: straight-line or one of two accelerated depreciation methods. Once you choose your method, you're stuck with it for the entire life of the asset.

In addition, you must use the same method for all property of the same class that you purchase during the year. For example, if you use the straight-line method to depreciate a computer, you must use that method to depreciate all other property in the same class as computers. Computers fall within the five-year class, so you must use the straight-line method for all other five-year property you buy during the year, such as office equipment.

Straight-Line Method

The straight-line method requires you to deduct an equal amount each year over the useful life of an asset. However, if the midyear convention applies, you deduct only a half-year's worth of depreciation in the first year. You make up for this by adding an extra one-half year of depreciation at the end. You can use the straight-line method to depreciate any type of depreciable property.

> EXAMPLE: Sally buys a $1,000 printer-fax-copy machine for her real estate business in 2012. It has a useful life of five years. (See the "Depreciation Periods" chart, above, in "IRS Depreciation Periods.") She bought more than 60% of her depreciable property for the year before September 30, so she can use the midyear convention. Using the straight-line method, she can depreciate the asset over six years. Her annual depreciation deductions are as follows:

2012	$100
2013	200
2014	200
2015	200
2016	200
2017	100
Total	$1,000

If the midquarter convention applies, you don't get one-half year's worth of depreciation the first year. Instead, your first year depreciation amount depends on the month of the year when you bought the property. For example, if Sally bought her machine in September, she would only get $75 deprecation in 2012, $200 in 2013 through 2016, and then $125 in 2017. If she bought it in December, she would get $25 in 2012 and $175 in 2017. If she bought it in January, she would get $175 in 2012 and $25 in 2017.

Accelerated Depreciation Methods

There is nothing wrong with straight-line depreciation, but the tax law provides an alternative that most businesses prefer: accelerated depreciation. As the name implies, this method provides faster depreciation than the straight-line method. It does not increase your total depreciation deduction, but it permits you to take larger deductions in the first few years after you buy an asset. You make up for this by taking smaller deductions in later years.

The fastest and most commonly used form of accelerated depreciation is the double-declining balance method. This is a confusing name, but all it means is that you get double the deduction that you would get for the first full year under the straight-line method. You then get less in later years. However, in later years, you may switch to the straight-line method (which will give you a larger deduction). This is built into the IRS depreciation tables. This method may be used to depreciate all property within the three-, five-, seven-, and ten-year classes, excluding farm property. This covers virtually all the tangible personal property you buy for your business.

EXAMPLE: Sally decides to use the double-declining balance method to depreciate her $1,000 printer-fax-copier machine. Her annual depreciation deductions are as follows:

2012	$200.00
2013	320.00
2014	192.00
2015	115.20
2016	115.20
2017	57.60
Total	$1,000.00

By using this method, she gets a $200 deduction in the first year, instead of the $100 deduction she'd get using straight-line depreciation. But starting two years later, she'll get smaller deductions than she would using the straight-line method.

The table below prepared by the IRS shows you the percentage of the cost of an asset that you may deduct each year using the double-declining balance method.

Depreciation Tables

Figuring out your annual depreciation deduction might seem to require some complicated math, but actually it's not that difficult. Of course, if you use a tax professional to do your taxes, he or she will do the math for you. Tax preparation software can also do this. However, if you want to do it yourself, you can use depreciation tables prepared by the IRS. These tables factor in the depreciation convention and method. They are all available in IRS Publication 946, *How to Depreciate Property* (available at the IRS website at www.irs.gov).

How to Depreciate Listed Property

The IRS imposes special rules on listed property—items that can easily be used for personal as well as business purposes. (See "Listed Property," above, for more.) If you use listed property for business more than

200% Declining Balance Depreciation Method Convention: Half-year						
	If the recovery period is:					
Year	3-year	5-year	7-year	10-year	15-year	20-year
1	33.33%	20.00%	14.29%	10.00%	5.00%	3.750%
2	44.45%	32.00%	24.49%	18.00%	9.50%	7.219%
3	14.81%	19.20%	17.49%	14.40%	8.55%	6.677%
4	7.41%	11.52%	12.49%	11.52%	7.70%	6.177%
5		11.52%	8.93%	9.22%	6.93%	5.713%
6		5.76%	8.92%	7.37%	6.23%	5.285%
7			8.93%	6.55%	5.90%	4.888%
8			4.46%	6.55%	5.90%	4.522%
9				6.56%	5.91%	4.462%
10				6.55%	5.90%	4.461%
11				3.28%	5.91%	4.462%
12					5.90%	4.461%
13					5.91%	4.462%
14					5.90%	4.461%
15					5.91%	4.462%
16					2.95%	4.461%
17						4.462%
18						4.461%
19						4.462%
20						4.461%
21						2.231%

50% of the time, you may deduct its cost just like any other long-term business property using Section 179 or under normal depreciation rules.

However, if your business use of property is 50% or less, you may not deduct its cost under Section 179 or use bonus depreciation or accelerated regular depreciation. Instead, you must use the slowest method of regular depreciation: straight-line depreciation. In addition, you are not allowed to use the normal depreciation periods allowed under the MACRS depreciation system. Instead, you must use the depreciation periods provided for by the Alternative Depreciation System (ADS for short). These are generally longer than the ordinary MACRS periods. However, you may still depreciate cars, trucks, and computers over five years. The main ADS depreciation periods for listed property are provided in the following chart.

ADS Depreciation Periods

Property	Depreciation Period
Cars and light trucks	5 years
Computers and peripheral equipment	5 years
Communication equipment	10 years
Personal property with no class life	12 years

If you start out using accelerated depreciation and in a later year your business use drops to 50% or less, you have to switch to the straight-line method and ADS period for that year and subsequent years. In addition, you are subject to depreciation recapture for the prior years—that is, you must calculate how much more depreciation you got in the prior years by using accelerated depreciation and count that amount as ordinary taxable income for the current year. This will, of course, increase your tax bill for the year.

Computer Software

Most real estate professionals buy computer software; some also create it themselves. The tax law favors the latter group.

Software You Buy

The software you buy comes in two basic types for tax purposes: software that comes already installed on a computer that you buy and software you purchase separately and install yourself (often called off-the-shelf software). Software that comes with a computer you buy and is included in the price—for example, your operating system—is depreciated as part of the computer, unless you're billed separately for the software. Off-the-shelf software must be depreciated over three years using the straight-line method. You can also use bonus depreciation for off-the-shelf software.

In the past, Section 179 expensing was not available for computer software because it is intangible property. Congress temporarily changed the law in 2003 to permit off-the-shelf software to be currently deducted under Section 179. However, this exception applies only to software placed in service from January 1, 2003 through December 31, 2012. Starting in 2013, Section 179 once again was prohibited for off-the-shelf software (unless, of course, the law is changed again).

If you acquire software that is not off-the-shelf software by buying another business or its assets, the rules discussed above don't apply. This software must be depreciated over 15 years using the straight-line method; this type of depreciation is called amortization. (IRC § 197.)

Software You Create

If, instead of buying off-the-shelf software, you create it yourself, you can currently deduct the cost under Section 174 of the Internal Revenue Code. This section allows deductions for research and experimentation expenses incurred in developing an invention, patent, process, prototype, formula, technique, or similar product.

You may currently deduct the costs under Section 174 whether the software is developed for your own use or to sell or license to others. (Rev. Proc. 2000-50.) For a detailed discussion of Section 174, see *What Every Inventor Needs to Know About Business & Taxes*, by Stephen Fishman (Nolo).

Real Property

Land cannot be depreciated because it never wears out. However, this doesn't mean you don't get a tax deduction for it. When you sell land, you may deduct the cost of the land from the sale price to determine your taxable gain, if any. The cost of clearing, grading, landscaping, or demolishing buildings on land is not depreciable. It is added to the tax basis of the land—that is, to its cost—and subtracted from the money you get when you sell the land.

Unlike land, buildings do wear out over time and therefore may be depreciated. This means that when you buy property with buildings on it, you must separate out the cost of the buildings from the total cost of the property to calculate your depreciation.

As you might expect, the depreciation periods for buildings are quite long (after all, buildings usually last a long time). The depreciation period for nonresidential buildings placed in service after May 12, 1993 is 39 years. You must use the straight-line method to depreciate real property. This means you'll be able to deduct only a small fraction of its value each year—1/39th of its value each year if the 39-year period applies.

Home Office Depreciation

If you have an office or other workplace you use solely for business in your home, you are entitled to depreciate the business portion of the home. For example, if you use 10% of your home for business, you may depreciate 10% of its cost (excluding the cost of the land). In the unlikely event your home has gone down in value since you bought it, you must use its fair market value on the date you began using your home office as your tax basis. You depreciate a home office over 39 years—the term used for nonresidential property. A home office is nonresidential property because you don't live in it.

Improvements to Leased Property

If you lease your office, as many real estate professionals do, you may depreciate any improvements you make (and pay for)—for example, installing new carpeting. Ordinarily, such improvements must be depreciated over 39 years, but a special rule permits many leasehold improvements to be depreciated over 15 years using the straight-line method.

Depreciation Recapture

To currently deduct long-term property under Section 179 or depreciate listed property using bonus depreciation or accelerated regular deprecia-tion, you must use the property for your business at least 51% of the time. If your business use falls under 51%, you'll have to give back part of the Section 179 or bonus or accelerated depreciation deductions you received. This is called "recapture" because the IRS is getting back—recapturing—part of your deduction. (See "Recapture Under Section 179," earlier in this chapter, for more on recapture.)

Recapture is required for listed property (personal use property) when your business use falls below 51% and for any property for which you took a Section 179 deduction. It is not required for nonlisted property for which you took no Section 179 deduction.

Recapture of all or part of the depreciation and/or Section 179 deduction previously allowed is also triggered when you sell any long-term, nonlisted asset for a gain—that is, for more than your adjusted basis.

> **EXAMPLE:** Sam buys a copy machine for his real estate business for $5,000. He takes $3,470 in depreciation deductions over the next two years. This leaves him with an adjusted basis of $1,530, at which point he decides to sell the machine. He gets $2,500 for the sale, which gives him a $970 gain. This gain is taxable as ordinary income.

You can't avoid recapture by not taking a Section 179 or depreciation deduction to which you were entitled. The IRS will treat you as though you took the deduction for recapture purposes, even if you really didn't.

> **EXAMPLE:** If Sam fails to depreciate his copy machine and then sells it two years later for $2,500, the IRS will figure that his adjusted

basis is $1,530, because he could have taken $3,470 in depreciation for it. So, he still has a taxable gain of $970.

Special Rules for Deducting Automobiles and Other Vehicles

If you use an automobile or other vehicle in your real estate business, you can deduct the cost in one of two ways: you can use the standard mileage rate deduction which permits you to deduct a specified amount for each business mile you drive (55.5 cents per mile in 2012); or you can deduct what you actually spend on the vehicle. If you use the standard mileage rate, you get no separate depreciation or Section 179 deduction because it is in included in the standard mileage rate deduction (see Chapter 4). If you're using the standard mileage rate, you don't need to read the rest of this section.

If you use the actual expense method, you are allowed to separately deduct the cost of your vehicle, as well as what you spend on gas, oil, repairs, and similar expenses. Although the general concept of depreciation and Section 179 expensing is the same for every type of property, special rules apply to depreciation and expensing deductions for cars. These rules give you a lower deduction for cars than you'd be entitled to using the normal depreciation and expensing rules.

Is Your Vehicle a Passenger Automobile?

First, you must figure out whether your vehicle is a passenger automobile as defined by the IRS. A passenger automobile is any four-wheeled vehicle made primarily for use on public streets and highways that has an unloaded gross weight of 6,000 pounds or less. The vehicle weight includes any part or other item physically attached to the automobile or usually included in the purchase price of an automobile. This definition includes virtually all automobiles.

However, if your vehicle is classified as a truck or van by the manufacturer, it is a passenger automobile only if it has a gross loaded vehicle weight of 6,000 pounds or less. The truck or van classification can apply not only to traditional trucks or vans, but to other vehicles such as SUVs, mini-vans, and crossover vehicles. This is based on Department of Transportation rules that all car manufacturers must follow. The gross loaded weight is based on how much the manufacturer says the vehicle can carry and is different from unloaded weight—that is, the vehicle's weight without any passengers or cargo.

You can find out your vehicle's gross loaded and unloaded weight by looking at the metal plate in the driver's side door jamb, looking at your owner's manual, checking the manufacturer's website or sales brochure, or asking an auto dealer. The gross loaded weight is usually called the Gross Vehicle Weight Rating (GVWR for short). The gross unloaded weight is often called the "curb weight."

Broker's Minivan Weighed More than 6,000 Pounds

Michelle Chiou, a real estate broker, purchased a Honda minivan for her business. The minivan's gross vehicle weight was 5,953 pounds. However, Chiou purchased the minivan with five accessories: all-season floor mats that weighed 18 pounds, cargo boards that weighed ten pounds, a cargo tray that weighed six pounds, a third-row sunshade that weighed eight pounds, and a cargo mat that weighed ten pounds. The combined weight of the five accessories was 52 pounds, and when added to the minivan's gross vehicle weight of 5,953 pounds, the total was 6,005 pounds. As a result, the minivan was not a passenger vehicle for tax purposes. (*Engle v. Comm'r*, 2009 TC Summ. Op. 138 (2009).)

Passenger Automobiles Are Listed Property

All passenger automobiles are listed property—property that is often used for personal purposes. As explained above, the IRS imposes more stringent requirements on deductions for listed property to discourage fraudulent deduction claims. Because passenger automobiles are listed property, you must keep mileage records showing how much you use your car for business and personal purposes and you must file IRS Form

4562, *Depreciation and Amortization*, with your annual tax return. (See Chapter 4.)

What You Can Depreciate

You can depreciate and/or expense your entire investment in a car (also called your basis). If you buy a passenger automobile and use it for business that same year, your basis is its cost. You may depreciate the entire cost, even if you financed part of the purchase with a car loan. The cost also includes sales taxes, destination charges, and other fees the seller charges. It does not, however, include auto license and registration fees. This assumes you use the car 100% for business. If you use it less than 100%, you may only depreciate or expense an amount equal to your percentage of business use. For example, if you use your car 60% for business, you may depreciate or expense only 60% of the cost.

If you trade in your old car to a dealer to purchase a new car, your basis in the car you purchase is equal to the adjusted basis of the trade-in car, plus the cash you pay (whether out of your own pocket or financed with a car loan).

> EXAMPLE: Brenda buys a new car for her consulting practice. The car has a $20,000 sticker price. She trades in her old car and pays the dealer $15,000, all of which she finances with a car loan from her bank. Her trade-in has an adjusted basis of $7,000. Her basis in the new car is $22,000 ($7,000 + $15,000), even though the sticker price on the new car was only $20,000.

If you convert a car that you previously owned for personal use to a business car, your basis in the car is the lower of what you paid for it (at the time you purchased it for personal use) or its fair market value at the time you convert it to business use. Your basis will usually be its fair market value, as this is usually the lower number. You can determine the fair market value by checking used car value guides, such as the *Kelley Blue Book*.

Deduction Limits for Passenger Automobiles

Depreciating and/or expensing a passenger automobile is unique in one very important way: The annual depreciation and expensing deduction for automobiles is limited to a set dollar amount each year. The annual limit applies to all passenger vehicles, no matter how much they cost. Because the limits are so low, it can take many years to fully deduct the cost of a car, far longer than the six years it takes to depreciate other assets with a five-year recovery period.

Starting in 2003, the IRS established two different sets of deduction limits for passenger automobiles: one for passenger automobiles other than trucks and vans, and slightly higher limits for trucks and vans that qualify as passenger automobiles (based on their weight) and are built on a truck chassis. This includes minivans and sport utility vehicles built on a truck chassis (as long as they meet the weight limit).

The charts below show the maximum annual depreciation deduction allowed for passenger automobiles and trucks and vans placed in service in 2012. The second chart shows the limits for passenger automobiles that are trucks and vans as defined above. Both charts assume 100% business use of the vehicle. You can find all the deduction limits in IRS Publication 946, *How to Depreciate Property*, and Publication 463, *Travel, Entertainment, Gift, and Car Expenses.*

Depreciation Limits for Passenger Automobiles Placed in Service During 2012	
1st tax year	$11,160 ($3,160 + $8,000 bonus depreciation)
2nd tax year	$5,100
3rd tax year	$3,050
Each succeeding year	$1,875

Depreciation Limits for Trucks and Vans Qualifying as Passenger Automobiles Placed in Service During 2012	
1st tax year	$11,360 ($3,360 + $8,000 bonus depreciation)
2nd tax year	$5,300
3rd tax year	$3,150
Each succeeding year	$1,875

The depreciation limits are not reduced if a car is in service for less than a full year. This means that the limit is not reduced when the automobile is either placed in service or disposed of during the year.

These figures are the maximum amount you can deduct each year, regardless of what depreciation method you use or whether you use first-year bonus depreciation or Section 179 expensing.

> EXAMPLE: Mario pays $50,000 for a new passenger automobile on June 1, 2012 and uses it 100% for his real estate business. He may deduct a maximum of $11,160 in 2012, $5,100 in 2013, $3,050 in 2014, and $1,875 each year thereafter.

The first-year deduction limit is so large (compared to the other years) because of first-year bonus depreciation (see above). For passenger automobiles, the first-year bonus allows you to add $8,000 to the regular depreciation limit of $3,160. However, if you don't qualify for bonus depreciation or decide not to opt out (it isn't required), your first-year deduction limit will be reduced to the regular $3,160 level. To take bonus depreciation, you must buy a new car and use it more than 50% of the time for your business during 2012.

> EXAMPLE: Mario buys a used car instead of a new one. He may not take first-year bonus depreciation for the car, so his first-year deduction is limited to $3,160.

The deduction limits in the above table are based on 100% business use of the vehicle. If you don't use your car solely for business, the limits are reduced based on your percentage of personal use.

EXAMPLE: Mario uses his new passenger car 60% for business. His first-year deduction is limited to $6,696 (60% × $11,160).

You may combine Section 179 expensing with bonus and regular depreciation, in that order. However, your total deduction cannot exceed the annual limits listed in the charts above. You reduce the depreciable basis in the auto after each deduction is taken.

Given the fact that the maximum Section 179 deduction for 2012 is $139,000, it may not be necessary to use bonus or regular depreciation because the Section 179 deduction alone will be enough to equal the maximum allowed deduction.

EXAMPLE: In February 2012, Mario buys a new $20,000 car, which he uses 100% for his real estate business. His business earned $100,000 for the year. He may deduct a maximum of $11,160 of the cost for 2012. He decides to deduct the entire $11,160 of the cost the first year using Section 179. This leaves him with a depreciable basis of $8,840 to depreciate in future years under the regular depreciation rules (subject to the annual limits noted above).

However, in some cases it may not be possible or advisable to take advantage of Section 179 because it is subject to important limitations. First, for an automobile to qualify, you must use it for business over 50% of the time for six years (the IRS useful life for automobiles). If you qualify for Section 179 the first year but your business usage falls below 51% in a later year, you'll have to give back to the IRS any extra deduction you got the first year by using Section 179 instead of or in addition to regular depreciation—a process known as recapture (see above). So don't use Section 179 unless you're sure you'll use the car over half the time for business over the next six years.

In addition, there is an income limit: Your Section 179 deduction for the year may not exceed your business's annual income. If you have no income, or a very small one, you'll get little or no Section 179 deduction that year. You'll have to carry forward the deduction and use it on your next year's taxes. In addition, you cannot use Section 179 if you convert a personal passenger automobile to business use.

In contrast, depreciation (whether regular or bonus) is not subject to an income limit. Thus, you get a full deduction for the current year even if it exceeds the income from your business or you have no income. Any resulting net operating loss for the year may be used to reduce your taxable income from other sources—for example, income from a job, your spouse's income, or investment income. Any remaining loss can be used to obtain a refund for part of the tax you paid in previous years, or can be applied to future years.

> EXAMPLE: Assume that Mario from the above example lost money from his real estate business during 2012. Nevertheless, he purchases a $25,000 car he uses 100% for the business. He can still deduct $11,160 of the cost of the car for 2012. However, if he uses Section 179 to deduct all or part of the cost, he won't be able to deduct any of it that year. Mario will have to carry it forward to deduct the following year. On the other hand, he can take full bonus and regular depreciation deductions, even though his business earned no money. He first takes bonus depreciation, which permits him to deduct 50% of the cost of the car. This amounts to $12,500, which exceeds the $11,160 auto depreciation limit for the year. By using bonus deprecation alone, Mario gets to deduct $11,160 as a business deduction. This and his other business deductions give him a $20,000 business loss for the year which he uses to help offset his wife's income that year (he and his wife file a joint return).

If a car is relatively inexpensive, there may be some room left under the $11,160 cap after bonus deprecation is taken. You can depreciate this amount using the regular depreciation rules. Usually, people use the fastest form of depreciation, the 200% declining balance method. Under this method, 20% of an automobile's cost could be depreciated in the first year.

> EXAMPLE: Assume that Mario's business car that he uses 100% for business cost $20,000 in 2012. He first deducts $10,000 using bonus depreciation. Using regular depreciation, he can take an additional deduction of $2,000 for the remaining $10,000

(20% × $10,000 = $2,000). However, because of the $11,160 annual cap, he can only deduct $1,160 of this amount, giving him a total deduction of $11,160. He then uses regular depreciation in later years to deduct the remaining basis, subject to the annual caps.

In many cases, it won't be possible to use bonus depreciation—for example, if you use the car less than 51% for business or if you bought the car used. In this event, you must depreciate the entire cost under the regular rules. You'll have to use the slowest method of depreciation (the straight-line method) if you use the car less than 51% for business, and you'll have to continue with this method even if your business use rises over 50% in later years.

Depreciation Methods

The following table shows how much of the cost of an automobile may be depreciated each year using the three different depreciation methods and applying the midyear convention. (If more than 40% of all the depreciable property you placed in service during the year was placed in service during the last quarter of the year, you'll have to use the midquarter convention; see above.) You must use the slower straight-line method if you use your car less than 51% for business and you must continue to use this method even if your business use rises over 50% in later years. Although automobiles have a five-year recovery period, they are depreciated over six calendar years.

Year	200% Declining Balance Method (midyear convention)	150% Declining Balance Method (midyear convention)	Straight-Line Method (midyear convention)
1	20%	15%	10%
2	32%	25.5%	20%
3	19.2%	17.85%	20%
4	11.5%	16.66%	20%
5	11.5%	16.66%	20%
6	5.76%	8.33%	10%

EXAMPLE: Assume that Mario buys a new car for $25,000 in 2012 that he uses 20% for business. His low business use of the car means that it does not qualify for bonus depreciation or Section 179. He must depreciate the car under regular deprecation, using the straight-line method. This gives him a deduction for the first year equal to 10% of his depreciable basis. Since his depreciable basis is $5,000 (20% of $25,000 = $5,000), he qualifies for only a $500 depreciation deduction that year (10% × $5,000 = $500).

How Long Do You Depreciate an Auto?

Because of the annual limits on depreciation and Section 179 deductions for passenger automobiles, you often won't be able to deduct the entire cost of a car over the six-year recovery period. Don't worry—as long as you continue to use your car for business, you can keep taking annual deductions after the six-year recovery period ends, until you recover your full basis in the car. The maximum amount you can deduct each year is determined by the date you placed the car in service and your business use percentage.

EXAMPLE: In 2012, Kim pays $50,000 for a car she uses 100% for her real estate business. Her depreciable basis in the car is $50,000. Her maximum depreciation deductions for the car over the next six years are as follows:

2012	$11,160
2013	$5,100
2014	3,050
2015	1,875
2016	1,875
2017	1,875
Total	$24,935

At the end of the depreciation period, she has $24,935 in unrecovered basis. Even though the depreciation period is over, she may continue to deduct $1,875 each year until she recovers the remaining $25,065 (assuming she continues to use the car 100% for business). This will take another 13 years.

Heavy Deductions for Heavy Metal: Expensing SUVs and Other Weighty Vehicles

The depreciation limits discussed above apply only to passenger automobiles—that is, vehicles with a gross unloaded weight of less than 6,000 pounds. However, in the case of trucks and vans, the 6,000 pound weight limit is based on gross loaded weight. (See "Is Your Vehicle a Passenger Automobile?" above.) Vehicles that weigh more than this are not subject to the limits. Using bonus depreciation and/or Section 179, this means you may be able to deduct all or most of the cost of such a vehicle in a single year—a potentially enormous deduction for real estate professionals who purchase heavy SUVs and similar vehicles for their business.

Bonus Depreciation

If an over-6,000-pound vehicle is placed in service in 2012, it will qualify for 50% first-year bonus depreciation. This means you can deduct 50% of the cost in one year if you use the vehicle 100% for business.

Section 179

Until 2004, people who purchased SUVs and other heavy vehicles they used over 50% for business could claim the full Section 179 deduction. However, allowing these huge deductions for Hummers and other SUVs bought for business purposes caused such an uproar that Congress limited the Section 179 deduction for SUVs to $25,000. The limit applies to any SUV placed in service after October 22, 2004. For these purposes, an SUV is any four-wheeled vehicle primarily designed or used to carry passengers over public streets, roads, or highways that has a gross vehicle weight of 6,000 to 14,000 pounds.

Auto Repairs and Improvements

Auto repairs and maintenance costs are fully deductible in the year they are incurred. You add these costs to your other annual expenses when you use the actual expense method. (You get no extra deduction for repairs when you use the standard mileage rate.) If you fix your car yourself, you may deduct the cost of parts and depreciate or deduct tools, but you get no deduction for your time or labor.

Unlike repairs, improvements to your car are capital expenses and must be depreciated over several years, not deducted all in the year when you pay for them. What's the difference between a repair and an improvement? Good question. Unlike a repair, an improvement:

- makes the vehicle much better than it was before
- restores the vehicle to operating condition after it has fallen into disrepair, or
- adapts the vehicle to a new use.

> EXAMPLE: Doug spends $100 to flush the carburetor on his business car. This expense simply keeps the vehicle in good running order. It does not make the car substantially better, restore it, or adapt it to a new use. Thus, the expense is a repair that may be currently deducted in the year in which it was incurred.

On the other hand, money you spend that makes the vehicle substantially better than it was before must be treated as an improvement and depreciated over time instead of expensed.

> EXAMPLE: Doug spends $2,500 for a brand-new engine for his car. This is an improvement because it makes the vehicle much better than it was before. Doug may not deduct the expense in a single year. Instead, he must depreciate it over five years.

Improvements are depreciated separately from the vehicle itself—that is, they are treated as a separate item of depreciable property. The same rules, however, apply to depreciating improvements as for regular auto depreciation. Depreciation of the original automobile and the later improvements are combined for purposes of the annual depreciation limits. The recovery period begins when the improvement is placed in service.

Tax Reporting and Record Keeping for Section 179 and Depreciation

Depreciation and Section 179 deductions are reported on IRS Form 4562, *Depreciation and Amortization*. If you have more than one business for which you're claiming depreciation, you must use a separate Form 4562 for each business. You need to file Form 4562 only for the first year a deduction is claimed.

If you're a sole proprietor (or owner of an LLC taxed as a sole proprietorship), you carry over the amount of your depreciation and Section 179 deductions to your Schedule C and subtract them from your gross business income along with your other business expenses.

LLCs and partnerships report their depreciation deductions on IRS Form 1065. These deductions are subtracted from the entity's income, along with all other deductions. The resulting profits or losses are passed through to the owners' individual returns. S corporations use Form 1065S, but the principle is the same. If a Section 179 deduction is taken by an entity taxed as a partnership or S corporation, it must be separately stated on the Schedule K-1 forms given to each owner. C corporations take all of their deductions, including deprecation, on their own tax returns, IRS Form 1120.

You need to keep accurate records for each asset you depreciate or expense under Section 179, showing:

- a description of the asset
- when and how you purchased the property
- the date it was placed in service
- its original cost
- the percentage of time you use it for business
- whether and how much you deducted under Section 179
- the amount of depreciation you took for the asset in prior years, if any
- its depreciable basis
- the depreciation method used
- the length of the depreciation period, and
- the amount of depreciation you deducted for the year.

If you have an accountant or bookkeeper, he or she should prepare these records for you. If you do your taxes yourself, you can use tax preparation software to create a worksheet containing this information. You can also use an accounting program, such as *QuickBooks*, to keep track of your depreciating assets. (Simple checkbook programs like *Quicken* are not designed to keep track of depreciation.) You may also use a spreadsheet program to create your own depreciation worksheet. Spreadsheet templates are available for this purpose. Of course, you can also do the job by hand. The Instructions to IRS Form 4562 contain a worksheet you can use.

For listed property, you'll also have to keep records showing how much of its use is for business and how much is personal. You should also keep proof of the amount you paid for the asset—receipts, canceled checks, and purchase documents. You need not file these records with your tax return, but you must have them available to back up your deductions if you're audited.

Deciding Between Leasing and Buying

When you're acquiring a long-term asset for your real estate business, you should consider whether it makes more sense to lease the item rather than purchase it. Almost everything a real estate professional needs can be leased—automobiles, computers, office furniture, telephones, and other equipment. And leasing can be an attractive alternative to buying. However, it's important to understand the tax consequences of leasing when making your decision.

Leasing Versus Purchasing

So which is better, leasing or buying? It depends. Leasing equipment can be a better option for real estate professionals who have limited capital or who want to upgrade their equipment every few years. Purchasing equipment can be a better option for real estate professionals with ample capital or who intend to keep their equipment for a long time. Each real estate professional's situation is different and the decision to buy or lease must be made on a case-by-case basis.

The following chart summarizes the major tax and nontax differences between leasing and buying equipment.

Leasing Versus Buying		
	Leasing	**Buying**
Tax Treatment	Lease payments are a currently deductible business operating expense. No depreciation or Section 179 deductions.	Up to $139,000 (2012) in equipment purchases can be deducted in one year under Section 179 (if requirements satisfied). Otherwise, cost is depreciated over several years (usually 5 to 7). Interest on loans to buy equipment is currently deductible.
Initial Cash Outlay	Small. No down payment required. Deposit ordinarily required.	Large. At least a 20% down payment usually required. Bank loan may be required to finance the remaining cost.
Ownership	You own nothing at end of lease term.	You own the equipment.
Costs of Equipment Obsolescence	Borne by lessor because it owns equipment. Lessee may lease new equipment when lease expires.	Borne by buyer because buyer owns equipment, which may have little resale value.

Before deciding whether to purchase or lease an expensive item, it's a good idea to determine the total actual costs of each option. This depends on many factors, including:

- the cost of the lease
- the purchase price for the item
- the item's useful life
- the interest rate on a loan to purchase the item
- the item's residual value—how much it will be worth at the end of the lease term
- whether you will purchase the item at the end of the lease and how much this will cost

- how much it would cost to dispose of the item
- your income tax bracket
- whether the item qualifies for one-year Section 179 expensing or bonus depreciation, or must be deducted using regular depreciation, and
- if the item must be depreciated, the length of the depreciation period.

There are several lease-versus-buy calculators on the Internet that you can use to compare the cost of leasing versus buying, including www.lease-vs-buy.com and www.chooseleasing.org. Commercial software and computer spreadsheets can also be used for this purpose.

Leases Versus Installment Purchases

An installment purchase (also called a conditional sales contract) is different from a lease—although the two can seem very similar. With an installment purchase, you end up owning all or part of the property, whereas with a lease you own nothing when the lease ends.

The distinction between a lease and an installment purchase is important because installment purchases are treated very differently for tax purposes. Installment purchase payments are not rent and cannot be deducted as a business operating expense. The purchaser may deduct installment purchase payments under Section 179 or by using bonus depreciation (if applicable) or deduct the property's value over several years using regular depreciation, except that any portion of the payments that represents interest may be currently deducted as an interest expense.

You can't simply label a transaction a lease or installment purchase depending on which is more advantageous. A lease must really be a lease (often called a true lease or tax lease) to pass muster with the IRS. A lease that is really just a way of financing a purchase is a "financial lease," not a true lease, and will be treated as an installment purchase by the IRS.

Whether a transaction is a lease or installment purchase depends on the parties' intent. The IRS will conclude that a conditional sales contract exists if *any of the following* is true:

- The agreement applies part of each payment toward an ownership interest that you will receive.

- You get title to the property upon the payment of a stated amount required under the contract.
- The amount you pay to use the property for a short time is a large part of the amount you would pay to get title to the property.
- You pay much more than the current fair rental value for the property.
- You have an option to buy the property at a nominal price compared to the value of the property when you may exercise the option.
- You have an option to buy the property at a nominal price compared to the total amount you have to pay under the lease.
- The lease designates some part of the payments as interest, or part of the payments are easy to recognize as interest.

A transaction will also look like an installment purchase to the IRS (even if it's labeled a lease) if:

- the lease term is about equal to the functional or economic life of the property
- the lease may not be canceled, and
- the lessee is responsible for maintaining the property.

CHAPTER

10

Getting Going: Deducting Start-Up Expenses

Every real estate broker and agent knows that it costs money to get a new real estate business up and running or to buy an existing business. What many don't know is that these costs (called start-up expenses) are subject to special tax rules. This chapter explains what types of expenditures are start-up expenses and how you can deduct these costs as quickly as possible.

What Are Start-Up Expenses?

Diana obtains a real estate agent license in January of 2012. After investigating several real estate brokerage firms, she agrees to start working at the ABC Brokerage as an independent contractor agent on June 1. Before she moves into the office and opens for business, Diana incurs various expenses, including payment of advance rent to ABC, leasing office furniture, purchasing a computer and digital camera, obtaining insurance, paying for business cards and other promotional materials, and fees to join the local Multiple Listing Service. She spends $5,000 of her savings to get her real estate agent business up and running.

Both Diana and you may be surprised to learn that these $5,000 in expenses she incurred before starting her real estate agent business are not currently deductible business operating expenses. In order to have currently deductible business expenses, you must already be in business. Instead, these are business start-up expenses—expenses incurred before a business begins.

Why is this distinction important? Because, as a general rule, business start-up expenses are not deductible until you sell or otherwise dispose of the business. Start-up expenses are considered capital expenses—that is, they are costs you incur to acquire an asset (a business) that will benefit you for more than one year.

Fortunately, however, there is a special tax rule designed to help small businesses get started. It allows you to deduct up to $5,000 in start-up expenses in the first year you are in business, and then deduct the remainder in equal amounts over the next 15 years. (IRC § 195.)

Once your real estate business begins, the same expenses that were start-up expenses before your business began become currently deductible business operating expenses. For example, rent you pay for office space after your real estate practice starts is a currently deductible operating expense, but rent you pay before your practice begins is a start-up expense.

Starting a New Real Estate Business

Most of the money you spend investigating whether, where, and how to start a new real estate business, as well as the cost of actually creating it, are deductible business start-up expenses. The tax law is much more generous with deductions for start-up costs if you are creating a new business as opposed to buying an existing business.

Common Start-Up Expenses

Here are some common types of deductible start-up expenses:

- the cost of investigating what it will take to create a successful business, including market research
- advertising costs, including advertising for your business's opening
- costs for employee training before the practice begins
- travel expenses related to finding a suitable business location
- expenses related to obtaining financing, suppliers, and clients
- business licenses, permits, and other fees
- fees paid to lawyers, accountants, consultants, and others for professional services, and
- operating expenses incurred before the business begins, such as rent, insurance, telephone, utilities, office supplies, and repairs.

Costs That Are Not Start-Up Expenses

There are some costs related to opening a business that are not considered start-up expenses. Many of these costs are still deductible, but different rules and restrictions apply to the way they are deducted.

Only Business Operating Expenses Qualify

You can deduct as start-up expenses only those costs that would be currently deductible as business operating expenses after your real estate business begins. This means the expenses must be ordinary, necessary, directly related to the business, and reasonable in amount. For example, you can't deduct the cost of pleasure travel or entertainment *unrelated* to your business. These expenses would not be deductible as operating expenses by an ongoing business, so you can't deduct them as start-up expenses either. (In fact, you can't deduct them at all.)

Long-Term Assets

Long-term assets are things you purchase for your business that will last for more than one year, such as computers, office equipment, cars, and cell phones. Long-term assets you buy before your real estate business begins are not considered part of your start-up costs. Instead, you treat these purchases like any other long-term asset you buy *after* your business begins—you must either depreciate the item over several years or deduct the cost in one year under IRS Section 179. (Chapter 9 explains how to deduct long-term assets.) However, you can't take depreciation or Section 179 deductions until after your business begins.

Taxes and Interest

Any tax and interest that you pay before your business begins is not a start-up expense. Instead, these costs are currently deductible as business operating expenses once your business begins. There are a few exceptions to this rule. Sales tax you pay for long-term assets for your business is added to the cost of the asset for purposes of depreciation or Section 179 deduction. (See Chapter 9.) And money you borrow to buy an interest in an S corporation, partnership, or LLC must be allocated among the company's assets. Interest on money you borrow to buy stock in a C corporation is treated as investment interest and may be currently deducted as a personal itemized deduction. (See Chapter 9.)

Organizational Costs

Costs you incur to form a partnership, limited liability company, or corporation are not part of your start-up costs. However, they are deductible in the same amounts as start-up expenses under a separate tax rule.

Education Expenses

You cannot deduct education expenses you incur to qualify for a new business or profession. You also can't deduct fees you must pay to become accredited to initially practice a profession. Thus, you may not deduct your costs of studying for and taking your state's real estate licensing exam.

However, after you begin working as a real estate agent or broker, you may currently deduct your annual real estate licensing fees as an operating expense.

Buying an Existing Real Estate Business

Different rules apply if you buy an existing business rather than create a new one. If you are buying a practice, you can deduct as start-up expenses only the costs you incur to decide *whether* to purchase a practice and *which* practice you should buy.

You don't have to make an offer, sign a letter of intent, or enter into a binding legal agreement to purchase an existing business for your expenses to cease being start-up expenses. You just have to make up your mind to purchase a specific business and focus on acquiring it. (Rev. Rul. 1999-23.)

> EXAMPLE: Sean obtains a real estate broker license and wants to purchase an existing real estate brokerage firm. He hires Duane, a business broker, to help him. Duane evaluates several real estate brokerages for sale, including Acme Realty. Sean decides he would like to buy Acme and hires accountant Al to conduct an in-depth review of its books and records to determine a fair acquisition price. Sean then enters into an acquisition agreement with Acme to purchase all its assets. The fees Sean paid to Duane are start-up expenses because they were paid to help Sean determine whether to purchase an existing business and which business to buy. The fees Sean paid to Al are not start-up expenses because they were incurred to help Sean purchase a specific existing business—the Acme Realty Co.

The money you pay to actually purchase an existing business is neither a start-up expense nor a currently deductible business operating expense. Instead, it is a capital expense. If you purchase an incorporated business by buying its stock, or buy an LLC, or partnership by purchasing the LLC or partnership interests, the cost becomes part of the tax basis of your stock or LLC or partnership interest. If and when you sell your stock or LLC or partnership interest, you will be able to deduct this amount from any profit you make on the sale before taxes are assessed. If, instead of buying the legal entity that owns a real estate business, you simply purchase its individual assets, you may depreciate the cost of tangible assets and amortize the cost of any intangible assets you purchase. (See Chapter 9.)

Expanding an Existing Business

What if you already have an existing real estate business and decide to expand it? The cost of expanding an existing business is considered a business operating expense, not a start-up expense. As long as these costs are ordinary and necessary, they are currently deductible.

> EXAMPLE: Sam, a successful real estate broker who works out of his home, decides to expand his business. He rents office space, takes on several real estate agents, and hires two employees to help run the business. The costs of renting and moving to the new office and training the new employees are currently deductible as ordinary and necessary operating expenses.

However, even though you perform the same services, you are not expanding an existing business when you create a new business entity for your real state business.

> EXAMPLE: Art and Nicole are real estate brokers who each own their own small firms. They decide to merge their offices into a new single entity. They form an LLP, with themselves as the partners. Although Art and Nicole are performing the same services as before, the new firm is a new business for tax purposes, not an expansion of an existing business. Thus, Art and Nicole's start-up costs would not be currently deductible operating expenses.

When Does a Real Estate Business Begin?

The date when your real estate business begins for tax purposes marks an important turning point. Operating expenses you incur once your business starts are currently deductible, while expenses you incur before this crucial date may have to be deducted over many years.

The general rule is that a new business begins for tax purposes when it starts to function as a going concern and performs the activities for which it was organized. (*Richmond Television Corp. v. U.S.*, 345 F.2d 901 (4th Cir. 1965).) The IRS says that a venture becomes a going concern when it acquires all of the assets necessary to perform its intended functions and puts those assets to work. In other words, your real estate practice begins when you start doing business, whether or not you are actually earning any money.

Applying this rule, a real estate sales business begins when you first offer your services to the public. You don't have to actually obtain any listings or sell properties. You just have to be available for hire by clients. Thus, for example, a real estate broker's business begins when he or she opens an office and is ready to list and sell properties.

If you purchase an existing business, it begins when the purchase is completed—that is, when you take over ownership.

Proving to the IRS That You're in Business

Because your business start date is so important for tax purposes, you should be able to prove to the IRS the exact date it began. There are many ways you can do this. Being able to show the IRS a copy of an advertisement for your business is a great way to prove you were open for business. You can also mail out brochures or other promotional materials. But you don't have to advertise to show you are open—simply handing out business cards is sufficient. Give your first business cards to friends and associates who could testify for you if you're audited by the IRS. Establish your office to show you are ready to take on clients. Take a photo of it with a digital camera (which will be date-stamped).

How to Deduct Start-Up Expenses

You can deduct $5,000 in start-up expenses the first year you're in business. Any expenses you have in excess of the first-year limit you'll have to deduct in equal amounts over the first 180 months (15 years) you're in business. This process is called amortization. One hundred and eighty months is the minimum amortization period; you can choose a longer period if you wish (almost no one does).

If you have more than $50,000 in start-up expenses, you are not entitled to the full first-year deduction. You must reduce your deduction by the amount that your start-up expenditures exceed the annual threshold amount. For example, if you have $53,000 in start-up expenses in 2012, you may deduct only $2,000 the first year, instead of the normal $5,000 threshold amount. If you have $55,000 or more in start-up expenses, you get no current deduction for start-up expenses. Instead, the whole amount must be deducted over 180 months.

> EXAMPLE: Tom, a real estate broker, incurred $25,000 in start-up expenses during 2012, the year he opened his brokerage firm. He may deduct $5,000 of his expenses that year. He can deduct the remaining $20,000 over the first 15 years (180 months) he's in business (including his first year)—or $111 per month ($20,000 ÷ 180 months = $111). He was in business for only two months in 2012, so his total start-up expense deduction for that first year is $5,222. He'll get a $1,333 deduction the next year and each year thereafter until he has deducted the entire $20,000.

In the past, you had to attach a separate written statement to your return electing to claim start-up expenses as a current deduction. However, this is no longer required. Instead, you are automatically deemed to have made the election for the year in which your business began. All you need do is list your start-up costs as "Other expenses" on your Schedule C (or other appropriate return if you are not a sole proprietor). You need not specifically identify the deducted amounts as start-up expenditures for the election to be effective.

One major reason for this change is that it is impossible to include a separate written statement with a return that is filed electronically and the IRS wants to encourage electronic filing.

If you don't want to currently deduct your first year of start-up expenses, you may choose to forgo the deemed election by clearly electing to capitalize your start-up on your federal income tax return for the tax year in which your business began. Your tax return must be timely filed (including any extensions). This election is irrevocable and your start-up costs become part of the tax basis of your business.

Who Gets Start-Up Deductions

If, like most real estate professionals, you're a sole proprietor (or have a one-person LLC taxed as a sole proprietorship), you'll deduct your start-up expenses on your Schedule C along with your other business expenses. It makes no practical difference if you use personal funds or money from a separate business account for start-up expenses.

Things are different if you have a corporation, partnership, LLP, or LLC. Deductions for start-up expenses belong to the business entity, not to you personally. If you pay for them out of your personal funds, you should seek reimbursement from the entity. (See Chapter 2 for a detailed discussion.)

If Your Business Doesn't Last 15 Years

Not all real estate businesses last for 15 years. If your start-up expenses exceeded the $5,000 first-year limit, you don't lose the value of your deductions if you sell or close your business before you have had a chance to deduct all of your start-up expenses. You can deduct any leftover start-up expenses as ordinary business losses. (IRC § 195(b)(2).) This means that you may be able to deduct them from any income you have that year, deduct them in future years, or deduct them from previous years' taxes.

If you sell your business or its assets, your leftover start-up costs will be added to your tax basis in the business. This is just as good as getting a tax deduction. If you sell your business at a profit, the remaining start-up costs will be subtracted from your profits before taxes are assessed, which reduces your taxable gain. If you sell at a loss, the start-up costs will be added to the money you lost—because this shortfall is deductible, a larger loss means lower taxes.

Keep Good Expense Records

Whether you intend to start a new real estate business or buy an existing one, you should keep careful track of every expense you incur before the business begins. Obviously, you should keep receipts and canceled checks. You should also keep evidence that will help show that the money went to investigate a new business—for example, correspondence and emails with accountants, attorneys, business brokers, and consultants; marketing or financial reports; and copies of advertisements. You will need these records to calculate your deductions and to prove your expenses to the IRS if you face an audit.

Organizational Expenses

Many real estate professionals form business entities, such as a corporation, partnership, or limited liability company. (See Chapter 2 for a discussion of different possible business structures.) The costs of forming an entity to run your business are deductible. These organizational expenses are not considered start-up expenses, although they are deducted in much the same way.

If you form a corporation, you can deduct the cost of creating the corporation, including legal fees for drafting articles of incorporation, bylaws, minutes of organizational meetings and other organizational documents, and accounting fees for setting up the corporation and its books. You can also deduct state incorporation fees and other filing fees. However, you may not deduct the cost of transferring assets to the corporation or fees associated with issuing stock or securities—for example, commissions and printing costs. These are capital expenses.

If you form a partnership or LLC with two or more members, you may deduct the cost of negotiating and drafting a partnership or LLC agreement, accounting services to organize the partnership, and LLC filing fees.

Organizational expenses are deducted in the same way as start-up costs. You may deduct the first $5,000 the first year you are in business, and any excess over the first 180 months. Again, your first-year deduction is reduced by the amount by which your organizational expenditures exceed $50,000. You must file IRS Form 4562, *Depreciation and Amortization*, with your tax return (along with a statement listing the cost).

CHAPTER

11

If You Get Sick: Medical Deductions

When you own your own business, you must pay for your own health insurance and other medical expenses—you don't have an employer to pay all or part of these costs for you. As we all know, the cost of health insurance keeps going up. However, as business owners, real estate professionals have an advantage that most others don't have with regard to these rising health care costs: They can deduct many of their health insurance costs from their taxes. In addition, you may be able to deduct a wide variety of medical expenses that are normally not covered by health insurance, including nonprescription medications, acupuncture, and eyeglasses.

The Impact of Health Care Reform

In March 2010, Congress enacted a massive health care reform bill called the Patient Protection and Affordable Care Act. Among other things, this law contained several important tax changes for small businesses. In mid-2012 the United States Supreme Court found that the Act was constitutional; thus it will go into effect over the next several years unless Congress acts to repeal it.

The most significant change created by the new law is the requirement that all Americans have health insurance coverage by 2014. Currently, there is no federal law requiring individuals to have health coverage; nor are employers required to provide it for their employees. This is all scheduled to change starting in 2014. By that year, all Americans must have at least minimal health coverage or they will have to pay a penalty to the IRS. To help everyone obtain coverage, starting in 2014, health insurers will not be allowed to deny coverage because of preexisting medical conditions.

The mandatory health coverage requirement will affect all businesses, large and small. But they will be affected in different ways. Larger employers—those with 50 or more full-time employees—will be required to provide their employees with minimum health coverage or pay a penalty to the IRS. Owners of smaller businesses with fewer than 50 employees will not be required to provide health coverage to their employees. But, to encourage them to do so, the law entitles small businesses with 25 or fewer employees to a substantial health care insurance tax credit until 2016.

Because of these changes, for the first time, starting in 2014, all small business owners will have to have at least minimal health insurance coverage for themselves and their families—either through their business or on their own—or pay a penalty to the IRS. This is true whether you're a self-employed sole proprietor, partner in a partnership or limited liability company, or employee of your own small corporation. For most taxpayers, the annual penalty for each family member (up to three) will be $95 in 2014, $325 in 2015, and $695 in 2016 and later. The penalty is not applicable to people who can't afford coverage.

To help individuals and small businesses be able to afford health coverage, each state will be required to establish a health insurance exchange by 2014. These exchanges will be a competitive insurance marketplace where small businesses and individuals who might not otherwise be able to afford it, can buy qualified health benefit plans. The exchanges will offer a choice of health plans that meet certain benefits and cost standards. To help lower-income people obtain coverage, a refundable premium assistance credit will be available for those who purchase health insurance from a state exchange and whose income is between 100% and 400% of the federal poverty line.

For more information on the new health care reform law, see www.healthcare.gov.

The Personal Deduction for Medical Expenses

All taxpayers—whether or not they own a business—are entitled to a personal income tax deduction for medical and dental expenses for themselves and their dependents. Eligible expenses include both health insurance premiums and out-of-pocket expenses not covered by insurance. However, there are two significant limitations on the deduction, which make it virtually useless (unusable) for most taxpayers.

To take the personal deduction, you must comply with both of the following requirements:

You must itemize your deductions on IRS Schedule A. (You can itemize deductions only if all of your itemized deductions exceed the standard deduction for the year: $11,900 for joint returns and $5,950 for single returns in 2012.)

You can deduct only the amount of your medical and dental expenses that is more than 7.5% of your adjusted gross income (AGI). (Your AGI is your net business income and other taxable income, minus deductions for retirement contributions and one-half of your self-employment taxes, plus a few other items (as shown at the bottom of your Form 1040).) Starting in 2013, the threshold for the itemized medical expense deduction is scheduled to go up to 10% of AGI. However, people 65 or older will be exempt from the increase until 2017.

> EXAMPLE: Al is an independent contractor real estate agent whose adjusted gross income for 2012 is $100,000. He pays $500 per month for health insurance for himself and his wife. He spends another $2,000 in out-of-pocket medical and dental expenses for the year. Al may deduct his medical expenses only if all of his itemized deductions exceed the $11,900 standard deduction for the year. If they do exceed the standard deduction, his personal medical expense deduction is limited to the amount he paid that's more than $7,500 (7.5% × $100,000 = $7,500). Because he paid a total of $8,000 in medical expenses for the year, his deduction is limited to $500.

As you can see, unless your medical expenses are substantial, the 7.5% limitation eats up most or all of your deduction. The more money you make, the less you can deduct. For this reason, most agents and brokers need to look elsewhere for meaningful medical expense deductions.

Deducting Health Insurance Costs

Health insurance premiums are the largest medical expense most people pay. There are several ways that business owners can deduct these costs.

Personal Income Tax Deduction for the Self-Employed

Self-employed people are allowed to deduct health insurance premiums (including dental and long-term care coverage) for themselves, their spouses, and their dependents. You can deduct not only the cost of regular private health insurance, but any Medicare premiums you pay for yourself and/or your spouse as well—this includes all Medicare Parts. This insurance can cover your children up to age 27 (26 or younger as of the end of the year), whether or not they are dependents. For these purposes, a child includes a son, daughter, stepchild, adopted child, or eligible foster child. Sole proprietors, partners in partnerships, LLC members, and S corporation shareholders who own more than 2% of the company stock can use this deduction. Basically, any business owner, other than the owner of a regular C corporation, can take this deduction. And you get the deduction whether you purchase your health insurance policy as an individual or have your business obtain it. It's important to understand, however, that this is not a business deduction. It is a special personal deduction for the self-employed. This deduction applies only to your federal, state, and local income taxes, not to your self-employment taxes.

Self-Employment Tax Primer

Self-employment taxes are the Social Security and Medicare taxes that business owners must pay. They consist of a 12.4% Social Security tax and a 2.9% Medicare tax, for a total tax of 15.3%. (However, for 2011 and 2012, the Social Security tax is 10.4%, thus the total tax is 13.3%.) The tax is paid on net self-employment income, which is your net income from your business, not including deductions for retirement contributions. The Social Security tax is subject to an income ceiling that is adjusted each year for inflation. In 2012, the ceiling was $110,100 in self-employment income. There is no ceiling on the 2.9% Medicare tax. Thus, if you earn more than the ceiling, being able to deduct your health insurance costs from your self-employment income will not give you a very significant tax savings, because you would have had to pay only a 2.9% tax on that income.

EXAMPLE: Kim is a sole proprietor real estate agent who pays $12,000 each year for health insurance for herself, her husband, and her three children. Her business earns far more than this amount in profit each year. Every year, she may deduct her $12,000 annual health insurance expenses from her gross income for federal and state income tax purposes. Because her combined federal and state income tax rate is 30%, this saves her $3,600 in income taxes each year. Because of this deduction, she is effectively paying $700 per month for health insurance, rather than $1,000 per month.

Business Income Limitation

There is a significant limitation on the health insurance deduction for the self-employed: You may deduct only as much as you earn from your business. If your business earns no money or incurs a loss, you get no deduction. Thus, for example, if Kim from the above example earned only $3,000 in profit from her business, her self-employed deduction would be limited to that amount; she wouldn't be able to deduct the remaining $9,000 in premiums she paid for the year.

If your business is organized as an S corporation, your deduction is limited to the amount of wages you are paid by your corporation.

If you have more than one business, you cannot combine the income from all your businesses for purposes of the income limit. You may only use the income from a single business you designate to be the health insurance plan sponsor.

Designating Your Plan Sponsor

If you purchase your health insurance plan in the name of one of your businesses, that business will be the sponsor. However, the IRS says you may purchase your health coverage in your own name and still get the self-employed health insurance deduction. (IRS Chief Counsel Memo 200524001.) This may be advantageous because it allows you to pick which of your businesses will be the sponsor at the start of each year. Obviously, you should pick the business you think will earn the most money that year.

No Other Health Insurance Coverage

You may not take the self-employed health insurance deduction if you are eligible to participate in a health insurance plan maintained by your employer or your spouse's employer. This rule applies separately to plans that provide long-term care insurance and those that do not. Thus, for example, if your spouse has employer-provided health insurance that does not include long-term care, you may purchase your own long-term care policy and deduct the premiums.

Tax Reporting

Because the self-employed health insurance deduction is a personal deduction, you take this deduction directly on your Form 1040 (it does not go on your Schedule C if you're a sole proprietor). If you itemize your deductions and do not claim 100% of your self-employed health insurance costs on your Form 1040, you may include the rest with all other itemized medical expenses on Schedule A, subject to the 7.5% limit. You would have to do this, for example, if your health insurance premiums exceed your business income.

Deducting Health Insurance as a Business Expense

You can deduct health insurance costs as a currently deductible business expense if your business pays them on behalf of an employee. The benefit to treating these costs as a business expense is that you can deduct them from your business income for tax purposes. The premiums are an employee fringe benefit and are not taxable income for the employee. Thus, if you are an employee of your real estate business, you can have your business pay your health insurance premiums and then deduct the cost as a business expense, reducing both your income and your self-employment taxes.

> EXAMPLE: Mona, a sole proprietor real estate broker, hires Milt to work as her assistant. She pays $250 per month to provide Milt with health insurance. The payments are a business expense that she can deduct from her business income. Milt need not count the value of the insurance as income or pay any tax on it. Mona deducts her $3,000 annual payments for Milt's insurance from her business income for both income tax and self-employment tax purposes. The $3,000 deduction saves her $750 in income taxes (she's in the 25% income tax bracket; 25% × $3,000 = $750). She also saves $459 in self-employment taxes (15.3% × $3,000 = $459).

Sole Proprietors, LLCs, S Corporations, Partnerships, and LLPs

Unfortunately, if (like the vast majority of real estate agents and brokers) you are a sole proprietor, partner in a partnership, LLC member, or S corporation shareholder with more than 2% of the company stock, you cannot be an employee of your own business for health insurance purposes. If your partnership, LLC, or S corporation buys health insurance on your behalf, it may deduct the cost as a business expense, but it must also add the amount to your taxable income.

If your business is organized as a partnership or LLC, the premiums are ordinarily treated as a guaranteed payment. The business lists the payment on the Schedule K-1 it provides the IRS and you showing your income from the business. You'll then have to pay income and self-employment tax on the amount.

You can still take the self-employed health insurance tax deduction discussed above, which will effectively wipe out the extra income tax you had to pay. But the self-employed health insurance deduction is a personal deduction, not a business deduction, and thus does not reduce your business income for self-employment tax purposes.

> EXAMPLE: Jim is a co-owner of a real estate brokerage firm organized as an LLC. The firm spends $10,000 for health insurance for Jim. It treats the money as a guaranteed payment and lists it as income to Jim on the K-1 form it provides the IRS. The LLC gets to deduct the payment as a business expense. Jim must pay income and self-employment tax on the $10,000. However, he may also deduct the $10,000 from his income tax as a personal deduction using the self-employed health insurance deduction. The net result is that Jim only pays self-employment tax on the $10,000. The same result would have been achieved if Jim had purchased his health insurance himself.

Partnerships, LLCs, and LLPs can avoid having to report health insurance payments as income if they don't take a tax deduction for them. This will have the same tax result and make things simpler.

If your business is an S corporation, the insurance costs are added to your employee compensation and are deducted as such by the corporation. However, you have to pay only income taxes on that amount, not employment taxes or unemployment tax. Again, if you qualify, you may take the self-employed health insurance deduction and wipe out the extra income tax you had to pay. To qualify for the deduction, your medical insurance must be either: (1) established by your S corporation, in its own name, and paid for with its funds, or (2) if purchased in your own name, your S corporation either directly pays for the health insurance, or reimburses you for it, and includes the premium payments as wages in the your IRS Form W-2, *Wage and Tax Statement.* (IRS Notice 2008-1.) You cannot qualify for the deduction if your S corporation neither pays for the insurance directly with its own funds nor reimburses you for your payments.

C Corporations

If your real estate business is organized as a C corporation, you ordinarily will work as its employee and will be entitled to the full menu of tax-free employee fringe benefits, including health insurance. This means the corporation can purchase health insurance for you, deduct the cost as a business expense, and not have to include the cost in your employee compensation. Your health insurance is completely tax-free.

If you want to convert your health insurance premiums to a tax-free fringe benefit and you don't have a C corporation, you must form one to run your real estate business and have the corporation hire you as its employee. You can do this even if you're running a one-person real estate business.

As an employee of a C corporation, you must be paid a salary, and your corporation must pay Social Security and Medicare taxes on your behalf. Your corporation deducts your health insurance premiums from its taxes—you don't deduct them from your personal taxes. Because you own the corporation, you get the benefit from the deduction.

There are disadvantages to incorporating, however. Incorporating costs money, you'll have to comply with more burdensome bookkeeping requirements, and you will have a more complex tax return. You'll also have to pay state and federal unemployment taxes for yourself—a tax you don't need to pay if you're not an employee of your business. And, depending on your state's requirements, you may have to provide yourself with workers' compensation coverage.

Because your health insurance is 100% deductible from your income taxes, it may not be worthwhile to incorporate just to save on Social Security and Medicare taxes. This is particularly true if your employee income would substantially exceed the Social Security tax ceiling: $110,100 in 2012. If you're in this situation, think about obtaining a Health Savings Account instead. (See "Adopting a Medical Reimbursement Plan," below.)

Disability Insurance

Disability insurance pays a monthly benefit to employees who are unable to work due to sickness or injury. You may provide disability insurance to your employees, including your spouse, as an employee benefit and deduct the premiums as a business expense. If your real estate business is a C corporation, it may deduct disability payments made for you, its employee. However, any employees who collect disability benefits must include them in their taxable income.

Employing Your Spouse

If you're a sole proprietor or have formed an entity other than an S corporation to run your business, there's another way you can deduct health insurance costs as a business expense: Hire your spouse to work in your business as an employee and provide him or her with health insurance. The insurance should be purchased in the name of the spouse-employee, not in the employer's name. The policy can cover your spouse, you, your children, and other dependents as well. Moreover, as of March 30, 2010, this insurance can cover your children up to age 27 (26 or younger as of the end of the year), whether or not they are your dependents. Then you can deduct the cost of the health insurance as a business expense.

> EXAMPLE: Joe, a real estate broker, hires his wife, Martha, to work as his employee assistant. He pays her $25,000 per year and provides her with a health insurance policy covering both of them and their two children. The annual policy premiums are $5,000. Joe may deduct the $5,000 as a business expense for his real estate business, listing it as an expense on his Schedule C. He gets to deduct the $5,000 not only from his $80,000 income for income

tax purposes, but also from his self-employment income for Social Security and Medicare tax purposes.

If you do this and you're self-employed, you should not take the health insurance deduction for self-employed people discussed above. You're better off tax-wise deducting all your health insurance premiums as a business expense, because a business deduction reduces the amount of your income subject to self-employment taxes. The self-employed health insurance deduction is a personal deduction, not a business deduction, and thus does not reduce your business income for self-employment tax purposes.

There are a couple of catches to this deduction. This method ordinarily doesn't work if you have an S corporation because your spouse is deemed to be a shareholder of the corporation along with you and can't also be a corporate employee. In addition, your spouse must be a bona fide employee. In other words, he or she must do real work in your business, you must pay applicable payroll taxes, and you must otherwise treat your spouse like any other employee. (See Chapter 14 for a detailed discussion.)

You'll probably want to pay your spouse as low a salary as possible, because both of you will have to pay Social Security and Medicare taxes on that salary (but not on employee benefits like health insurance and medical expense reimbursements). You should, however, regularly pay your spouse at least some cash wages, or the IRS could claim your spouse is not a real employee. You can make the cash wages a relatively small part of your spouse's total compensation—wages plus fringe benefits like your medical reimbursement plan.

No matter how you pay your spouse, his or her total compensation must be reasonable—that is, you can't pay more than your spouse's services are worth. For example, you can't pay your spouse at a rate of $100 per hour for simple clerical work. Total compensation means the sum of the salary plus all the fringe benefits you pay your spouse, including health insurance and medical expense reimbursements, if any. (See "Adopting a Medical Reimbursement Plan," below.)

EXAMPLE: Tina's husband, Tim, works part time as an office assistant in her real estate brokerage. Tina calls a couple of employment agencies and learns that other real estate brokers in the area pay people like Tim about $10 per hour, so she decides to pay him at this rate. Tim will work 500 hours per year (10 hours per week, 50 weeks per year), so his total compensation should be about $5,000 (500 hours × $10 per hour = $5,000). Tina wants to provide Tim with a health insurance policy covering him and his family (including Tina) and a medical reimbursement plan. She would like to purchase a health insurance policy for $7,500 per year, but she knows she can't justify this expense, since Tim's total annual compensation can't be more than about $5,000. Instead, Tina has her business provide Tim with $3,500 worth of health insurance, $500 of medical reimbursements, and $1,000 in salary. Tina and Tim must pay Social Security and Medicare tax on his $1,000 in wages. But Tina gets to deduct the wages and the $4,000 in health insurance and medical reimbursement costs as a business expense. This saves her (and Tim) $1,500 in federal and state taxes for the year.

Your Spouse May Not Be Your Partner

A marriage may be a partnership, but you can't be partners with your spouse in your business and also claim he or she is your employee for purposes of health insurance deductions. If your spouse co-owns the business with you, he or she is treated as self-employed—not an employee—for purposes of health insurance. Your spouse is a co-owner if you file partnership returns for your business (IRS Form 1065) listing him or her as a partner, or if your spouse has made a substantial financial investment in your business with the spouse's own money.

Alternatively, spouses who jointly own a business may elect to be taxed as a "qualified joint venture." When this is done, both spouses are treated as sole proprietors for tax purposes.

Of course, if you're single, you won't be able to hire a spouse to take advantage of this method for turning health insurance costs into a business expense. However, if you're a single parent, you could hire your child and deduct the cost of your child's health insurance as a business expense. But your child's policy cannot also cover you or other family members.

Tax Credits for Employee Health Insurance

The previous section explained how you can deduct health insurance costs for employees—including your spouse—as a business expense. Tax deductions are all well and good, but there is something even better: tax credits. Unlike a deduction, a tax credit is a dollar-for-dollar reduction in the taxes you owe the IRS. In other words, a $1,000 credit saves you $1,000 on your taxes. How much a $1,000 deduction saves you depends on your top tax bracket, but it will be no more than $350 as of 2012, since the top federal income tax bracket (for 2012) is 35%.

The massive health insurance reform enacted by Congress in 2010 created a brand new tax credit for small employers who pay for health insurance for their employees. From 2010 through 2013, employers who qualify can claim a tax credit of up to 35% of their contributions to their employees' health insurance premiums, subject to certain limits. The percentage increases to 50% for 2014 and 2015. The credit ends in 2016. Obviously, if you qualify for the credit, you can save substantial taxes.

Currently, less than half of all employers with three to nine employees provide their workers with health insurance. One big reason is the cost. Small employers face higher premiums, broker fees, and administrative costs than large firms. As a result, small businesses pay up to 18% more per worker than large firms for the same health insurance policy. The small employer tax credit is intended to level the playing field and enable more small businesses to provide health insurance for their employees.

To qualify for the health insurance credit, you must satisfy three requirements. See the IRS's *3 Simple Steps* guide for an excellent chart you can use to determine whether you qualify for the credit (available at www.irs.gov/pub/irs-utl/3_simple_steps.pdf).

Requirement #1: You Must Have Employees

You can qualify for the health insurance credit only if your real estate business has nonowner employees who are not your relatives. You can forget about getting the credit if you're running a one-person operation—for example, you're a sole proprietor real estate agent with no employees.

Who Is An Employee

For these purposes, an employee is a person who works full or part time for your real estate business. As is the case with the business tax deduction for health expenses, business owners don't count as employees for these purposes and don't qualify for the tax credit. This includes sole proprietors, partners in partnerships, shareholders owning more than 2% of an S corporation, and any owner of more than 5% of the business. In addition, family members don't count as employees. This includes a spouse, child (or descendant of a child); a sibling or stepsibling; a parent (or ancestor of a parent); a stepparent; a niece or nephew; an aunt or uncle; or a son-in-law, daughter-in-law, father-in-law, mother-in-law, brother-in-law, or sister-in-law. Thus, you can't hire any of these people to work as employees in your business and qualify for the credit.

Ten or Fewer Employees

The credit is designed for smaller businesses. The full credit is available only to businesses with ten or fewer full-time employees. It is gradually phased out if you have more than ten full-time employees: It is reduced to 6.67% for each full-time employee over ten. Thus, it is phased out completely for a business with 25 full-time employees (15 × 6.67% = 100%).

Requirement #2: Employee Compensation Must Average Less Than $50,000

The tax credit is intended to help employers pay for health insurance for employees with relatively low salaries. To qualify for the credit, the average annual wages of your employees for the year must be less than $50,000 per full-time employee. The credit is reduced by 4% for each $1,000 that the person's average annual compensation exceeds $25,000. Thus, the credit is completely phased out if your employees are paid $50,000 or more in annual wages.

Requirement #3: You Must Pay at Least 50% of Employee Health Insurance Premiums

Finally, you must pay at least 50% of the annual premiums for your employees' health insurance. Health insurance for purposes of the credit can take a variety of forms. It's up to the employer to decide what type of coverage to provide. You can pay for the insurance directly or reimburse your employees for their payments. The coverage can be under any hospital or medical service policy, or a health maintenance organization (HMO) contract offered by a health insurance company. Employers also have the option of providing dental or vision coverage, long-term care, nursing home care, home health care, community-based care, or any combination of these. Medicare supplemental health insurance also qualifies for the credit.

Only the health insurance premiums paid by the employer are counted in calculating the credit. If an employer pays only a portion of the premiums (with employees paying the rest), only that portion is counted. For example, if an employer pays 80% of the premiums for employees' coverage, only that 80% is counted in calculating the credit.

Amount of the Credit

For 2010 through 2013, the credit is equal to 35% of the employer's health insurance payments for its employees. This amount is increased to 50% for 2014 and 2015.

However, there is a cap on the amount of premiums that can be used to calculate the credit. This prevents employers from providing their employees with "Cadillac" health care plans and reaping huge tax credits. The cap is equal to the average premium charged in the state's small group health insurance market. This amount is determined by the Department of Health and Human Services (HHS). The instructions for IRS Form 8941 list the average premium for the small group market in each state. You can find it on the IRS website. For California, for example, the average premium for employee-only coverage is $4,790 per year, with $11,493 for family coverage. These are the maximum amounts that can be used to calculate the credit for California employers.

EXAMPLE: During 2012, Acme Realty, Inc., has four full-time employees with average annual wages of $23,000 per employee. Acme pays $24,000 in health care premiums for its employees (which does not exceed the average premium cost for the small group market in Acme's state) and otherwise meets the requirements for the credit. Acme's health insurance credit for 2012 equals $8,400 (35% × $24,000 = $8,400). This means Acme may reduce its total tax liability for 2012 by $8,400.

The health credit is a general business credit you claim on your tax return. If the credit exceeds your tax liability for the year, the unused credit amount can be carried back one year and carried forward 20 years.

It's important to understand that when you take the health credit, your tax deduction for employee health insurance expenditures is reduced by the amount of the credit. For example, Acme Realty (above), took an $8,400 credit; it can deduct only $15,600 of the $24,000 it paid for employee health insurance as a business expense in 2012. It can't also deduct the $8,400 amount that it got as a credit.

Adopting a Medical Reimbursement Plan

Health insurance usually doesn't cover all your medical expenses. For example, it doesn't cover preexisting conditions or deductibles or co-payments—that is, amounts you must pay yourself before your insurance coverage kicks in. Many costs aren't covered at all, including ongoing physical therapy, fertility treatment, and optometric care. One way to deduct these expenses is to establish a medical reimbursement plan. Another way is to use a Health Savings Account (discussed below).

What Is a Medical Reimbursement Plan?

A medical reimbursement plan is an arrangement under which an employer reimburses its employees for health or dental expenses. These plans are usually self-funded—that is, the employer pays the expenses out of its own pocket, not through insurance.

Why would an employer do this? One good reason is that the reimbursements are tax deductible business expenses for the employer.

Also, the employee doesn't have to include the reimbursements as taxable income (as long as the employee has not taken a deduction for these amounts as a personal medical expense).

So how does this help you? Again, your spouse (if you have one) comes to the rescue. You can hire your spouse as your employee and provide him or her with a medical reimbursement plan. The plan may cover not only your spouse, but also you, your children, and other dependents. This allows your business to reimburse your and your family's out-of-pocket medical expenses and deduct the amounts as a business expense. And you need not include the reimbursements in your own taxable income. The IRS has ruled that this is perfectly legal. (Tax Advice Memo 9409006.)

> EXAMPLE: Jennifer, a real estate broker, hires her husband Paul as an employee to work as her part-time assistant. She establishes a medical reimbursement plan covering Paul, herself, and their young child. Paul spends $6,000 on medical expenses. Jennifer reimburses Paul for the $6,000 as provided by their plan. Jennifer may deduct the $6,000 from her business income for the year, meaning she pays neither income nor self-employment tax on that amount. Paul need not include the $6,000 in his income—it's tax-free to him. The deduction saves Jennifer and Paul $2,000 in taxes for the year.

CAUTION

Your spouse must be a legitimate employee. Your spouse must be a legitimate employee for your medical reimbursement plan to pass muster with the IRS. You can't simply hire your spouse on paper—he or she must do real work in your business. If you can't prove your spouse is a legitimate employee, the IRS will disallow your deductions in the event of an audit. If you're audited, the IRS will be particularly suspicious if your spouse is your only employee. You should have your spouse sign an employment contract and keep impeccable time records.

Again, the medical expense reimbursement plan deduction is available only to your employees, not to you (the business owner). The only way you can qualify as an employee is if your real estate business is a C corporation. (See "Deducting Health Insurance as a Business Expense," above.) However, if you don't have a spouse to employ, you could employ your child and provide him or her with a reimbursement plan. But the plan may not cover you or any other family members.

What Expenses May Be Reimbursed?

One of the great things about medical reimbursement plans is that they can be used to reimburse employees for a wide variety of health-related expenses. Indeed, deductible medical expenses include any expense for the diagnosis, cure, mitigation, treatment, or prevention of disease, or any expense paid to affect the structure or function of the human body. (IRS Reg. 1.213.1(e).)

This includes, of course, premiums in health and accident insurance and health insurance deductibles and co-payments. But it also includes expenses for acupuncture, chiropractors, eyeglasses and contact lenses, dental treatment, laser eye surgery, psychiatric care, and treatment for learning disabilities. (See "Withdrawing HSA Funds," below, for a list of expenses that can and cannot be deducted.) You can draft your plan to include only those expenses you wish to reimburse. Presumably, though, you'd want to include as many expenses as possible if the plan covers only your spouse, yourself, and your family.

Plan Requirements

If you decide to adopt a medical expense reimbursement plan, the plan must be in writing, it may not discriminate in favor of highly compensated employees, and it must reimburse employees only for medical expenses that are not paid for by insurance.

The nondiscrimination rule will affect you only if you have employees other than your spouse or children. If you do, a medical reimbursement plan may be too expensive for you, because you'll have to provide coverage to nonfamily members as well. A plan is nondiscriminatory under IRS rules if it:

- covers at least 70% of all employees
- covers at least 80% of all employees eligible to benefit from the plan, provided that 70% or more of all employees are eligible, or

- is found to be nondiscriminatory by the IRS based on the facts and circumstances.

EXAMPLE: Acme Realty, Inc., employs 12 people. Two work only 20 hours per week. To be nondiscriminatory, Acme's medical expense reimbursement plan must cover 80% of the ten employees eligible to participate—in other words, it must cover eight of the ten full-time employees.

However, the plan may exclude employees who:

- work fewer than 25 hours a week
- are not yet 25 years old
- work for you fewer than seven months in a year, or
- have worked for you less than three years.

If a plan is found to be discriminatory by the IRS, all or part of the medical benefits paid to highly compensated employees under the plan will be taxable to the employee. Highly compensated employees include:

- anyone among the top 25% highest-paid employees
- the five highest-paid corporate officers (if your business is incorporated), and
- shareholders who own more than 10% of the corporation stock.

How to Establish a Plan

If a medical expense reimbursement plan sounds attractive to you, you should act to establish one as early in the year as possible, because it only applies to medical expenses incurred after the date the plan is adopted. (Rev. Rul. 2002-58.) Forget about using a plan to reimburse your spouse or yourself for expenses you have already incurred. If you do, the reimbursement must be added to your spouse's income for tax purposes, and you must pay employment tax on it.

A written medical reimbursement plan must be drawn up and adopted by your business. If your business is incorporated, the plan should be adopted by a corporate resolution approved by the corporation's board of directors. You can find a form for this purpose in *The Corporate Records Handbook*, by Anthony Mancuso (Nolo).

12 Steps to Audit-Proof Your Medical Reimbursement Plan for Your Spouse

Your medical reimbursement plan is subject to attack by the IRS if it doesn't look like a legitimate business expense. Your spouse must be a real employee, you must treat him or her as such, and you must manage your plan in a businesslike manner.

1. Have your spouse sign a written employment agreement specifying his or her duties and work hours.
2. Adopt a written medical reimbursement plan for your business.
3. Use time sheets to keep track of the hours your spouse works.
4. Make sure your spouse's total compensation is reasonable.
5. Have your spouse open a separate bank account to use when he or she pays medical expenses or receives reimbursements from your business.
6. Comply with all payroll tax, unemployment insurance, and workers' compensation requirements for your spouse-employee.
7. Reimburse your spouse for covered expenses by check from a separate business bank account or pay the health care provider directly from your business account. Make a notation on the check that the payment is made under your medical reimbursement plan.
8. Never pay your spouse in cash.
9. Have your spouse submit all bills to be reimbursed or paid by your business at least twice a year, or monthly or quarterly if you prefer. Keep all documentation showing the nature and amounts of the medical expenses paid for by your plan—receipts, cancelled checks, and so on—to show that you didn't reimburse your spouse too much and that the payments were for legitimate medical expenses.
10. Don't pay for expenses incurred before the date you adopted your plan.
11. If you have employees other than your spouse, make sure you meet the nondiscrimination requirements.
12. Claim your deduction on the correct tax form:
    - sole proprietors—Schedule C, line 14, "Employee benefit programs;"
    - LLCs and partnerships—Form 1065, line 19, "Employee benefit programs;"
    - C corporations—Form 1120, Line 24, "Employee benefit programs."

Sample Plan

A sample medical expense reimbursement plan is provided below. It's self-explanatory, except that you need to decide certain components as described below.

Eligibility

If you have employees other than your spouse (or think you may have them in the future), you must decide whether to place limitations on which employees may be covered by your plan. You may cover all your employees or exclude certain classes of employees, as described in "Plan Requirements," above. It's up to you. But, be careful about whom you exclude from your plan—make sure you don't eliminate your spouse. For example, if your plan excludes all employees who work fewer than 25 hours per week, your spouse will have to work at least 25 hours to qualify for your plan. If your spouse will only work 15 hours per week, your plan should exclude only those employees who work fewer than 15 hours.

Dollar Limits

You also have the option of placing an annual dollar limit on the reimbursements you'll make. If your spouse is your only employee, you probably won't want a limit. But if you have other employees—or may have them in the future—a limit may be advisable.

Claims Submission

Finally, you must decide how often the employee must submit claims for reimbursement. Twice a year is fine, but you can make it more frequent if you wish.

Medical Expense Reimbursement Plan

Effective [*date*], [*your business name*] ("Employer") will reimburse all eligible employees for medical expenses incurred by themselves and their dependents, subject to the conditions and limitations set forth below.

Uninsured Expenses

Employer will reimburse eligible employees and their dependents only for medical expenses that are not covered by health or accident insurance.

Medical Expenses Defined

Medical expenses are those expenses defined by Internal Revenue Code § 213(d). They consist of any expense for the diagnosis, cure, mitigation, treatment, or prevention of disease; or any expense paid to affect the structure or function of the human body. Medical expenses include both prescription and nonprescription drugs and medicines.

Dependent Defined

Dependent is defined by IRC § 152. It includes any member of an eligible employee's family for whom the employee and his or her spouse provides more than half of the financial support.

Eligibility

[*Choose Alternative A or B.*]

Alternative A:

The Plan shall be open to all employees.

Alternative B:

The Plan shall be open to all employees who:

[*Check applicable boxes—you may check any number.*]

- ☐ work more than [*specify—25 hrs/week is maximum*] hours per week
- ☐ are at least [*specify—25 is maximum*] years of age
- ☐ have completed [*specify—3 years is maximum*] years of service with Employer
- ☐ work [*specify—7 months is maximum*] months per year

Limitation (*Optional*)

Employer shall reimburse any eligible employee no more than [*dollar amount*] in any calendar year for medical expenses.

Submission of Claims

Any eligible employee seeking reimbursement under this Plan shall submit to Employer, [*choose one*] ☐ monthly ☐ quarterly ☐ at least twice a year on [*date*] and [*date*], all bills for medical care, including those for accident or health insurance. Such bills and other claims for reimbursement shall be verified by Employer prior to reimbursement. Employer, in its sole discretion, may terminate the employee's right to reimbursement if the employee fails to comply.

Direct Payments

At its option, Employer may pay all or part of a covered employee's medical expenses directly, instead of making reimbursements to the employee. Such a direct payment shall relieve Employer of all further liability for the expense.

Termination

Employer may terminate this Plan at any time. Medical expenses incurred prior to the date of termination shall be reimbursed by Employer. Employer is under no obligation to provide advance notice of termination.

Benefits Not Taxable

Employer intends that the benefits under this Plan shall qualify under IRC § 105 so as to be excludable from the gross income of the employees covered by the Plan.

______________________________ ______________
Employer's Signature Date

______________________________ ______________
Employee's Signature Date

Health Savings Accounts

There is yet another tax-advantaged method of buying health insurance: Health Savings Accounts (HSAs). HSAs can save you taxes, but they're not for everybody.

What Are Health Savings Accounts?

The HSA concept is very simple: Instead of relying on health insurance to pay small or routine medical expenses, you pay them yourself.
To help you do this, you establish a Health Savings Account with a health insurance company, bank, or other financial institution. Your contributions to the account are tax deductible, and you don't have to pay tax on the interest or other money you earn on the money in your account. You can withdraw the money in your HSA to pay almost any kind of health-related expense, and you don't have to pay any tax on these withdrawals.

In case you or a family member gets really sick, you must also obtain a health insurance policy with a high deductible—for 2012, at least $1,200 for individuals and $2,400 for families. The money in your HSA can be used to pay this large deductible and any co-payments you're required to make.

Using an HSA can save you money in two ways:

- You'll get a tax deduction for the money you deposit in your account.
- The premiums for your high-deductible health insurance policy may be lower than those for traditional comprehensive coverage policies or HMO coverage (perhaps as much as 40% lower).

Establishing Your HSA

To participate in the HSA program, you need two things:

- a high-deductible health plan that qualifies under the HSA rules, and
- an HSA account.

HSA-Qualified Plans

You can't have an HSA if you're covered by health insurance other than a high-deductible HSA plan—for example, if your spouse has family coverage for you from his or her job. So you may have to change your existing coverage. However, you may get your own HSA if you are not covered by your spouse's health insurance. In addition, people eligible to receive Medicare may not participate in the HSA program.

You need to obtain a bare-bones health plan that meets the HSA criteria (is "HSA-qualified"). You may obtain coverage from a health maintenance organization, preferred provider organization, or traditional plan. The key feature of an HSA-qualified health plan is that it has a relatively high annual deductible (the amount you must pay out of your own pocket before your insurance kicks in). In 2012, the minimum annual deductible for a single person was $1,200, and $2,400 for families.

Family Deductibles

One attractive feature of HSA plans is that the annual deductible applies to the entire family, not each family member separately. With such a per-family deductible, expenses incurred by each family member accumulate and are credited toward the one family deductible. For example, a family of four would meet the $2,400 maximum annual deductible if each family member paid $600 in medical expenses during the year (4 × $600 = $2,400). This is a unique feature of HSA plans.

You can have a higher deductible if you wish, but there is an annual ceiling on the total amount you can have for your deductible plus other out-of-pocket expenses you're required to pay before your health plan provides coverage. (Such out-of-pocket expenses include co-payments, but do not include health insurance premiums.) For example, in 2012 the annual ceiling for an individual HSA plan was $6,050. This means that your annual deductible and other out-of-pocket expenses you're required to pay before your insurance kicks in cannot exceed that amount. Thus, if your annual deductible was $3,000, your other annual out-of-pocket expenses would have to be limited to $3,050. In 2012, the maximum limits were $6,050 for a single person and $12,100 for families. All these numbers are adjusted for inflation each year.

In addition, your health insurance plan must be "HSA-qualified." To become qualified, the insurer must agree to participate in the HSA program and give the roster of enrolled participants to the IRS. If your insurer fails to report to the IRS that you are enrolled in an HSA-qualified insurance plan, the IRS will not permit you to deduct your HSA contributions.

HSA-qualified health insurance policies should be clearly labeled as such on the cover page or declaration page of the policy. It might be possible to convert a high-deductible health insurance policy you already have to an HSA-qualified health insurance policy; ask your health insurer for details.

You'll be able to obtain an HSA-qualified health plan from health insurers that participate in the program. The U.S. Treasury has an informative website on HSAs at www.treas.gov/offices/public-affairs/hsa. You can also contact your present health insurer.

Special Rule for Preventive Care

A special rule permits high-deductible health plans to provide coverage for preventive health care before the annual deductible is satisfied. Preventive health care is care that doesn't treat a preexisting condition. It includes, but is not limited to:

- periodic health evaluations, including tests and diagnostic procedures ordered in connection with routine examinations, such as annual physicals
- routine prenatal and well-child care
- child and adult immunizations
- tobacco cessation programs
- obesity weight-loss programs, and
- health screening services. (IRS Notice 2004-23.)

For example, your plan can pay for your annual physical even though you have not met the annual deductible.

The premiums you pay for an HSA-qualified health plan are deductible to the same extent as any other health insurance premiums. This means that, if you're self-employed, you may deduct your entire premium from your federal income tax as a special personal deduction.

You can also deduct your contribution if your business is an LLC or partnership or if you've formed an S corporation. If your partnership or LLC makes the contribution for you, it must be reported as a distribution to you on your Schedule K-1. You still get the self-employed health insurance deduction but will have to pay tax on the distribution if it exceeds your basis (the value of your investment) in your LLC or partnership. Contributions by an S corporation to a shareholder-employee's HSA are treated as guaranteed payments. The S corporation may deduct them, but they must be included in the shareholder-employee's gross income and are subject to income tax. (IRS Notice 2005-8.)

If you've formed a C corporation and work as its employee, your corporation can make a contribution to your HSA and deduct the amount as employee compensation. The contribution is not taxable to you. (See "HSAs for Employees," below.)

HSA Account

Once you have an HSA-qualified health insurance policy, you may open your HSA account. An HSA must be established with a trustee. The HSA trustee keeps track of your deposits and withdrawals, produces annual statements, and reports your HSA deposits to the IRS.

Any person, insurance company, bank, or financial institution already approved by the IRS to be a trustee or custodian of an IRA is approved automatically to serve as an HSA trustee. Others may apply for approval under IRS procedures for HSAs.

Health insurers can administer both the health plan and the HSA. However, you don't have to have your HSA administered by your insurer. You can establish an HSA with banks, insurance companies, mutual funds, or other financial institutions offering HSA products.

Whoever administers your account will usually give you a checkbook or debit card to use to withdraw funds from the account. You can also make withdrawals by mail or in person.

Look at the plans offered by several companies to see which offers the best deal. Compare the fees charged to set up the account, as well as any other charges (some companies may charge an annual service fee, for example). Ask about special promotions and discounts. And find out how the account is invested.

Making Contributions to Your HSA

When you have your HSA-qualified health plan and HSA account, you can start making contributions to your account. There is no minimum amount you are required to contribute each year; you may contribute nothing if you wish. If your business is a corporation, partnership, or LLC, you don't have to make all the contributions to your HSA from your personal funds. All or part of your annual contribution can be paid for by your business from its funds. But, as described in the following section, this changes how the contributions are deducted.

There are maximum limits on how much you may contribute each year:

- If you have individual coverage, the maximum you may contribute to your HSA each year is $3,100.
- If you have family coverage, the maximum you may contribute to your HSA each year is $6,250.

These maximums are for 2012 and are adjusted for inflation each year.

Taxpayers who have HSAs may make a one-time tax-free rollover of funds from their Individual Retirement Accounts (IRAs) to their HSA. The rollover amount is limited to the maximum HSA contribution for the year (minus any HSA contributions you've already made for the year).

Catch-Up Contributions

Individuals who are 55 to 65 years old can make additional optional tax-free catch-up contributions to their HSA accounts of up to $1,000 (see the chart below). This rule is intended to compensate for the fact that older folks won't have as many years to fund their accounts as younger taxpayers. If you're in this age group, it's wise to make these contributions if you can afford them, so your HSA account will have enough money to pay for future health expenses.

	Self Only	Family
Maximum Contribution	$3,100	$6,250
Catch-Up Contribution (55 and over)	$1,000	$1,000
Minimum Deductible	$1,200	$2,400
Maximum Out-of-Pocket Payments	$6,050	$12,100

Where to Invest Your HSA Contributions

The contributions you make to your HSA account may be invested just like IRA contributions. You can invest in almost anything: money market accounts, bank certificates of deposit, stocks, bonds, mutual funds, Treasury bills, and notes. However, you can't invest in collectibles such as art, antiques, postage stamps, or other personal property. Most HSA funds are invested in money market accounts and certificates of deposit.

Deducting HSA Contributions

The amounts contributed each year to HSA accounts, up to the annual limit, are deductible from federal income taxes.

Individual Contributions

You can deduct HSA contributions made with your personal funds as a personal deduction on the first page of your IRS Form 1040. You deduct the amount from your gross income, just like a business deduction. This means you get the full deduction whether or not you itemize your personal deductions.

> EXAMPLE: In 2012, Martin, a real estate agent, establishes an HSA for himself and his family with a $2,400 deductible. He contributes the maximum amount to his HSA account—$6,250. Because he is in the 25% federal income tax bracket, this saves him $1,563 in federal income tax for 2012.

Contributions by Your Business

If your real estate business is a partnership or LLC and it makes an HSA contribution for you as a distribution of partnership or LLC funds, it is reported as a cash distribution to you on your Schedule K-1 (Form 1065). You may take a personal deduction for the HSA contribution on your tax return (IRS Form 1040) and the contribution is not subject to income or self-employment taxes.

However, the tax result is very different if the contribution is made as a guaranteed payment to the partner or LLC member. A guaranteed payment is like a salary paid to a partner or LLC member for services performed for the partnership or LLC. The amount of a guaranteed payment is determined without reference to the partnership's or LLC's income. The partnership or LLC deducts the guaranteed payment on its return and lists it as a guaranteed payment to you on your Schedule K-1 (Form 1065). You must pay income and self-employment tax on the amount. You may take a personal income tax deduction on your Form 1040 for the HSA contribution.

Contributions by an S corporation to a shareholder-employee's HSA are treated as wages subject to income tax, but they normally are not subject to employment taxes. The shareholder can deduct the contribution on his or her personal tax return (IRS Form 1040) as an HSA contribution.

If you've formed a C corporation and work as its employee, your corporation can make a contribution to your HSA and deduct the amount as employee compensation. The contribution is not taxable to you. However, if you have other employees, similar contributions must be made to their HSAs. You may also make contributions from your own fund.

Withdrawing HSA Funds

If you or a family member needs health care, you can withdraw money from your HSA to pay your deductible or any other medical expenses. You pay no federal tax on HSA withdrawals used to pay qualified medical expenses. However, you cannot deduct qualified medical expenses as an itemized deduction on Schedule A (Form 1040) that are equal to the tax-free distribution from your HSA.

Qualified medical expenses are broadly defined to include many types of expenses ordinarily not covered by health insurance—for example, dental or optometric care. This is one of the great advantages of the HSA program over traditional health insurance. (The lists in "What HSA Funds Can Be Used For," below, show the type of health expenses that can and cannot be paid with an HSA.)

No Approval Required

HSA participants need not obtain advance approval from their HSA trustee (whether their insurer or someone else) that an expense is a qualified medical expense before they withdraw funds from their accounts. You make that determination yourself. The trustee will report any distribution to you and the IRS on Form 1099-SA, *Distributions From an HSA, Archer MSA, or Medicare Advantage MSA*. You should keep records of your medical expenses to show that your withdrawals were for qualified medical expenses and are therefore excludable from your gross income.

> EXAMPLE: Jane, a self-employed real estate agent and single mother, obtains family health insurance coverage with a $2,500 deductible. She sets up an HSA at her bank and deposits $2,500 every year for three years. She deducts each contribution from her gross income for the year for income tax purposes. Jane pays no taxes on the interest she earns on the money in her account, which is invested in a money market fund. By the end of three years, she has $7,750 in the account. Jane becomes ill after the third year and is hospitalized. She withdraws $2,500 from her HSA to pay her deductible. She also withdraws $3,000 to pay for speech therapy for her son, which is not covered by her health insurance. She pays no federal tax on these withdrawals.

However, you may not use HSA funds to purchase nonprescription medications. The only way to deduct these is to hire your spouse and establish a medical reimbursement plan. (See "Adopting a Medical Reimbursement Plan," above.)

Tax-Free Withdrawals

If you withdraw funds from your HSA to use for something other than qualified medical expenses, you must pay the regular income tax on the withdrawal plus a 20% penalty. For example, if you were in the 25% federal income tax bracket, you'd have to pay a 45% tax on your nonqualified withdrawals.

Once you reach the age of 65 or become disabled, you can withdraw your HSA funds for any reason without penalty. If you use the money for nonmedical expenses, you will have to pay regular income tax on the withdrawals. When you die, the money in your HSA account is transferred to the beneficiary you've named for the account. The transfer is tax free if the beneficiary is your surviving spouse. Other transfers are taxable.

If you elect to leave the HSA program, you can continue to keep your HSA account and withdraw money from it tax-free for health care expenses. However, you won't be able to make any additional contributions to the account.

What HSA Funds Can Be Used For

Health insurance ordinarily may not be purchased with HSA funds. However, there are three exceptions to this general rule. HSA funds can be used to pay for:

- a health plan during any period of continuation coverage required under any federal law—for example, when you are terminated from your job and purchase continuing health insurance coverage from your employer's health insurer, which the insurer is legally required to make available to you under COBRA
- long-term health care insurance, or
- health insurance premiums you pay while you are receiving unemployment compensation.

You can use HSA funds to pay for the following health expenses:

- abdominal supports
- abortion
- acupuncture
- air conditioner (when necessary for relief from an allergy or for difficulty in breathing)

- alcoholism treatment
- ambulance
- arch supports
- artificial limbs
- birth control pills (by prescription)
- blood tests
- blood transfusions
- braces
- breast reconstruction surgery
- cardiographs
- chiropractor
- Christian Science practitioner
- contact lenses
- contraceptive devices (by prescription)
- convalescent home (for medical treatment only)
- crutches
- dental treatment
- dentures
- dermatologist
- diagnostic fees
- diathermy
- drug addiction therapy
- elastic hosiery (prescription)
- eyeglasses
- fees paid to health institute prescribed by a doctor
- fertility treatment
- fluoridation unit
- guide dog
- healing services
- hearing aids and batteries
- hospital bills
- hydrotherapy
- insulin treatments
- lab tests
- laser eye surgery
- lead paint removal
- legal fees to authorize treatment for mental illness

- lodging while away from home for outpatient care
- medical conference expenses (only if the conference concerns the chronic illness of yourself, your spouse, or a dependent)
- metabolism tests
- neurologist
- nursing services
- nursing home
- obstetrician
- operating room costs
- ophthalmologist
- optician
- optometrist
- oral surgery
- organ transplant (including donor's expenses)
- orthopedic shoes
- orthopedist
- osteopath
- oxygen and oxygen equipment
- pediatrician
- physician
- physiotherapist
- podiatrist
- postnatal treatments
- practical nurse for medical services
- prenatal care
- prescription medicines
- psychiatrist
- psychoanalyst
- psychologist
- radium therapy
- sex therapy
- special education costs for the handicapped
- splints
- sterilization
- stop-smoking programs (not including nonprescription drugs)
- surgeon
- telephone or TV equipment to assist the hard of hearing

- therapy equipment
- transportation expenses to obtain health care
- ultraviolet ray treatment
- vaccines
- vitamins (if prescribed)
- weight-loss program (only if it is a treatment for a specific disease diagnosed by a doctor—for example, obesity; cost of reduced-calorie foods is not deductible)
- wheelchair, and
- X-rays.

HSA funds cannot be used to pay for the following health-related expenses:

- advance payment for services to be rendered next year
- athletic club membership
- bottled water
- child care for a healthy child
- commuting expenses of a disabled person
- cosmetic surgery and procedures
- cosmetics, hygiene products, and similar items
- diaper service
- domestic help
- funeral, cremation, or burial expenses
- health programs offered by resort hotels, health clubs, and gyms
- illegal operations and treatments
- illegally procured drugs
- maternity clothes
- nutritional supplements (unless recommended by a medical practitioner to treat a specific illness diagnosed by a doctor)
- nonprescription medication
- premiums for life insurance, income protection insurance, disability insurance, and loss of limbs, sight, or similar insurance benefits
- Scientology counseling
- social activities
- specially designed car for the handicapped other than an autoette or special equipment
- swimming pool or swimming lessons

- travel for general health improvement
- tuition and travel expenses to send a child to a particular school, or
- veterinary fees.

Are HSAs a Good Deal?

Should you get an HSA? It depends. HSAs appear to be a very good deal if you're young or in good health and don't go to the doctor often or take many expensive medications. You can purchase a health plan with a high deductible, pay substantially lower premiums, and have the security of knowing you can dip into your HSA if you get sick and have to pay the deductible or other uncovered medical expenses.

If you don't tap into the money, it will keep accumulating free of taxes. You also get the benefit of deducting your HSA contributions from your income taxes. And you can use your HSA funds to pay for many health-related expenses that aren't covered by traditional health insurance.

If you enjoy good health while you have your HSA and don't have to make many withdrawals, you may end up with a substantial amount in your account that you can withdraw without penalty for any purpose once you turn 65. Unlike all other existing tax-advantaged savings or retirement accounts, HSAs provide a tax break when funds are deposited and when they are withdrawn. No other account provides both a "front end" and a "back end" tax break. With IRAs, for example, you must pay tax either when you deposit or when you withdraw your money. This feature can make your HSA an extremely lucrative tax shelter—a kind of super IRA.

On the other hand, HSAs are not for everybody. You could be better off with traditional comprehensive health insurance if you or a member of your family has substantial medical expenses. When you are in this situation, you'll likely end up spending all or most of your HSA contributions each year and earn little or no interest on your account (but you'll still get a deduction for your contributions). Of course, whether traditional health insurance is better than an HSA depends on its cost, including the deductibles and co-payments you must make. In addition, depending on your medical history and where you live, the cost of an HSA-qualified health insurance plan may be too great to make the program cost-effective for you. However, if your choice is an HSA or nothing, get an HSA.

HSAs for Employees

Employers may provide HSAs to their employees. Any business, no matter how small, may participate in the HSA program. The employer purchases an HSA-qualified health plan for its employees, and they establish their own individual HSA accounts. The employer may pay all or part of its employees' insurance premiums and make contributions to their HSA accounts. Employees may also make their own contributions to their individual accounts. The combined annual contributions of the employer and employee may not exceed the limits listed above.

HSAs are portable when an employee changes employers. Contributions and earnings belong to the account holder, not the employer. Employers are required to report amounts contributed to an HSA on the employee's Form W-2.

Health insurance payments and HSA contributions made by businesses on behalf of their employees are currently deductible business expenses. The employees do not have to report employer contributions to their HSA accounts as income. Employers deduct them on the "Employee benefit programs" line of their business income tax return. If filing Schedule C, this is in Part II, line 14.

If you've formed a C corporation and work as its employee, your corporation may establish an HSA on your behalf and deduct its contributions on its own tax return. The contributions are not taxable to you, but you get no personal deduction for them. You do get a deduction, however, if you make contributions to your HSA account from your personal funds. You can't do this if you have an S corporation, LLC, or partnership, because owners of these entities are not considered employees for employment benefit purposes.

Hiring Your Spouse

If you're a sole proprietor or have formed any business entity other than an S corporation, you may hire your spouse as your employee and have your business pay for an HSA-qualified family health plan for your spouse, you, and your children and other dependents. Moreover, your HSA-qualified health plan can cover your children up to age 27 (26 or younger as of the end of the year), whether or not they are your dependents. Your spouse then establishes an HSA, which your business may fully fund each year. The money your business spends for your spouse's health insurance premiums and to fund the HSA is a fully deductible business expense. This allows you to reduce both your income and your self-employment taxes. (See "Personal Income Tax Deduction for the Self-Employed," above.)

Nondiscrimination Rules

If you have employees other than yourself, your spouse, or other family members, you'll need to comply with nondiscrimination rules—that is, you'll have to make comparable HSA contributions for all employees with HSA-qualified health coverage during the year. Contributions are considered comparable if they are either of the same amount or the same percentage of the deductible under the plan. The rule is applied separately to employees who work fewer than 30 hours per week. Employers who do not comply with these rules are subject to a 35% excise tax.

Tax Reporting for HSAs

You must report to the IRS each year how much you deposit to and withdraw from your HSA. You make the report using IRS Form 8889, *Health Savings Accounts*. You'll also be required to keep a record of the name and address of each person or company whom you pay with funds from your HSA.

CHAPTER

12

Deductions That Can Help You Retire

When you own your own business, it's up to you to establish and fund your own pension plan to supplement the Social Security benefits you'll receive when you retire. The tax law helps you do this by providing tax deductions and other income tax benefits for your retirement account contributions and earnings.

This chapter provides a general overview of the retirement plan choices you have as a small business owner. Choosing what type of account to establish is just as important as deciding what to invest in once you open your account—if not more so. Once you set up your retirement account, you can always change your investments within the account with little or no difficulty. But changing the type of retirement account you have may prove difficult and costly. So it's best to spend some time up front learning about your choices and deciding which plan will best meet your needs.

RESOURCE

For additional information on the tax aspects of retirement, see:

- *Nolo's Essential Retirement Tax Guide,* by John Suttle and Twila Slesnick (Nolo)
- *IRAs, 401(k)s & Other Retirement Plans,* by Twila Slesnick and John C. Suttle (Nolo)
- IRS Publication 560, *Retirement Plans for Small Business,* and
- IRS Publication 590, *Individual Retirement Arrangements.*

Two easy-to-understand guides on retirement investing are:

- *Get a Life: You Don't Need a Million to Retire Well,* by Ralph Warner (Nolo), and
- *Retire Happy: What You Can Do NOW to Guarantee a Great Retirement,* by Richard Stim and Ralph Warner (Nolo).

CAUTION

You should get professional help with your plan if you have employees (other than a spouse). Having employees makes it much more complicated to set up a retirement plan. (See "Having Employees Complicates Matters—Tremendously," below.) Because of the many complex issues raised by having employees, any business owner with employees should turn to a professional consultant for help in choosing, establishing, and administering a retirement plan.

Why You Need a Retirement Plan (or Plans)

In all likelihood, you will receive Social Security benefits when you retire. However, Social Security will probably cover only half of your needs—possibly less, depending upon your retirement lifestyle. You'll need to make up this shortfall with your own retirement investments.

As small business owners, real estate professionals are better off than employees of most companies when it comes to retirement. This is because the government allows small businesses to set up retirement accounts specifically designed for small business owners. These accounts provide enormous tax benefits that are intended to maximize the money you can save during your working years for your retirement years. The amount you are allowed to contribute each year to your retirement account depends upon the type of account you establish and how much money you earn. If your real estate business doesn't earn money, you won't be able to make any contributions—you need income to fund retirement accounts.

The two biggest benefits that most of these plans provide—tax deductions for plan contributions and tax deferral on investment earnings—are discussed in more detail below.

How Much Money Will You Need When You Retire?

How much money you'll need when you retire depends on many factors, including your lifestyle. You could need anywhere from 50% to 100% of the amount you were earning while you were employed. The average is about 70% to 80% of preretirement earnings.

Tax Deduction

Retirement accounts that comply with IRS requirements are called "tax-qualified." You can deduct the amount you contribute to a tax-qualified retirement account from your income taxes (except for Roth IRAs and Roth 401(k)s). If you are a sole proprietor, partner in a partnership, or

LLC member, you can deduct from your personal income contributions you make to a retirement account. If you have incorporated your business, the corporation can deduct as a business expense contributions that it makes on your behalf. Either way, you or your business gets a substantial income tax savings with these contributions.

> EXAMPLE: Art, a sole proprietor real state agent, contributes $10,000 this year to a qualified retirement account. He can deduct the entire amount from his personal income taxes. Because Art is in the 28% tax bracket, he saves $2,800 in income taxes for the year (28% × $10,000), and he has also saved $10,000 toward his retirement.

Tax Deferral

In addition to the tax deduction you receive for putting money into a retirement account, there is another tremendous tax benefit to retirement accounts: tax deferral. When you earn money on an investment, you usually must pay taxes on those earnings in the same year that you earn the money. For example, you must pay taxes on the interest you earn on a savings account or certificate of deposit in the year when the interest accrues. And when you sell an investment at a profit, you must pay income tax in that year on the gain you receive. For example, you must pay tax on the profit you earn from selling stock in the year that you sell the stock.

A different rule applies, however, for earnings you receive from a tax-qualified retirement account. You do not pay taxes on investment earnings from retirement accounts until you withdraw the funds. Because most people withdraw these funds at retirement, they are often in a lower income tax bracket when they pay tax on these earnings. This can result in substantial tax savings for people who would have had to pay higher taxes on these earnings if they paid as the earnings accumulated.

> EXAMPLE: Bill and Brian both invest in the same mutual fund. Bill has a taxable individual account, while Brian invests through a tax-deferred retirement account. They each invest $5,000 per year. They earn 8% on their investments each year and pay income tax at the

28% rate. At the end of 30 years, Brian has $566,416. Bill only has $272,869. Reason: Bill had to pay income taxes on the interest his investments earned each year, while Brian's interest accrued tax-free because he invested through a retirement account. Brian must pay tax on his earnings only when he withdraws the money (but he'll have to pay a penalty tax if he makes withdrawals before age 59½, subject to certain exceptions).

The following chart compares the annual growth of a tax-deferred account and a taxable account.

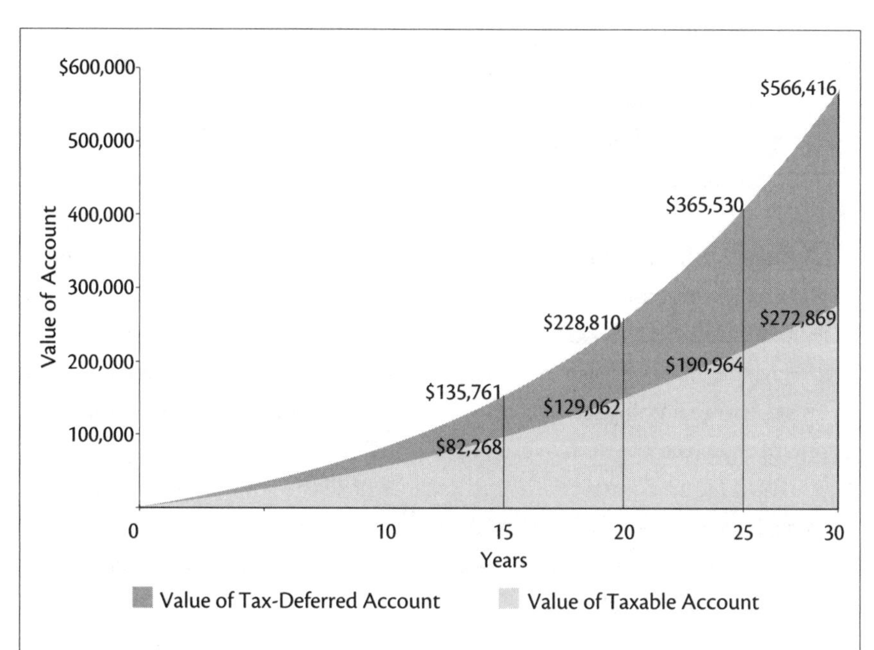

Assumptions:

- Investments earn 8% annually.
- $5,000 is invested annually in the tax-deferred account.
- $3,600 (what's left after $5,000 is taxed at 28%) is invested annually in the non-tax-deferred account.
- Income on the non-tax-deferred account is taxed annually at 28%, and recipient does not pay state income tax.

Having Employees Complicates Matters—Tremendously

If you have no employees (other than your spouse), you can probably choose, establish, and administer your own retirement plan with little or no assistance. The instant you add employees to the mix, however, virtually every aspect of your plan becomes more complex. This is primarily due to something called nondiscrimination rules. These rules are designed to ensure that your retirement plan benefits all employees, not just you. In general, the laws prohibit you from doing the following:

- making disproportionately large contributions for some plan participants (like yourself) and not for others
- unfairly excluding certain employees from participating in the plan, and
- unfairly withholding benefits from former employees or their beneficiaries.

If the IRS finds the plan to be discriminatory at any time (usually during an audit), the plan could be disqualified—that is, determined not to satisfy IRS rules. If this happens, you and your employees will owe income tax and probably penalties, as well.

Having employees also increases the plan's reporting requirements. You must provide employees with a summary of the terms of the plan, notification of any changes you make, and an annual report of contributions. And you must file an annual tax return. Because of all the complex issues raised by having employees, any real estate professional with employees (other than a spouse) should seek professional help when creating a retirement plan.

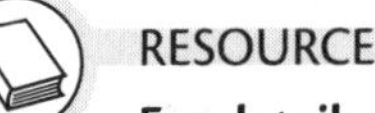

RESOURCE

For detailed guidance on distributions from retirement accounts, refer to *IRAs, 401(k)s & Other Retirement Plans: Taking Your Money Out,* by Twila Slesnick and John C. Suttle (Nolo).

CAUTION

Retirement accounts have restrictions on withdrawals. The tax deferral benefits you receive by putting your money in a retirement account come at a price: You're not supposed to withdraw the money until you are 59½ years old; and, after you turn 70½, you must withdraw a certain minimum amount each year and pay tax on it. Stiff penalties are imposed if you fail to follow these rules. So, if you aren't prepared to give up your right to use this money freely, you should think about a taxable account instead where there are no restrictions on your use of your money. You should also consider a Roth IRA or Roth 401(k)—you can withdraw your contributions to these accounts (but not earnings) at any time without penalty (see below).

Individual Retirement Accounts—IRAs

The simplest type of tax-deferred retirement account is the individual retirement account, or IRA. An IRA is a retirement account established by an individual, not a business. You can have an IRA whether you're a business owner or an employee in someone else's business. Moreover, you can establish an IRA for yourself as an individual and also set up one or more of the other types of retirement plans discussed below, which are just for businesses.

An IRA is a trust or custodial account set up for the benefit of an individual or his or her beneficiaries. The trustee or custodian administers the account. The trustee can be a bank, mutual fund, brokerage firm, or other financial institution (such as an insurance company).

IRAs are extremely easy to set up and administer. You need a written IRA agreement but don't need to file any tax forms with the IRS. The financial institution you use to set up your account will usually ask you to complete IRS Form 5305, *Traditional Individual Retirement Trust Account*, which serves as an IRA agreement and meets all of the IRS requirements. Keep the form in your records—you don't file it with the IRS.

Most financial institutions offer an array of IRA accounts that provide for different types of investments. You can invest your IRA money in just about anything: stocks, bonds, mutual funds, treasury bills and notes, and bank certificates of deposit. However, you can't invest in collectibles such as art, antiques, stamps, or other personal property.

You can establish as many IRA accounts as you want, but there is a maximum combined amount of money you can contribute to all of your IRA accounts each year. This amount goes up every year. Maximum contributions for 2012 are shown in the chart below. The limit is adjusted each year for inflation in $500 increments.

There are different limits for workers who are at least 50 years old. Anyone at least 50 years old at the end of the year can make increased annual contributions of $1,000 per year. This rule is intended to allow older people to catch up with younger folks, who will have more years to make contributions at the higher levels.

Annual IRA Contribution Limits

Tax Year	Under Age 50	Aged 50 or Over
2012	$5,000	$6,000

If you are married, you can double the contribution limits. For example, a married couple in 2012 can contribute up to $5,000 per spouse into their IRAs, or a total of $10,000. This is true even if one spouse isn't working. To take advantage of doubling, you must file a joint tax return, and the working spouse must earn at least as much as the combined IRA contribution.

There are two different types of IRAs that you can choose from:

- traditional IRAs, and
- Roth IRAs.

Traditional IRAs

Traditional IRAs have been around since 1974. Anybody who has earned income (from a job, business, or alimony) can have a traditional IRA. As stated above, you can deduct your annual contributions to your IRA from your taxable income. If neither you nor your spouse (if you have one) has another retirement plan, you may deduct your contributions no matter how high your income is.

However, there are income limits on your deductions if you (or your spouse, if you have one) are covered by another retirement plan. For these purposes, being covered by another plan means you have one of the self-employed plans described below (or are covered by an employer plan).

These limits are based on your and your spouse's annual modified adjusted gross income (MAGI for short). Your MAGI is your adjusted gross income before it is reduced by your IRA contributions and certain other more unusual items. These limits are set forth in the following chart.

Annual Income Limits for IRA Deductions

Tax Year	Married Filing Jointly		Single Taxpayer	
	Full Deduction	Partial Deduction	Full Deduction	Partial Deduction
2012	Under $92,000	$92,000–$112,000	Under $58,000	$58,000–$68,000

If your income is in the partial deduction "phase-out" range, you can use an online calculator at http://screen.morningstar.com/IRA/IRACalculator.html to determine how much you may deduct.

You can still contribute to an IRA even if you can't take a deduction. This is called a nondeductible IRA. Your money will grow in the account tax free; and, when you make withdrawals, you'll only have to pay tax on your account earnings, not the amount of your contributions (which have already been taxed). However, figuring out how much is taxable and how much is tax free can be a big accounting headache.

You may not make any more contributions to a traditional IRA after you reach age 70½. Moreover, you'll have to start making distributions from the account after you reach that age.

There are time restrictions on when you can (and when you must) withdraw money from your IRA. You are not supposed to withdraw any money from your IRA until you reach age 59½, unless you die or become disabled. Under the normal tax rules, you are required to start withdrawing at least a minimum amount of your money by April 1 of the year after the year you turn 70. Once you start withdrawing money from your IRA, the amount you withdraw will be included in your regular income for income tax purposes.

As a general rule, if you make early withdrawals, you must pay regular income tax on the amount you take out, plus a 10% federal tax penalty. There are some exceptions to this early withdrawal penalty (for example, if you withdraw money to purchase a first home or pay educational expenses, the penalty doesn't apply—subject to dollar limits). To learn about these and other exceptions in detail, see *IRAs, 401(k)s & Other Retirement Plans: Taking Your Money Out*, by Twila Slesnick and John Suttle (Nolo).

Roth IRAs

Like traditional IRAs, Roth IRAs are tax-deferred and allow your retirement savings to grow without any tax burden. Unlike traditional IRAs, however, your contributions to Roth IRAs are not tax-deductible. Instead, you get to withdraw your money from the account tax-free when you retire.

Once you have established your account, your ability to contribute to it will be affected by changes in your income level. If you are single and your income reaches $110,000, your ability to contribute to your Roth IRA will begin to phase out. Once your income reaches $125,000, you will no longer be able to make contributions. If you are married and filing a joint return with your spouse, your ability to contribute to your account will start to phase out when your income reaches $173,000, and you will be prohibited from making any contributions at all when your income reaches $183,000. These are the 2012 limits. The limits are adjusted for inflation each year.

You can withdraw the money you contributed to a Roth IRA penalty-free anytime—you already paid tax on it so the government doesn't care. But the earnings on your investments in a Roth IRA are a different matter. You can't withdraw these until after five years. Early withdrawals of your earnings are subject to income tax and early distribution penalties. You are not, however, required to make withdrawals when you reach age 70½. Because Roth IRA withdrawals are tax-free, the government doesn't care if you leave your money in your account indefinitely. However, your money will be tax-free on withdrawal only if you leave it in your Roth IRA for at least five years.

Is the Roth IRA a good deal? If your tax rate when you retire is higher than your tax rate before retirement, you'll probably be better off with a Roth IRA than a traditional IRA because you won't have to pay tax on your withdrawals at the higher rates. The opposite is true if your taxes go down when you retire. The catch is that nobody can know for sure what their tax rate will be when they retire. You can find several online calculators that will help you compare your results with a Roth IRA versus traditional IRA at www.choosetosave.org/calculators. Much more information on Roth IRAs can be found at www.rothira.com.

Roth IRA Conversions

If the Roth IRA sounds attractive to you, and you already have a traditional IRA, you may convert it to a Roth IRA. This can vastly increase the amount of money in your Roth IRA. There used to be an income limit on such conversions; but, starting in 2010, everyone became allowed to convert to a Roth IRA, no matter what their income.

However, when you convert to a Roth IRA, you'll have to pay income tax on the amount of the conversion. For example, if you convert $20,000 from your traditional IRA to a Roth IRA, you'll have to add $20,000 to your taxable income for the year. If you were in the 25% bracket, this would add $5,000 to your income taxes. One way to keep these taxes down is to convert only a portion of your traditional IRAs into a Roth each year for several years instead of doing it all at once.

Whether a Roth conversion is a good idea or not depends on many factors, including your age, your current tax rate, and your tax rate upon retirement. You can find an online calculator at www.dinkytown.com/java/RothTransfer.html that allows you to compare the results when you convert to a Roth versus leaving your traditional IRAs alone.

Employer IRAs

You can establish an employer IRA as long as you are in business and earn a profit. You don't have to have employees working for you, and it doesn't matter how your real estate business is organized: You can be a sole proprietor, partner in a partnership, member of a limited liability company, or owner of a regular or S corporation.

The great advantage of employer IRAs is that you can contribute more than you can with traditional IRAs and Roth IRAs, both of which have lower annual contribution limits. And as long as you meet the requirements for establishing an employer IRA, you can have this type of IRA in addition to one or more individual IRAs.

There are two kinds of employer IRAs to choose from: SEP-IRAs and SIMPLE IRAs.

SEP-IRAs

SEP-IRAs are designed for the self-employed. Any person who receives self-employment income from providing a service can establish a SEP-IRA. It doesn't matter whether you work full time or part time. You can even have a SEP-IRA if you are covered by a retirement plan at a full-time employee job.

A SEP-IRA is a simplified employee pension. It's very similar to an IRA, except that you can contribute more money under this plan. Instead of being limited to a $5,000 to $6,000 annual contribution (2012), you can invest up to 20% of your net profit from self-employment every year, up to a maximum of $50,000 a year in 2012. You don't have to make contributions every year, and your contributions can vary from year to year. As with other IRAs, you can invest your money in almost anything (stocks, bonds, notes, mutual funds).

You can deduct your contributions to SEP-IRAs from your income taxes, and the interest on your SEP-IRA investments accrues tax-free until you withdraw the money. Withdrawals from SEP-IRAs are subject to the same rules that apply to traditional IRAs. This means that if you withdraw your money from your SEP-IRA before you reach age 59½, you'll have to pay a 10% tax penalty plus regular income taxes on your withdrawal, unless an exception applies. And you must begin to withdraw your money by April 1 of the year after the year you turn 70.

SIMPLE IRAs

Self-employed people and companies with fewer than 100 employees can set up SIMPLE IRAs. If you establish a SIMPLE IRA, you are not allowed to have any other retirement plans for your business (although you may still have an individual IRA). SIMPLE IRAs are easy to set up and administer and will enable you to make larger annual contributions than a SEP or Keogh plan if you earn less than $10,000 per year from your real estate business.

SIMPLE IRAs may only be established by an employer on behalf of its employees. If you are a sole proprietor, you are deemed to employ yourself for these purposes and may establish a SIMPLE IRA in your own name as the employer. If you are a partner in a partnership, LLC member, or owner of an incorporated business, the SIMPLE IRA must be established by your business, not you personally.

Contributions to SIMPLE IRAs are divided into two parts. You may contribute:

- up to 100% of your net income from your business up to an annual limit—the contribution limit is $11,500 for 2012 ($14,000 if you were born before 1955), and
- a matching contribution which can equal 3% of your net business income.

If you're an employee of your incorporated business, your first contribution (called a salary reduction contribution) comes from your salary, and the matching contribution is paid by your business.

The limits on contributions to SIMPLE IRAs might seem very low, but they could work to your advantage if you earn a small income from your business—for example, if you only work at it part time. This is because you can contribute an amount equal to 100% of your earnings, up to the $11,500 or $14,000 limits. Thus, for example, if your net earnings are only $10,000, you could contribute the entire amount (plus a 3% employer contribution). You can't do this with any of the other plans because their percentage limits are much lower. For example, you may contribute only 20% of your net self-employment income to a

SEP-IRA or Keogh, so you would be limited to a $2,000 contribution if you had a $10,000 profit.

The money in a SIMPLE IRA can be invested like any other IRA. Withdrawals from SIMPLE IRAs are subject to the same rules as traditional IRAs, with one big exception: Early withdrawals from SIMPLE IRAs are subject to a 25% tax penalty if the withdrawal is made within two years after the date you first contributed to your account. Other early withdrawals are subject to a 10% penalty, the same as traditional IRAs, unless an exception applies.

Keogh Plans

Keogh plans—named after the Congressman who sponsored the legislation that created them—are only for business owners who are sole proprietors, partners in partnerships, or LLC members. You can't have a Keogh if you incorporate your real estate business.

Keoghs require more paperwork to set up than employer IRAs, but they also offer more options: You can contribute more to these plans and still get an income tax deduction for your contributions.

Types of Keogh Plans

There are two basic types of Keogh plans:

- defined contribution plans, in which benefits are based on the amount contributed to and accumulated in the plan, and
- defined benefit plans, which provide for a set benefit upon retirement.

There are two types of defined contribution plans: profit sharing plans and money purchase plans. These plans can be used separately or in tandem with one another.

Setting Up a Keogh Plan

As with individual IRAs and employer IRAs, you can set up a Keogh plan at most banks, brokerage houses, mutual funds, and other financial institutions, as well as trade or professional organizations. You can also choose among a huge array of investments for your money.

To set up your plan, you must adopt a written Keogh plan and set up a trust or custodial account with your plan provider to invest your funds. Your plan provider will ordinarily have an IRS-approved master or prototype Keogh plan for you to sign. You can also have a special plan drawn up for you, but this is expensive and unnecessary for most small business owners.

Profit-Sharing Plans

You can contribute up to 20% of your net self-employment income to a profit-sharing Keogh plan, up to a maximum of $50,000 per year in 2012. You can contribute any amount up to the limit each year or not contribute at all.

Money Purchase Plans

In a money purchase plan, you contribute a fixed percentage of your net self-employment earnings every year. You decide how much to contribute each year. Make sure you will be able to afford the contributions each year because you can't skip them, even if your business earns no profit for the year. In return for giving up flexibility, you can contribute a higher percentage of your earnings with a money purchase plan: the lesser of 25% of your compensation or $50,000 in 2012 (the same maximum amount as the profit-sharing plan).

Withdrawing Your Money

You may begin to withdraw your money from your Keogh plan after you reach age 59½. If you have a profit-sharing plan, early withdrawals are permitted without penalty in cases of financial hardship, if you become disabled, or if you have to pay health expenses in excess of 7.5% of your adjusted gross income. If you have a money purchase plan, early withdrawals are permitted if you become disabled, leave your business after you turn 55, or make child support or alimony payments from the plan under a court order. Otherwise, early withdrawals from profit-sharing and money purchase Keogh plans are subject to a 10% penalty.

Solo 401(k) Plans

Most people have heard of 401(k) plans—they are retirement plans established by businesses for their employees. 401(k)s are a type of profit-sharing plan in which a business's employees make plan contributions from their salaries and the business makes a matching contribution. These plans are complex to establish and administer and are generally used only by larger businesses. Until recently, self-employed people and businesses without employees rarely used them, because they offered no benefit over other profit-sharing plans that are much easier to set up and run.

However, things have changed. Now, any business owner who has no employees (other than a spouse) can establish a solo self-employed 401(k) plan (also called a one-person or individual 401(k)). Solo 401(k) plans are designed specifically for business owners without employees.

Solo 401(k) plans have the following advantages over other retirement plans:

You can make very large contributions—as much as 20% of your net profit from self-employment, plus an elective deferral contribution of up to $17,000 in 2012. The maximum contribution per year is $50,000 (2012) (the same maximum amount as for profit-sharing and money purchase plans discussed in "Keogh Plans," above). Business owners over 50 may make additional catch-up contributions of up to $5,000 per year that are not counted toward the $50,000 limit.

You can borrow up to $50,000 from your solo 401(k) plan, as long as you repay the loan within five years (you cannot borrow from a traditional IRA, Roth IRA, SEP-IRA, or SIMPLE IRA).

As with other plans, you must pay a 10% penalty tax on withdrawals you make before age 59½, but you may make penalty-free early withdrawals for reasons of personal hardship (defined as an "immediate financial need" that can't be met any other way).

You can set up a solo 401(k) plan at most banks, brokerage houses, mutual funds, and other financial institutions and invest the money in a variety of ways. You must adopt a written plan and set up a trust or custodial account with your plan provider to invest your funds. Financial institutions that offer solo 401(k) plans have preapproved ready-made plans that you can use.

CAUTION

Beware of retirement account deadlines. If you want to establish any of the retirement accounts discussed in this chapter and take a tax deduction for the year, you must meet specific deadlines. The deadlines vary according to the type of account you set up, as shown in the following chart. Once you establish your account, you have until the due date of your tax return for the year (April 15 of the following year, plus any filing extensions) to contribute to your account and take a deduction.

Retirement Account Deadlines

Plan Type	Deadline for Establishing Plan
Traditional IRA	Due date of tax return (April 15 plus extensions)
Roth IRA	Due date of tax return (April 15 plus extensions)
SEP-IRA	Due date of tax return (April 15 plus extensions)
SIMPLE IRA	October 1
Keogh Profit Sharing Plan	December 31
Keogh Money Purchase Plan	December 31
Keogh Defined Benefit Plan	December 31
401(k) Plan	December 31

CHAPTER 13

Business Operating Expenses and Other Deductions

Business operating expenses are the bread and butter expenses that every business incurs for things like rent, supplies, and salaries. Some of these deductions—like rent and other office expenses—are covered in other chapters in the book (see Chapter 8). This chapter looks at some of the most common deductible operating expenses that real estate agents and brokers are likely to incur in the normal course of running their operations, such as advertising expenses, insurance, and legal fees. You can deduct these costs as business operating expenses as long as they are ordinary, necessary, and reasonable in amount and meet the additional requirements discussed below.

Advertising

Advertising is often the largest operating expense for real estate agents. Indeed, the average brokerage spends 15% to 20% of its budget on advertising. There are two basic types of real estate advertising: specific and institutional. Specific advertising focuses on selling a particular property or properties. Institutional advertising promotes the real estate company and its agents, rather than a particular property. Both forms of advertising are a currently deductible business operating expense if they are reasonable in amount and bear a reasonable relation to your business. Moreover, the cost of advertising is currently deductible even though you expect it to benefit your business over several years.

Advertising includes expenses for:

- business cards
- direct mail, including mailing lists
- newspaper advertising
- Internet advertising, including pay per click advertising programs
- flyers
- home spec sheets and floor plans
- presentation materials and supplies
- food, beverage, and other costs for holding open houses
- advertisements in the local yellow pages
- radio and television advertisements
- producing online virtual home tours
- photographs

- magazine advertisements
- advertisements on the Internet
- greeting cards
- fees you pay to advertising and public relations agencies
- billboards
- newsletters
- postcards
- logo clothing and other imprinted items, and
- signs and display racks.

However, advertising to influence government legislation is never deductible. "Help wanted" ads you place to recruit workers are not advertising costs, but you can deduct them as ordinary and necessary business operating expenses.

Broker's Castle Not an Advertising Expense

Not everything can be an advertising expense. There must be a direct relationship between the expense and the business of realty. Case in point: Georgia broker Daniel Kenerly who built a 30-room home in the style of a Moorish castle. This was not just any castle; it included three brick turrets up to 60 feet high, a drawbridge, and an airplane hanger. As one might expect, the castle aroused public interest: It was written up in some newspapers and the public was even allowed to tour it. But the castle was never directly used in any advertising for Kenerly's realty business and he could not show that it had any advertising or promotional effect for the business. The tax court concluded, therefore, that the castle's cost did not qualify as a deductible advertising expense. (*Kenerly v. Comm'r*, 47 TCM 1244 (1984).)

Good Will Advertising

If it relates to business you reasonably expect to gain in the future, you can usually deduct the cost of institutional or "good will" advertising meant to keep your or your company's name before the public. Examples of good will advertising include:

- advertisements that encourage people to contribute to charities, such as the Red Cross or similar causes, or
- sponsoring a Little League baseball team, bowling team, or golf tournament.

However, you can't deduct time and labor that you give away as an advertising expense, even though doing so promotes good will. You must actually spend money to have an advertising expense.

Giveaway Items

Giveaway items that you use to publicize your business (such as pens, coffee cups, T-shirts, refrigerator magnets, calendars, tote bags, and key chains) are deductible. However, you are not allowed to deduct more than $25 in business gifts to any one person each year. This limitation applies to advertising giveaway items unless they:

- cost $4 or less
- have your name clearly and permanently imprinted on them, and
- are one of a number of identical items you distribute widely.

EXAMPLE 1: Acme Realty orders 1,000 ballpoint pens with its name and company logo printed on them and makes them freely available to its clients. Each pen costs $1. The pens do not count toward the $25 gift limit. Acme may deduct the entire $1,000 expense for the pens.

EXAMPLE 2: Acme buys a $200 fountain pen and gives it to its highest producing agent. The pen is a business gift to an individual, so Acme can deduct only $25 of the cost.

Signs, display racks, and other promotional materials that you give away to other businesses to use on their premises do not count as gifts.

Permanent Signs

Signs that have a useful life of less than one year—for example, paper or cardboard signs—are currently deductible as business operating expenses. However, a metal or plastic sign that has a useful life of more than one year is a long-term business asset, which you cannot currently deduct as a business operating expense. Instead, you must either depreciate the cost over several years or deduct it in one year under Section 179. This means that yard signs must ordinarily be depreciated. (See Chapter 9 for more on deducting long-term assets.)

Broker Fees Charged to Agents

The broker-agent financial relationship can take a variety of forms. Real estate brokers often impose various charges or fees on the independent contractor real estate agents that they contract with. These may include desk rental fees, transaction fees, referral fees, insurance fees, franchise fees, charges for copying, advertising fees, delivery service fees, Multiple Listing Service fees, and training fees. These are all deductible business expenses for the agents. The broker should list all such charges and fees on a year-end statement.

Casualty Losses

Casualty losses are damage to property caused by fire, theft, vandalism, earthquake, storm, floods, terrorism, or some other "sudden, unexpected, or unusual event." There must be some external force involved for a loss to be a casualty loss. Thus, you get no deduction if you simply lose or misplace property or it breaks or wears out over time.

You may take a deduction for casualty losses to business property if, and only to the extent that, the loss is not covered by insurance. Thus, if the loss is fully covered, you'll get no deduction.

Amount of Deduction

How much you may deduct depends on whether the property involved was stolen or completely destroyed or only partially destroyed. However, you must always reduce your casualty losses by the amount of any insurance proceeds you actually receive or reasonably expect to receive. If more than one item was stolen or wholly or partly destroyed, you must figure your deduction separately for each and then add them all together.

Total Loss

If the property is stolen or completely destroyed, your deduction is figured as follows: Adjusted Basis – Salvage Value – Insurance Proceeds = Casualty Loss. (Your adjusted basis is the property's original cost, plus the value of any improvements, minus any deductions you took for depreciation or Section 179 expensing—see Chapter 9.) Obviously, if an item is stolen, there will be no salvage value.

> EXAMPLE: Sean's business computer is stolen from his apartment by a burglar. The computer cost $2,000. Sean has taken no tax deductions for it because he purchased it only two months ago, so his adjusted basis is $2,000. Sean is a renter and has no insurance covering the loss. Sean's casualty loss is $2,000. ($2,000 adjusted basis – $0 salvage value – $0 insurance proceeds = $2,000.)

Partial Loss

If the property is only partly destroyed, your casualty loss deduction is the lesser of the decrease in the property's fair market value or its adjusted basis, reduced by any insurance you receive or expect to receive.

> EXAMPLE: Assume that Sean's computer from the example above is partly destroyed due to a small fire in his home. Its fair market value in its partly damaged state is $500. Since he spent $2,000 for it, the decrease in its fair market value is $1,500. The computer's adjusted basis is $2,000. He received no insurance proceeds. Thus, his casualty loss is $1,500.

Personal Property

You can deduct uninsured casualty losses to personal property—that is, property you don't use for your business—from your income tax. In 2010 and later, these losses are an itemized deduction and are deductible only to the extent they exceed 10% of your adjusted gross income for the year. For example, if you have $10,000 in total casualty losses and 10% of your AGI is $7,000, your loss is limited to $3,000. In addition, your loss is deductible only to the extent it exceeds $100—in other words, you must reduce your loss by $100. This reduction applies to each total casualty or theft loss. It does not matter how many pieces of property are involved in an event. Only a single $100 reduction applies.

Damage to Your Home Office

If you take the home office deduction, you may deduct losses due to damage or destruction of your home office as part of your deduction. However, your loss is reduced by any insurance proceeds you receive or expect to receive.

You can deduct casualty losses that affect your entire house as an indirect home office expense. The amount of your deduction is based on your home office use percentage.

> EXAMPLE: Real estate agent Dana's home is completely destroyed by a fire. Her fire insurance only covered 80% of her loss. Her home office took up 20% of her home. She can deduct 20% of her total casualty loss as an indirect home office deduction.

You can fully deduct casualty losses that affect only your home office—for example, if only your home office is burned in a fire—as direct home office expenses. However, you can't deduct as a business expense casualty losses that don't affect your home office at all—for example, if your kitchen is destroyed by fire.

If the loss involves business property that is in your home office but is not part of your home—for example, a burglar steals your home office computer—it's not part of the home office deduction.

See Chapter 7 for a detailed discussion of the home office deduction.

Tax Reporting

You report casualty losses to business property on part B of IRS Form 4684, *Casualties and Thefts*, and then transfer the deductible casualty loss to Form 4797, *Sales of Business Property*, and the first page of your Form 1040. The amount of your deductible casualty loss is subtracted from your adjusted gross income for the year. However, casualty losses are not deducted from your self-employment income for Social Security and Medicare tax purposes. These reporting requirements are different from the reporting for other deductions covered in this chapter, which are reported on IRS Schedule C, Form 1040.

Partnerships, S corporations, and LLCs must also fill out Form 4797. The amount of the loss is taken into account when calculating the entity's total business income for the year. This amount is reported on the entity's information tax return (Form 1065 for partnerships and LLCs; Form 1120S for S corporations). C corporations deduct their casualty losses on their own tax returns (Form 1120).

If you take a casualty loss as part of your home office deduction, you must include it on Form 8829, *Expenses for Business Use of Your Home.*

Charitable Contributions

If, like the vast majority of real estate agents and brokers, you are a sole proprietor, partner in a partnership, LLC member, or an S corporation shareholder, the IRS treats any charitable contributions your business makes as a personal contribution by you and your co-owners. As such, the contributions are not business expenses—you can deduct them only as a personal charitable contribution. You may deduct these contributions only if you itemize deductions on your personal tax return; they are subject to certain income limitations.

RESOURCE

For detailed guidance on tax deductions for charitable contributions, refer to *Every Nonprofit's Tax Guide,* by Stephen Fishman (Nolo).

Clothing

You can deduct the cost of clothing only if:

- it is essential for your business
- it is not suitable for ordinary street wear, and
- you don't wear the clothing outside of business.

Thus, for example, you may deduct the cost of clothing with a company logo. But clothing that you can wear on the street is not deductible—for example, you can't deduct the cost of business suits. If your clothing is deductible, you may also deduct the cost of dry cleaning and other care.

Dues and Subscriptions

Dues you pay to professional, business, and civic organizations are deductible business expenses, as long as the organization's main purpose is not to provide entertainment facilities to members. This includes dues paid to:

- trade associations for real estate brokers and agents, including national, state, and local realtor associations, and other real estate associations
- local chambers of commerce and business leagues, and
- civic or public service organizations, such as a Rotary or Lions club.

You get no deduction for dues you pay to belong to other types of social, business, or recreational clubs—for example, country clubs or athletic clubs. For this reason, it's best not to use the word "dues" on your tax return, because the IRS may question the expense. Use other words to describe the deduction—for example, if you're deducting membership dues for a trade organization, list the expense as "trade association membership fees."

You may deduct as a business expense subscriptions to professional, technical, and trade journals that deal with your business field.

Education Expenses

The costs of education, including tuition, fees, books, and other learning materials, are deductible business expenses only if the education:

- helps maintain or improve skills required in your existing business, or
- is required by law or regulation to maintain your professional standing.

Thus, whether your educational expenses are deductible depends on when and why you incur the expenses.

Lifetime Learning Credit

Instead of taking a tax deduction for your business related education expenses, you may qualify for the lifetime learning credit. A tax credit is a dollar-for-dollar reduction in your tax liability, so it's even better than a tax deduction.

The lifetime learning credit can by used to help pay for any undergraduate or graduate level education, including nondegree education, to acquire or improve job skills (for example a continuing education course). If you qualify, your credit equals 20% of the first $10,000 of postsecondary tuition and fees you pay during the year, for a maximum credit of $2,000 per tax return. However, the credit is phased out and then eliminated at certain income levels: It begins to go down if your modified adjusted gross income is more than $52,000 ($102,000 for a joint return), and you cannot claim the credit at all if your MAGI is over $62,000 ($124,000 for a joint return). These are the limits for 2012. The limits are adjusted for inflation each year.

You can take this credit not only for yourself, but for a dependent child (or children) for whom you claim a tax exemption, or your spouse as well (if you file jointly). And it can be taken any number of times. However, you can't take the credit if you've already deducted the education cost as a business expense.

EXAMPLE: Bill, a self-employed real estate broker with a $40,000 AGI, spends $2,000 on continuing real estate education courses during 2012. He may take a $400 lifetime learning credit (20% × $2,000 = $400).

Studying for Real Estate Agent Exam

You cannot currently deduct education expenses you incur to qualify for a new business or profession. This means you cannot deduct the costs of education courses you take to help prepare for your state's real estate license exam. Nor is the fee to take the exam itself deductible. This rule applies even when a licensed real estate agent, salesperson, or sales associate pays for education to pass the state exam to become a real estate broker. Courts have reasoned that the tasks performed by licensed real estate brokers are so different from those performed by licensed real estate agents that courses taken to prepare for the broker's examination qualify an agent for a new trade or business. (*Goldstein v. Comm'r*, 52 TCM 1481 (1987).)

Educational Requirements to Become a Real Estate Agent or Broker

If your state imposes minimum educational requirements to become a real estate agent or broker, the cost of meeting them is not deductible. Similarly, the cost of going to law school or obtaining an accounting degree is not deductible.

Real Estate Continuing Education

Real estate agents and brokers may deduct the cost of undergoing mandatory continuing education to maintain their licenses.

> EXAMPLE: Sue, a real estate broker, is required by law to attend 12 hours of continuing education to keep her real estate license. The real estate seminars she attends to satisfy this requirement are deductible education expenses.

Education that is not required to maintain an agent's license is still deductible if it helps improve his or her skills.

College Education

It is usually not possible to deduct expenses incurred to obtain a bachelor's degree. This is because such degrees generally qualify the graduate for a new trade or business in some field, and that field would not necessarily be in the same area as that person was previously engaged in. (*Malek v. Commissioner* T.C. Memo. 1985-428 (1985).)

Traveling for Education

Local transportation expenses paid to get to and from a deductible educational activity are deductible. This includes transportation between either your home or business and the educational activity. Going to or from home to an educational activity does not constitute nondeductible commuting. If you drive, you may deduct your actual expenses or use the standard mileage rate. (See Chapter 4 for more on deducting car expenses.)

There's no law that says you must take your education courses as close to home as possible. You may travel outside your geographic area for education, even if the same or a similar educational activity is available near your home or place of business. Companies and groups that sponsor educational events are well aware of this rule and take advantage of it by offering courses and seminars at resorts and other enjoyable vacation spots such as Hawaii and California. Deductible travel expenses may include airfare or other transportation, lodging, and meals. (See Chapter 5 for more about travel expenses.)

Franchise Fees

Many real estate brokers choose to affiliate with a regional or national real estate franchise company, such as Century 21 Real Estate, RE/MAX, or Prudential Real Estate. Affiliating with such a franchise is expensive. An initial franchise fee must usually be paid up front—this can run up to $50,000 or more. Unfortunately, the IRS classifies initial franchise fees as intangible asset expenses that must be deducted over 15 years. This deduction is claimed ratably (in equal amounts) over 180 months (15 years) beginning on the first day of the month the franchise is acquired. For example, a broker who paid a $50,000 fee to affiliate with a franchise could deduct $3,333 per year. If the franchise was acquired on July 1, $1,667 could be deducted the first year.

In addition to up front fees, most franchise companies require their franchisees to pay them other recurring fees over the term of the agreement. These may include royalties (a percentage of your business income that must be paid to the franchisor each year), marketing fees, training fees, and various other fees. These recurring fees are currently deductible operating expenses.

Gifts

It's a common practice for real estate agents to send gifts to clients after a closing. Such gifts can take many forms—for example, a bottle of wine, customized mail box, or yard plant. One agent even hosted a spa night in which she paid for manicures and pedicures for 37 clients.

These and other business gifts are a deductible business expense. However, the deduction for business gifts is limited to $25 per person per year. Any amount over the $25 limit is not deductible. If this amount seems awfully low, that's because it was established in 1954!

> EXAMPLE: Real estate agent Lisa sends a $100 gift basket to a client who closes on new home. Lisa may deduct $25 of the cost.

A gift to a member of a client's family is treated as a gift to the client, unless you have a legitimate nonbusiness connection to the family member. If you and your spouse both give gifts, you are treated as one taxpayer—it doesn't matter if you work together or have separate businesses.

The $25 limit applies only to gifts to individuals. It doesn't apply if you give a gift to an entire company, unless the gift is intended for a particular person or group of people within the company. Such company-wide gifts are deductible in any amount, as long as they are reasonable.

> EXAMPLE: Bob, a commercial real estate broker, has the Acme Company as a client. Just before Christmas, he drops off a $200 cheese basket at the company's reception area for all of Acme's employees. He also delivers an identical basket to Acme's president. The first basket left in the reception area is a company-wide gift, not subject to the $25 limit. The basket for Acme's president is a personal gift and therefore is subject to the limit.

If you give gifts to clients, be sure to keep good records listing:

- the recipient's name
- description of gift
- cost of each gift
- date of the gift, and
- the business relationship between you and the recipient.

Referral Fees Are Not Gifts

Referral fees are not gifts and are not subject to the $25 limit. A gift occurs when you transfer property to someone and don't receive anything of value in return. Referral fees are not gifts because they are payments for something of value in return—bringing in new clients to the agent. For example, a real estate broker who paid $100 to $200 to former customers who referred new clients to him was not making gifts for tax purposes, even though he referred to them as such. (*Pacheco v. Comm'r*, 2009 T.C. Memo 112 (2009).)

Insurance for Your Real Estate Business

You can deduct the premiums you pay for any insurance you buy for your business as a business operating expense. This includes:

- medical insurance for your employees (see Chapter 11)
- fire, theft, and flood insurance for business property
- credit insurance that covers losses from business debts
- liability insurance
- errors and omissions insurance
- workers' compensation insurance you are required by state law to provide your employees (if you are an employee of an S corporation, the corporation can deduct workers' comp payments made on your behalf, but they must be included in your employee wages)
- business interruption insurance
- life insurance covering a corporation's officers and directors if you are not a direct beneficiary under the policy, and
- unemployment insurance contributions (either as insurance costs or business taxes, depending on how they are characterized by your state's laws).

Homeowners' Insurance for Your Home Office

If you have a home office and qualify for the home office deduction, you may deduct the home office percentage of your homeowners' or renters' insurance premiums. For example, if your home office takes up 20% of your home, you may deduct 20% of the premiums. You can deduct 100% of any special coverage that you add to your homeowners' or renters' policy for your home office and/or business property. For example, if you add an endorsement to your policy to cover business property, you can deduct 100% of the cost.

If you use the actual expense method to deduct your car expenses, you can deduct as a business expense the cost of insurance that covers liability, damages, and other losses for vehicles used in your business. If you use a vehicle only for business, you can deduct 100% of your insurance costs. If you operate a vehicle for both business and personal use, you can deduct only the part of the insurance premiums that applies to the business use of your vehicle. For example, if you use a car 60% for business and 40% for personal reasons, you can deduct 60% of your insurance costs. (See Chapter 9.)

If you use the standard mileage rate to deduct your car expenses, you get no separate deduction for insurance. Your insurance costs are included in the standard rate. (See Chapter 4.)

Interest on Business Loans

Interest you pay on business loans is usually a currently deductible business expense. It makes no difference whether you pay the interest on a bank loan, personal loan, credit card, line of credit, car loan, or real estate mortgage. Nor does it matter whether the collateral you used to get the loan was business or personal property. If you use the money for business, the interest you pay to get that money is a deductible business expense. It's how you use the money that counts, not how you get it. Borrowed money is used for business when you buy something with the money that's deductible as a business expense.

EXAMPLE: Max borrows $50,000 from a local bank to help start his real estate brokerage firm. He pays 6% interest on the loan. His annual interest is deductible on his Schedule C, Form 1040, because it is for a business loan.

Your deduction begins only when you spend the borrowed funds for business purposes. You get no business deduction for interest you pay on money that you keep in the bank. Money in the bank is considered an investment—at best, you might be able to deduct the interest you pay on the money as an investment expense. (See "How to Eliminate Nondeductible Personal Interest," below.)

How to Eliminate Nondeductible Personal Interest

Because interest on money you borrow for personal purposes—like buying clothes or taking vacations—is not deductible, you should avoid paying this type of interest whenever possible. If you own a business, you can do this by borrowing money to pay your business expense and then using the money your business earns to pay off your personal debt. By doing this, you "replace" your nondeductible personal interest expense with deductible business expenses.

Home Offices

If you are a homeowner and take the home office deduction, you can deduct the home office percentage of your home mortgage interest as a business expense. (See Chapter 7 for a detailed discussion of the home office deduction.)

Car Loans

If, like most real estate agents, you use your car for your real estate business, you can deduct the interest that you pay on your car loan as an interest expense. You can take this deduction whether you deduct your car expenses using the actual expense method or the standard mileage rate, because the standard mileage rate was not intended to encompass interest on a car loan.

If you use your car only for business, you can deduct all of the interest you pay. If you use it for both business and personal reasons, you can deduct the business percentage of the interest. For example, if you use your car 60% of the time for business, you can deduct 60% of the interest you pay on your car loan.

Loans to Buy a Business

If you borrow money to buy an interest in an S corporation, partnership, or LLC, it's wise to seek an accountant's help to figure out how to deduct the interest on your loan. It must be allocated among the company's assets and, depending on what assets the business owns, the interest might be deductible either as a business expense or as an investment expense, which is more limited. (See "How to Eliminate Nondeductible Personal Interest," above.)

Interest on money you borrow to buy stock in a C corporation is always treated as investment interest. This is true even if the corporation is small (also called closely held) and its stock is not publicly traded.

Loans From Relatives and Friends

If you borrow money from a relative or friend and use it for business purposes, you may deduct the interest you pay on the loan as a business expense. However, the IRS is very suspicious of loans between family members and friends. You need to carefully document these transactions. Treat the loan like any other business loan: Sign a promissory note, pay a reasonable rate of interest, and follow a repayment schedule. Keep your cancelled loan payment checks to prove you really paid the interest.

Interest You Can't Deduct

You can't deduct interest:

- on loans used for personal purposes
- on debts your business doesn't owe
- on overdue taxes (only C corporations can deduct this interest)
- that you pay with funds borrowed from the original lender through a second loan (but you can deduct the interest once you start making payments on the new loan)
- that you prepay if you're a cash basis taxpayer (but you may deduct it the next year)
- on money borrowed to pay taxes or fund retirement plans, or
- on loans of more than $50,000 that are borrowed on a life insurance policy on yourself or another owner or employee of your business.

Points and other loan origination fees that you pay to get a mortgage on business property are not deductible business expenses. You must add these costs to the cost of the building and deduct them over time using depreciation. The same is true for interest on construction loans if you are in the business of building houses or other real property.

Get Separate Credit Cards for Your Business and Car Expenses

If you use the same credit card for your business and nonbusiness expenses, you are theoretically entitled to a business deduction for the credit card interest on your business expenses. However, you'll have a very difficult time calculating exactly how much of the interest you pay is for business expenses. To avoid this problem, use a separate credit card for business. This can be a special business credit card, but it doesn't have to be. You can simply designate one of your ordinary credit cards for business use. If you use the actual expense method to take your car expense deduction, it's a good idea to use another credit card just for car expenses. This will make it much easier to keep track of what you spend on your car.

Always pay your personal credit cards first, because you can't deduct the interest you pay on those costs.

Legal and Professional Services

You can deduct fees that you pay to attorneys, accountants, consultants, and other professionals as business expenses if the fees are paid for work related to your business.

> EXAMPLE: Ira, a real estate broker, hires attorney Jake to represent him in a malpractice suit. The legal fees Ira pays Jake are a deductible business expense.

Legal and professional fees that you pay for personal purposes generally are not deductible. For example, you can't deduct the legal fees you incur if you get divorced or you sue someone for a traffic accident injury. Nor are the fees that you pay to write your will deductible, even if the will covers business property that you own.

Buying Long-Term Property

If you pay legal or other fees in the course of buying long-term business property, you must add the amount of the fee to the tax basis (cost) of the property. You may deduct this cost over several years through depreciation or deduct it in one year under IRC Section 179. (See Chapter 9 for more on depreciation.)

Starting a Business

Legal and accounting fees that you pay to start your real estate business are deductible only as business start-up expenses. You can deduct $5,000 of start-up expenses the first year you're in business and any excess amounts over 180 months. The same holds true for incorporation fees or fees that you pay to form a partnership or LLC. (See Chapter 10 for more on start-up expenses.)

Accounting Fees

You can deduct any accounting fees that you pay for your business as a deductible business expense—for example, fees you pay an accountant to set up or keep your business books, prepare your business tax return, or give you tax advice for your business.

Self-employed taxpayers may deduct the cost of having an accountant or other tax professional complete the business portion of their tax returns—Schedule C and other business tax forms—but they cannot deduct the time the preparer spends on the personal part of their returns. If you are self-employed and pay a tax preparer to complete your Form 1040 income tax return, make sure that you get an itemized bill showing the portion of the tax preparation fee allocated to preparing your Schedule C (and any other business tax forms attached to your Form 1040).

Multiple Listing Service Fees

Most parts of the country have some kind of Multiple Listing Service (MLS)—a database of all of current, pending, sold, and expired listings of every member brokerage firm in the area. In many areas of the country, the majority of residential listings are sold through the MLS. Real estate brokers can deduct any charges they pay to list property in the MLS.

Taxes and Licenses

Most taxes that you pay in the course of your real estate business are deductible.

Income Taxes

Federal income taxes that you pay on your business income are not deductible. However, a corporation or partnership can deduct state or local income taxes it pays. Individuals may deduct state and local income taxes only as an itemized deduction on Schedule A, Form 1040. This is a personal, not a business, deduction. However, an individual can deduct state tax on gross business income as a business expense—for example, Michigan has a business tax of 4.95% on business gross receipts over $350,000. This tax is a federally deductible business operating expense. Of course, you can't deduct state taxes from your income for state income tax purposes.

Self-Employment Taxes

If, like most real estate agents and brokers, you are a sole proprietor, partner in a partnership, or LLC member, you may deduct one-half of your self-employment taxes from your total net business income. This deduction reduces the amount of income on which you must pay personal income tax. It's an adjustment to gross income, not a business deduction. You don't list it on your Schedule C; instead, you take it on page one of your Form 1040.

The self-employment tax is a 15.3% tax (13.3% for 2012), so your deduction is equal to 7.65% of your income. To figure out your income after taking this deduction, multiply your net business income by 92.35% or 0.9235.

> EXAMPLE: Billie earned $60,000 from her real estate agent business and had $10,000 in business expenses. Her net business income was $50,000. She multiplies this amount by 0.9235 to determine her net self-employment income, which is $46,175. This is the amount on which Billie must pay federal income tax.

This deduction is intended to help ease the tax burden on the self-employed.

Employment Taxes

If you have employees, you must pay half of their Social Security and Medicare taxes from your own funds and withhold the other half from their pay. These taxes consist of a 12.4% Social Security tax, up to an annual salary cap ($110,100 in 2012), and a 2.9% Medicare tax on all employees' pay. For 2011 and 2012, the employee's portion of the Social Security tax was reduced by 2% to 4.2%; the employer's 6.2% Social Security tax contribution remains the same. You may deduct half of this amount as a business expense. You should treat the taxes you withhold from your employees' pay as wages paid to your employees on your tax return.

> EXAMPLE: You pay your employee $18,000 a year. However, after you withhold employment taxes, your employee receives $14,500. You also pay an additional $1,500 in employment taxes from your own funds. You should deduct the full $18,000 salary as employee wages and deduct the $1,500 as employment taxes paid.

Sales Taxes

You may deduct sales taxes that you pay when you purchase goods or services for your real estate business. The amount of the tax is added to the cost of the goods or services for purposes of your deduction for the item.

> EXAMPLE: Jean, a real estate broker, buys $100 worth of office supplies from the local stationery store. She has to pay $7.50 in state and local sales taxes on the purchase. She may take a $107.50 deduction for the supplies. She claims the deduction on her Schedule C as a purchase of supplies.

If you buy a long-term business asset, the sales taxes must be added to its basis (cost) for purposes of depreciation or expensing under IRC Section 179.

> EXAMPLE: Jean buys a $2,000 computer for her business. She pays $150 in state and local sales tax. The computer has a useful life of more than one year and is therefore a long-term business asset for tax purposes. She can't currently deduct the cost as a business operating expense. Instead, Jean must depreciate the cost over several years or expense the cost (deduct the full cost in one year) under Section 179. The total cost to be depreciated or expensed is $2,150.

Real Property Taxes

You can deduct your current year's state and local property taxes on business real property as business expenses. However, if you prepay the next year's property taxes, you may not deduct the prepaid amount until the following year.

Home Offices

If you are a homeowner and take the home office deduction, you may deduct the home office percentage of your property taxes. However, as a homeowner, you are entitled to deduct all of your mortgage interest and property taxes, regardless of whether you have a home office. Taking the home office deduction won't increase your income tax deductions for your property taxes, but it will allow you to deduct them from your income for the purpose of calculating your self-employment taxes. You'll save $153 in self-employment taxes for every $1,000 in property taxes you deduct (15.3% self-employment tax × $1,000 = $153).

> EXAMPLE: Suzy uses 20% of her three-bedroom Tulsa home as a home office. She pays $10,000 per year in mortgage interest and property taxes. By taking the home office deduction, she gets to deduct this amount from her income for self-employment tax purposes, which saves her $1,530.

Charges for Services

Water bills, sewer charges, and other service charges assessed against your business property are not real estate taxes, but they are deductible as business expenses. If you have a home office, you can deduct your home office percentage of these items.

However, real estate taxes imposed to fund specific local benefits such as streets, sewer lines, and water mains are not deductible as business expenses. Because these benefits increase the value of your property, you should add what you pay for them to the tax basis (cost for tax purposes) of your property.

Other Taxes

Other deductible taxes include:

- excise taxes—for example, Hawaii imposes a general excise tax on businesses ranging from 0.5% to 4% of gross receipts
- state unemployment compensation taxes or state disability contributions
- corporate franchise taxes
- occupational taxes charged at a flat rate by your city or county for the privilege of doing business, and
- state and local taxes on personal property—for example, equipment or machinery that you use in your business.

License Fees

License fees imposed on your business by your local or state government are deductible business expenses. This includes the cost of maintaining your state real estate license.

Website Development and Maintenance

The cost of developing and maintaining a website for a real estate business vary widely. It can be relatively inexpensive if you use a standard template you purchase from a template company. However, the cost will be much greater if you want to create a custom design for your website.

Many real estate (and other) businesses currently deduct all website development and ongoing maintenance expenses as an advertising expense. However, some tax experts believe that the cost of initially setting up a website is a capital expense, not a currently deductible business operating expense, because the website is a long-term asset that benefits the business for more than one year. Under normal tax rules, capital expenses must be deducted over several years. Three years is the most common deduction period used for websites, since this is the same period as for software.

However, even if website development costs are capital expenses, they may be currently deducted in a single year under Section 179, which allows businesses to deduct a substantial amount of capital expenses in a single year (see Chapter 9).

Most tax experts agree that ongoing website hosting, maintenance, and updating costs are a currently deductible operating expense. Money you spend to get people to view your website, such as SEO (search engine optimization) campaigns, is also a currently deductible advertising expense.

CHAPTER

14

Independent Contractors and Employees in Real Estate

The world of real estate professionals is dominated by independent contractors ("ICs")—people who are considered self-employed for tax purposes. One important reason is that most licensed real estate agents and brokers enjoy a special independent contractor status for tax purposes. This chapter explains why it's important to understand the differences between independent contractor and employee status and how to tell the difference between the two.

Employee or Independent Contractor: What's the Difference?

As far as the IRS is concerned, there are only two types of workers in the world: employees and independent contractors. Independent contractors—also called self-employed workers—are in business for themselves. Employees are people who work for someone else's business. Initially, it's up to the hiring party to decide how to classify a worker. But this classification is subject to review by various governmental agencies, including the IRS (see "Worker or IC—Who Decides?" below).

The tax rules are very different for each. With employees, the employer must:

- withhold federal income taxes from the employee's pay
- withhold Social Security and Medicare taxes from the employee's pay, and pay half of these taxes as well
- contribute to a state unemployment insurance fund on behalf of most types of employees
- provide workers' compensation insurance coverage for most types of employees, and
- must avoid violating employees' rights under a wide array of state and federal labor and antidiscrimination laws. Among other things, these laws, impose a minimum wage and require many employees to be paid time-and-a-half for overtime.

None of these requirements apply to independent contractors, which can benefit both the hiring party and the independent contractor.

In the real estate world, brokers can save substantial money by using IC agents. Agents also like being independent contractors for several reasons:

- IC agents make their own estimated tax payments to the IRS four times per year, instead of having their taxes withheld. The lack of withholding combined with control over estimated tax payments can result in improved cash flow for ICs.
- IC agents can take advantage of many business-related tax deductions that are limited or not available to employees. This may include, for example, office expenses, including those for home offices, travel expenses, entertainment and meal expenses, equipment and insurance costs, and more. In contrast to the numerous deductions available to the self-employed, an employee's work-related deductions are severely limited. Even those expenses that are deductible may only be deducted to the extent they exceed 2% of the employee's adjusted gross income. This means that most expenses related to employment cannot be fully deducted.
- IC agents can establish retirement plans such as solo 401(k) and SEP-IRAs that have tax advantages. These plans also allow them to shelter a substantial amount of their income until they retire.

Because of these tax benefits, IC agents often pay less tax than employees who earn similar incomes.

Special IC Status for Real Estate Agents

A special provision of the tax law (IRC Sec. 3508) provides that real estate agents automatically qualify as independent contractors for all federal tax purposes if they meet certain requirements. These agents are called statutory independent contractors or statutory nonemployees because their status is established by law. This usually makes classifying real estate agents for tax purposes far easier and more certain than it is for most other occupations—you can thank an effective real estate industry lobbying for getting this law adopted in 1992.

Rules Apply Only to Licensed Agents or Brokers

A real estate agent or broker must meet the following requirements to be classified as a statutory IC:

- the person must be a licensed real estate agent or broker (unlicensed assistants don't qualify)
- the agent's pay must be based on commissions earned, not the number of hours worked—proposed IRS regulations say that at least 90% of the agent's total pay must from commissions, and
- the agent must sign a written agreement that states that he or she will not be treated as an employee for federal tax purposes.

The vast majority of real estate agents are paid by commission, so it's usually easy to meet these requirements. The broker and agent just have to make sure that the broker signs an IC agreement that provides that the broker will not be treated as an employee for federal tax purposes. Sample IC forms for this purpose are available from many real estate organizations, such as the National Association of Realtors.

Rules Apply Only to Federal Taxes

It is very important to understand that the statutory IC rules for real estate agents apply only to federal taxes—that is, federal income, Social Security, and Medicare taxes. The statutory IC classification has no application to state income taxes, workers' compensation, state unemployment taxes, and pension plan rules.

The hiring firm must apply the common law right of control test or other tests used by various state and federal agencies to determine whether an agent is an independent contractor or employee for all purposes other than federal taxes. If the agent flunks the applicable test, he or she will have to be treated as an employee for that purpose. For example, if an agent must be classified as an employee under your state's workers' compensation laws, the hiring broker might have to provide him or her with workers' comp coverage. This is true even though the agent is a statutory IC.

The rules vary state to state. Some states have special rules for real estate agents. For example, California real estate brokers are required to provide workers' comp coverage for their salespeople, even though they are classified as statutory ICs under federal tax law. On the other hand, all states exclude from unemployment insurance coverage real estate agents who work on commission except for Indiana, Iowa, Nevada, South Dakota, and West Virginia.

The myriad state rules are beyond the scope of this book. For a detailed discussion of all the practical and legal issues hiring firms face when hiring independent contractors, see *Working With Independent Contractors*, by Stephen Fishman (Nolo).

Other Services by Person Not Covered

The statutory IC classification applies only when someone performs services as a licensed real estate agent. It does not apply to other types of services performed by the same person. Real estate agent services include all activities customarily performed to help sell real estate—for example, advertising or showing property, acquiring a lease to rent property, and recruiting, training, or supervising other real estate agents. Appraisal services by a licensed real estate agent are also included if performed in connection with the sale of real property. However, services performed as a real estate agent do not include property management.

> EXAMPLE: Alicia is a licensed real estate agent who performs services as a real estate agent for Acme Realty under a written IC contract and is paid for these services solely by commission. However, in addition to performing services as a real estate agent, Alicia provides bookkeeping services for Acme. Alicia is a statutory IC when she works as a real estate agent. However, her bookkeeping work does not qualify for this status. Whether she is an IC or employee when she performs bookkeeping services for Acme must be determined under the normal right of control test (see below).

Other Real Estate Professionals Not Covered

There are no special federal tax rules for workers other than licensed real estate agents or brokers. Mortgage brokers (loan officers) do not qualify as statutory ICs because the IRS says that placing loans for residential real estate sales and refinancing existing loans are not activities customarily performed by a real estate agent. A mortgage broker would have to qualify as an IC under the normal IRS right of control test (discussed below).

The same is true for any other unlicensed person hired to help in the business, such as an unlicensed assistant or a Web designer.

The Standard Test—Right of Control

The fact that an agent or other person who works in a real estate office doesn't qualify as a statutory IC does not necessarily mean he or she must be classified as an employee. Instead, you will have to use the standard IRS right of control test to classify the worker for federal tax purposes.

The difficulty in applying the right of control test is that control isn't always easy to determine. IRS auditors can't look into the minds of brokers and agents to see if there is a right of control. They rely instead on indirect or circumstantial evidence indicating control or lack of it—for example, whether the agent is given mandatory training, is required to attend meetings, is paid by the hour, and can be fired at any time. The chart below shows the primary factors used by the IRS and most other government agencies to determine if a hiring firm has the right to control an agent or other worker.

How would these factors apply to a real estate agent? An agent is likely to be considered an employee under the right of control test if he or she:

- is paid by the hour or other unit of time
- is given mandatory training
- is required to attend sales meetings
- is assigned mandatory floor time
- must work a specified number of hours
- is given employee-type bonuses
- is provided with health insurance or other employee-type benefits
- is required to satisfy a sales quota
- is required to work from the broker's office
- has expenses reimbursed
- cannot engage in outside employment.

Of course, if an agent qualifies as a statutory IC, he or she may be treated like an employee under the right of control test, but will still be an independent contractor for federal tax purposes.

IRS Test for Worker Status		
	Agents more likely to be ICs if:	**Agents more likely to be employees if:**
Behavioral Control	• they are not given instructions • they are not given training	• they are given instructions they must follow about how to do the work • they are given detailed training
Financial Control	• they have a significant investment in equipment and facilities • they pay business or travel expenses themselves • they make their services available to the public • they are paid by the job • they have opportunity for profit or loss	• they are provided with equipment and facilities free of charge • they are reimbursed for their business or travel expenses • they make no effort to market their services to the public • they are paid by the hour or other unit of time • they have no opportunity for profit or loss—for example, because they're paid by the hour and have all expenses reimbursed
Relationship Between Broker and Agent	• they don't receive employee benefits such as health insurance • they sign an IC agreement with hiring firm • they can't quit or be fired at will • they perform services that are not part of firm's regular business activities	• they receive employee benefits • they have no written client agreement • they can quit at any time without incurring any liability to firm • they can be fired at any time • they perform services that are part of firm's core business

Worker or IC—Who Decides?

Initially, it's up the broker and each agent that affiliates with him or her to decide how to characterize their relationship for tax purposes. However, their decision is subject to review by various government agencies, including:

- the IRS
- the state tax department
- the state unemployment compensation insurance agency, and
- the state workers' compensation insurance agency.

These agencies are mostly interested in whether workers classified as independent contractors should have been classified as employees. The reason is that employers must pay money to each of these agencies for employees, but not for independent contractors. The more workers you have classified as employees, the more money flows into the agencies' coffers. In the case of taxing agencies, employers must withhold tax from employees' paychecks and hand it over to the government; ICs pay their own taxes, which means the government must wait longer to get its money and faces the possibility that ICs won't declare their income or will otherwise cheat on their taxes. An agency that determines that you misclassified an employee as an IC may impose back taxes, fines, and penalties.

Scrutinizing agencies use various tests to determine whether a worker is an IC or an employee. The determining factor is usually whether the hiring firm has the right to control the worker. If the hiring firm has the right to direct and control the way a worker performs—both as to the final results and the details of when, where, and how the work is done—then the worker is an employee. On the other hand, if the hiring firm's control is limited to accepting or rejecting the final results the worker achieves, then that person is an IC.

Unfortunately, applying this "right of control" test can be very subjective and uncertain. Workers performing exactly the same functions have been found to be ICs in some cases, and employees in others. Fortunately for real estate professionals, the vast majority of real estate agents can be safely classified as ICs for federal tax purposes without having to apply the complicated right of control test. All brokers and IC agents need to understand this law.

Tax Reporting for ICs

If a real estate agent qualifies as an IC under the statutory IC rule or right of control test, the broker he or she contracts with need not withhold or pay any federal taxes on the agent's behalf. The IC agent is responsible for paying these taxes.

However, if an IC agent or any other independent contractor is paid $600 or more during the year for business-related services, the hiring firm must:

- file IRS Form 1099-MISC telling the IRS how much the IC agent was paid, and
- obtain the IC's taxpayer identification number.

The IRS may impose a $250 fine if a hiring firm intentionally fails to file a Form 1099.

Hiring Employees

Hiring employees costs money, but you may deduct most or all of what you pay them as a business expense. Thus, for example, if you pay an employee $50,000 per year in salary and benefits, you'll ordinarily get a $50,000 tax deduction. You should factor this in whenever you're thinking about hiring an employee or deciding how much to pay him or her.

Employee Pay

Employee pay may be in the form of salaries, sales commissions, bonuses, vacation allowances, sick pay (as long as it's not covered by insurance), or fringe benefits. For tax deduction purposes, it doesn't really matter how you measure or make the payments.

Most of the time, amounts you pay employees to work in your business will be business operating expenses. These expenses are currently deductible as long as they are:

- ordinary and necessary
- reasonable in amount
- paid for services actually performed, and
- actually paid or incurred in the year the deduction is claimed (as shown by your payroll records).

An employee's services are ordinary and necessary if they are common, accepted, helpful, and appropriate for your business; they don't have to be indispensable. An employee's pay is reasonable if the amount is in the range of what other businesses would pay for similar services. These requirements usually won't pose a problem when you hire an employee to perform any legitimate business function.

> EXAMPLE: Ken, a highly successful real estate broker, hires Kim to work as his assistant pays her $2,000 per month—what such workers are typically paid in the area. Ken can deduct Kim's $2,000 monthly salary as a business operating expense. If Kim works a full year, Ken will get a $24,000 deduction.

Payments to employees for personal services are not deductible as business expenses.

> EXAMPLE: Ken hires Samantha to work as a live-in nanny for his three children. Samantha is Ken's employee, but her services are personal, not related to his business. Thus, Ken may not deduct her pay as a business expense.

Special rules apply if you hire family members to work in your business or if you hire yourself. ("Employing Your Family or Yourself," below.)

Payroll Taxes

Whenever you hire an employee, you become an unpaid tax collector for the government. You are required to withhold and pay both federal and state taxes for the worker. These taxes are called payroll taxes or employment taxes. Federal payroll taxes consist of:

- Social Security and Medicare taxes—also known as FICA
- unemployment taxes—also known as FUTA, and
- federal income taxes—also known as FITW.

You must periodically pay FICA, FUTA, and FITW to the IRS, either electronically or by making federal tax deposits at specified banks, which transmit the money to the IRS. You are entitled to deduct as a business expense payroll taxes that you pay yourself. You get no deductions for taxes you withhold from employees' pay.

Every year, employers must file IRS Form W-2, *Wage and Tax Statement*, for each of their employees. The form shows the IRS how much the worker was paid and how much tax was withheld.

RESOURCE

Need more information? IRS Circular E, *Employer's Tax Guide*, provides detailed information on these requirements. You can download the guide from the IRS website at www.irs.gov.

Employer's FICA Contributions

FICA is an acronym for Federal Income Contributions Act, the law requiring employers and employees to pay Social Security and Medicare taxes. FICA consists of:

- a 12.4% Social Security tax on an employee's wages up to an annual ceiling or cap—in 2012, the cap was $110,100 per year, and
- a 2.9% Medicare tax on all employee wages paid.

This adds up to a 15.3% tax, up to the Social Security tax ceiling. (However, for 2011 and 2012, the employee tax rate for Social Security is 2% so the total tax is 13.3% instead of 15.3%.) Employers must pay half of this—7.65%—out of their own pockets. They must withhold the other portion from their employees' pay. Employers are entitled to deduct as a business expense the portion of the tax they pay.

The ceiling for the Social Security tax changes annually. You can find out what the Social Security tax ceiling is for the current year from IRS Circular E, *Employer's Tax Guide*; the amount is printed on the first page.

FUTA

FUTA is an acronym for the Federal Unemployment Tax Act, the law that establishes federal unemployment taxes. Most employers must pay both state and federal unemployment taxes. Even if you're exempt from the state tax, you may still have to pay the federal tax. Employers alone are responsible for FUTA—you may not collect or deduct it from employees' wages.

You must pay FUTA taxes if either of the following is true:

- You pay $1,500 or more to employees during any calendar quarter—that is, any three-month period beginning with January, April, July, or October.
- You had one or more employees for at least some part of a day in any 20 or more different weeks during the year. The weeks don't have to be consecutive, nor does it have to be the same employee each week.

Technically, the FUTA tax rate is 6%, but, in practice, you rarely pay this much. You are given a credit of 5.4% if you pay the applicable state unemployment tax in full and on time. This means that the actual FUTA tax rate is usually 0.6%. In 2012, the FUTA tax was assessed on the first $7,000 of an employee's annual wages. The FUTA tax, then, is usually $42 per year per employee. This amount is a deductible business expense.

FITW

FITW is an acronym for federal income tax withholding. You must calculate and withhold federal income taxes from your employees' paychecks. Employees are solely responsible for paying federal income taxes. Your only responsibility is to withhold the funds and remit them to the government. You get no deductions for FITW.

State Payroll Taxes

Employers in every state are required to pay and withhold state payroll taxes. These taxes include:

- state unemployment compensation taxes in all states
- state income tax withholding in most states, and
- state disability taxes in a few states.

Employers in every state are required to contribute to a state unemployment insurance fund. Employees make no contributions, except in Alaska, New Jersey, Pennsylvania, and Rhode Island, where employers must withhold small employee contributions from employees' paychecks. The employer contributions are a deductible business expense.

If your payroll is very small—below $1,500 per calendar quarter—you probably won't have to pay unemployment compensation taxes. In most states, you must pay state unemployment taxes for employees if you're paying federal FUTA taxes. However, some states have more strict requirements. Contact your state labor department for the exact rules and payroll amounts.

All states except Alaska, Florida, Nevada, South Dakota, Texas, Washington, and Wyoming have income taxation. If your state has income taxes, you must withhold the applicable tax from your employees' paychecks and pay it to the state taxing authority. Each state has its own income tax withholding forms and procedures. Contact your state tax department for information. Of course, employers get no deductions for withholding their employees' state income taxes.

California, Hawaii, New Jersey, New York, and Rhode Island have state disability insurance that provides employees with coverage for injuries or illnesses that are not related to work. Employers in these states must withhold their employees' disability insurance contributions from their pay. Employers must also make their own contributions in Hawaii, New Jersey, and New York—these employer contributions are deductible.

In addition, subject to some important exceptions, employers in all states must provide their employees with workers' compensation insurance to cover work-related injuries. Workers' compensation is not a payroll tax. Employers must purchase a workers' compensation policy from a private insurer or state workers' compensation fund. Your worker's compensation insurance premiums are deductible as a business insurance expense. (See Chapter 13 for more on deducting business insurance.)

CAUTION

Employers in California must withhold for parental leave. Employers in California are also required to withhold (as part of their disability program) a certain amount for parental leave. For more information on the program, go to www.edd.ca.gov.

Bookkeeping Expenses Are Deductible

Figuring out how much to withhold, doing the necessary record keeping, and filling out the required forms can be complicated. If you have a computer, computer accounting programs such as *QuickBooks* or *QuickPay* can help with all the calculations and print out your employees' checks and IRS forms. You can also hire a bookkeeper or payroll tax service to do the work. Amounts you pay a bookkeeper or payroll tax service are deductible business operating expenses. You can find these services in the phone book or on the Internet under payroll tax services. You can also find a list of payroll service providers on the IRS website at www.irs.gov.

Employee Fringe Benefits

There is no law that says you must provide your employees with any fringe benefits—not even health insurance (except in Hawaii and Massachusetts), sick pay, or vacation. However, starting in 2014, large employers (those with at least 50 or more full-time employees) will be required to provide health insurance to their full-time employees or pay a penalty to the IRS. In addition, the tax law encourages you to provide employee benefits by allowing you to deduct the cost as a business expense. (These expenses should be deducted as employee benefit expenses, not employee compensation.) Moreover, your employees do not have to treat the value of their fringe benefits as income on which they need pay tax. So you get a deduction, and your employees get tax-free goodies.

In contrast, if you're a business owner (a sole proprietor, partner in a partnership, 2% or more owner of an S corporation, or LLC member), you must include in your income and pay tax on the value of any fringe benefits your company provides to you—the only exception is for *de minimis* fringes.

Tax-free employee fringe benefits include:

- health insurance
- accident insurance

- Health Savings Accounts (see Chapter 11)
- dependent care assistance
- educational assistance
- group term life insurance coverage—limits apply based on the policy value
- qualified employee benefits plans, including profit-sharing plans, stock bonus plans, and money purchase plans
- employee stock options
- lodging on your business premises
- moving expense reimbursements
- achievement awards
- commuting benefits
- employee discounts on the goods or services you sell
- supplemental unemployment benefits
- de minimis (low-cost) fringe benefits such as low-value birthday or holiday gifts, event tickets, traditional awards (such as a retirement gift), other special occasion gifts, and coffee and soft drinks, and
- cafeteria plans that allow employees to choose among two or more benefits consisting of cash and qualified benefits.

Starting in 2011, small employers (those with 100 or fewer employees) can offer their employees a simple cafeteria plan—a plan not subject to the nondiscrimination requirements of traditional cafeteria plans.

Health insurance is by far the most important tax-free employee fringe benefit; it is discussed in detail in Chapter 11. See IRS Publication 15-B, *Employer's Tax Guide to Fringe Benefits*, for more information on the other types of benefits.

Employees may also be supplied with working condition fringe benefits. These are property and services you provide to an employee so that the employee can perform his or her job. A working condition fringe benefit is tax-free to an employee to the extent the employee would be able to deduct the cost of the property or services as a business or depreciation expense if he or she had paid for it. If the employee uses the benefit 100% for work, it is tax-free. But the value of any personal use of a working condition fringe benefit must be included in the employee's compensation, and he or she must pay tax on it. The employee must meet any documentation requirements that apply to the deduction.

One of the most common working condition fringe benefits is a company car. If an employee uses a company car part of the time for personal driving, the value of the personal use must be included in the employee's income. The employer determines how to value the use of a car, and there are several methods that may be used. The most common is for the employer to report a percentage of the car's annual lease value as determined by IRS tables. For a detailed discussion of these valuation rules, refer to IRS Publication 15-B.

Reimbursing Employees for Business-Related Expenditures

There may be times when an employee must pay for a work-related expense. Most commonly, this occurs when an employee is driving, traveling, or entertaining while on the job. Sometimes, depending on the circumstances, an employee could end up paying for almost any work-related expense; for example, an employee might pay for office supplies or parking at a client's office.

All these employee payments have important tax consequences, whatever form they take. The rules discussed below apply whether the expenses are incurred by an employee who is not related to the employer or by an employee who is the employer's spouse or child. They also apply to a business owner who has incorporated the business and works as its employee.

Accountable Plans

The best way to reimburse or otherwise pay employees for any work-related expenses is to use an accountable plan. When employees are paid for their expenses under an accountable plan, two great things happen:

- The employer doesn't have to pay payroll taxes on the payments.
- The employees won't have to include the payments in their taxable income.

Moreover, the amounts the employers pays will be deductible, just like your other business expenses, subject to the same rules.

EXAMPLE: The Acme Realty Co. decides that Manny, its office manager, should attend the Real Estate Management Expo in Las

Vegas. Manny pays his expenses himself. When he gets back, he fully documents his expenses as required by Acme's accountable plan. These amount to $2,000 for transportation and hotel and $1,000 in meal and entertainment expenses. Acme reimburses Manny $3,000. Acme may deduct as a business expense the entire $2,000 cost of Manny's flight and hotel and 50% of the cost of the meals and entertainment. Manny need not count the $3,000 reimbursement as income (or pay taxes on it), and Acme need not include the amount on the W-2 form it files with the IRS reporting how much Manny was paid for the year. Moreover, Acme need not withhold income tax or pay any Social Security or Medicare taxes on the $3,000.

Requirements for an Accountable Plan

An accountable plan is an arrangement in which the employer agrees to reimburse or advance employee expenses only if the employee:

- pays or incurs expenses that qualify as deductible business expenses for your business while performing services as your employee
- adequately accounts to you for the expenses within a reasonable period of time, and
- returns to you within a reasonable time any amounts received in excess of the actual expenses incurred.

These payments to employees can be made through advances, direct reimbursements, charges to a company credit card, or direct billings to the employer.

These strict rules are imposed to prevent employees from seeking reimbursement for personal expenses (or nonexistent phony expenses) under the guise that they were business expenses. Employees used to do this all the time to avoid paying income tax on the reimbursed amounts (employees must count employer reimbursements for their personal expenses as income, but not reimbursements for the employer's business expenses).

An accountable plan need not be in writing (although it's not a bad idea). All you need to do is set up procedures for your employees to follow that meet the requirements.

Employees Must Document Expenses

Employees must provide their employers the same documentation for work-related expenses that the IRS requires the employer to provide when it claims the expenses as a deduction. This documentation should be provided within 60 days after the expense was incurred.

Particularly thorough documentation is needed for car, travel, entertainment, and meal expenses—these are the expenses the IRS is really concerned about. (See Chapter 6 for more about deducting meal and entertainment expenses.) However, you can ease up on the documentation requirements if employees are paid a per diem (per day) allowance equal to or less than the per diem rates the federal government pays its workers while traveling. You can find these rates at www.gsa.gov (look for the link to "Per Diem Rates") or in IRS Publication 1542, *Per Diem Rates*. If this method is used, the IRS will assume that the amounts for lodging, meals, and incidental expenses are accurate without any further documentation. The employee need only substantiate the time, place, and business purpose of the expense. The same holds true if the employee is paid the standard mileage rate for an employee who uses a personal car for business. (See Chapter 4 for more about deducting car expenses.)

However, per diem rates may not be used for an employee who:

- owns more than 10% of the stock in an incorporated business, or
- is a close relative of a 10% or more owner—a brother, sister, parent, spouse, grandparent, or other lineal ancestor or descendent.

In these instances, the employee must keep track of the actual cost of all business-related expenses that he or she wants to get reimbursed by the employer. Any per diem rate reimbursement for a 10% or more owner or owner's relative must be counted as taxable wages for the employee.

The documentation requirements are less onerous for other types of expenses. Nevertheless, the employer must still document the amount of money spent and show that it was for your business. For example, an employee who pays for a repair to an office computer out of his or her own pocket should save the receipt and write "repair of office computer" or something similar to show the business purpose of the payment. It's not sufficient for an employee to submit an expense report with vague categories or descriptions such as "travel" or "miscellaneous business expenses."

Returning Excess Payments

Employees who are advanced or reimbursed more than they actually spent for business expenses must return the excess payments to the employer within a reasonable time. The IRS says a reasonable time is 120 days after an expense is incurred. Any amounts not returned are treated as taxable wages for the employee and must be added to the employee's income for tax purposes. This means that the employer must pay payroll tax on those amounts.

> EXAMPLE: Acme Realty gives an employee a $1,000 advance to cover her expenses for a short business trip. When she gets back, she gives Acme an expense report and documentation showing she only spent $900 for business while on the trip. If she doesn't return the extra $100 within 120 days after the trip, it will be considered wages for tax purposes and Acme will have to pay payroll tax on the amount.

Unaccountable Plans

Any payments you make to employees for business-related expenses that do not comply with the accountable plan rules are deemed to be made under an unaccountable plan. These payments are considered to be employee wages, which means all of the following:

- The employee must report the payments as income on his or her tax return and pay tax on them.
- The employee may deduct the expenses—but only as a miscellaneous itemized deduction. (See "Unreimbursed Employee Expenses," below.)
- The employer may deduct the payments as wages paid to an employee.
- The employer must withhold the employee's income taxes and share of Social Security and Medicare taxes from the payments.
- The employer must pay the employer's 7.65% share of the employee's Social Security and Medicare taxes on the payments.

This is a tax disaster for the employee and not a good result for the employer, either, because you will have to pay Social Security and Medicare tax that you could have avoided if the payments had been made under an accountable plan.

Unreimbursed Employee Expenses

Unless the employer has agreed to do so, it has no legal obligation to reimburse or pay employees for job-related expenses they incur. Employees are entitled to deduct from their own income ordinary and necessary expenses arising from their employment that are not reimbursed by their employers. In this event, the employer gets no deduction, because it hasn't paid for the expense.

CAUTION

Some states require reimbursement. Check with your state's labor department to find out the rules for reimbursing employee expenses. You might find that you are legally required to repay employees, rather than letting your employees deduct the expenses on their own tax returns. In California, for example, employers must reimburse employees for all expenses or losses they incur as a direct consequence of carrying out their job duties. (Cal. Labor Code § 2802.)

Employees may deduct essentially the same expenses as business owners, subject to some special rules. For example, there are special deduction rules for employee home office expenses (see Chapter 7). In addition, employees who use the actual expense method for car expenses may not deduct car loan interest.

However, it's much better for the employees to be reimbursed by the employer under an accountable plan and let the employer take the deduction. Why? Because employees can deduct unreimbursed employee expenses only if the employee itemizes his or her deductions and only to the extent these deductions, along with the employee's other miscellaneous itemized deductions, exceed 2% of his or her adjusted gross income. Adjusted gross income (AGI) is the employee's total income, minus deductions for IRA and pension contributions and a few other deductions (shown on Form 1040, line 35).

These rules apply to all employees, including family members who work as employees, and to a broker or agent who has incorporated his or her business and works as its employee.

An employee's unreimbursed expenses must be listed on IRS Schedule A, Form 1040, as a miscellaneous itemized deduction. Employees must also file IRS Form 2106 reporting the amount of the expenses.

Employing Your Family or Yourself

Whoever said "never hire your relatives" must not have read the tax code. The tax law promotes family togetherness by making it highly advantageous for small business owners to hire their spouses or children. If you're single and have no children, you're out of luck.

Employing Your Children

Believe it or not, your children can be a great tax savings device. If you hire your children as employees to do legitimate work in your real estate business, you may deduct their salaries from your business income as a business expense. Your child will have to pay tax on the salary only to the extent it exceeds the standard deduction amount for the year: $5,950 in 2012. Moreover, if your child is under 18, you won't have to withhold or pay any FICA (Social Security or Medicare) tax on the salary (subject to a couple of exceptions).

These rules allow you to shift part of your business income from your own tax bracket to your child's bracket, which should be much lower than yours (unless you earn little or no income). This can result in substantial tax savings.

> **EXAMPLE:** Carol hires Mark, her 16-year-old son, to perform website maintenance and updating services for a real estate brokerage firm which she owns as a sole proprietor. He works ten hours per week and she pays him $20 per hour (the going rate for such work). Over the course of a year, she pays him a total of $9,000. She need not pay FICA tax for Mark because he's under 18.

When she does her taxes for the year, she may deduct his $9,000 salary from her business income as a business expense. Mark pays tax only on the portion of his income that exceeds the $5,950 standard deduction—so he pays federal income tax only on $3,050 of his $9,000 salary. With such a small amount of income, he is in the lowest federal income tax bracket: 10%. He pays $305 in federal income tax for the year. Had Carol not hired Mark and done the work herself, she would have lost her $9,000 deduction and had to pay income tax and self-employment taxes on this amount—a 38.3% tax in her tax bracket (25% federal income tax + 13.3% self-employment tax = 38.3%). Thus, she would have had to pay an additional $3,447 in federal taxes. Depending on the state where Carol lives, she likely would have had to pay a state income tax as well.

No Payroll Taxes

As mentioned above, one of the advantages of hiring your child is that you need not pay FICA taxes if your child is under the age of 18 and works in your trade or business, or your partnership if it's owned solely by you and your spouse.

EXAMPLE: Lisa, a 16-year-old, does office work for her mother's real estate brokerage, which is operated as a sole proprietorship. Although Lisa is her mother's employee, her mother need not pay FICA taxes on her salary until she turns 18.

Moreover, you need not pay federal unemployment (FUTA) taxes for services performed by your child who is under 21 years old.

However, these rules do not apply—and you must pay both FICA and FUTA—if you hire your child to work for:

- your corporation, or
- your partnership, unless all the partners are parents of the child.

EXAMPLE: Ron works in a real estate office that is co-owned by his mother and her partner, Ralph, who is no relation to the family. FICA and FUTA taxes must be paid for Ron because he is working for a partnership and not all of the partners are his parents.

You need not pay FICA or FUTA if you've formed a one-member limited liability company and hire your child to work for it. For tax purposes a one-member LLC is a "disregarded entity"—that is, it's treated as if it didn't exist.

No Withholding

In addition, if your child has no unearned income (for example, interest or dividend income), you must withhold income taxes from your child's pay only if it exceeds the standard deduction for the year. The standard deduction was $5,950 in 2012 and is adjusted every year for inflation. Children who are paid less than this amount need not pay any income taxes on their earnings.

> EXAMPLE: Connie, a 15-year-old girl, is paid $4,000 a year to answer phones and perform other office work in her parents' brokerage firm. She has no income from interest or any other unearned income. Her parents need not withhold income taxes from Connie's salary because she has no unearned income and her salary was less than the standard deduction amount for the year.

However, you must withhold income taxes if your child has more than $300 in unearned income for the year and his or her total income exceeds $950 (in 2012).

Employing Your Spouse

You don't get the benefits of income shifting when you employ your spouse in your business, because your income is combined when you file a joint tax return. You'll also have to pay FICA taxes on your spouse's wages, so you get no savings there, either. You need not pay FUTA tax if you employ your spouse in your unincorporated business. This tax is usually only $42 per year, however, so this is not much of a savings.

The real advantage of hiring your spouse is in the realm of employee benefits. You can provide your spouse with any or all of the employee benefits discussed in "Employee Fringe Benefits," above. You'll get a tax deduction for the cost of the benefit, and your spouse doesn't have to declare the benefit as income, provided the IRS requirements are satisfied. This is a particularly valuable tool for health insurance—you can give your spouse health insurance coverage as an employee benefit. (See Chapter 11 for a detailed discussion.)

If you work at an outside office or other workspace, there is no law that says your spouse must work there too. After all, having your spouse spend all day with you at your office might constitute too much togetherness. Fortunately, your spouse can work at home—for example, by doing bookkeeping or marketing work for the family real estate business. All these activities can easily be conducted from a home office.

Having your spouse work at home has tax benefits as well. If you set up a home office for your spouse that is used exclusively for business purposes, you'll get a home office deduction. Your spouse has no outside office, so the home office will easily pass the convenience of the employer test. (See Chapter 7.) Moreover, you can depreciate or deduct under Section 179 the cost of office furniture, computers, additional phone lines, copiers, fax machines, and other business equipment you buy for your spouse's use on the job.

Rules to Follow When Employing Your Family

The IRS is well aware of the tax benefits of hiring a child or spouse, so it's on the lookout for taxpayers who claim the benefit without really having their family members work in their businesses. If the IRS concludes that your children or spouse aren't really employees, you'll lose your tax deductions for their salary and benefits. And they'll have to pay tax on their benefits. To avoid this, you should follow these simple rules.

Rule 1: Your Child or Spouse Must Be a Real Employee

First of all, your spouse or children must be bona fide employees. Their work must be ordinary and necessary for your business, and their pay must be for services actually performed. Their services don't have to be indispensable, only common, accepted, helpful, and appropriate for your business. Any real work for your business can qualify—for example, you could employ your child or spouse to clean your office, answer the phone, stuff envelopes, or input data. You get no business deductions when you pay your child for personal services, such as babysitting or mowing your lawn at home. On the other hand, money you pay for yard work performed on business property could be deductible as a business expense.

Hardworking Seven-Year-Old Was Parents' Employee

Walt and Dorothy Eller owned three trailer parks and a small strip mall in Northern California. They hired their three children, ages seven, 11, and 12, to perform various services for their businesses, including pool maintenance, landscaping, reading gas and electric meters, delivering leaflets and messages to tenants, answering phones, making minor repairs, and sweeping and cleaning trailer pads and parking lots. The children worked after school, on weekends, and during their summer vacations. The Ellers paid each of their children a total of $5,200, $4,200, and $8,400 respectively over a three-year period and deducted the amounts as business expenses. The IRS tried to disallow the deductions, claiming that the children's pay was excessive. The court allowed most of the deductions, noting that these hardworking children performed essential services for their parents' businesses.

The court found that the seven-year-old was a bona fide employee but ruled that he should earn somewhat less than his older brother and sister because 11- and 12-year-old children can generally handle greater responsibility and perform greater services than seven-year-old children. Thus, while the older siblings could reasonably be paid $5,700 for their services over the three years in question, the seven-year-old could only reasonably be paid $4,000. (*Eller v. Commissioner*, 77 TC 934 (1981).)

The IRS won't believe that an extremely young child is a legitimate employee. How young is too young? The IRS has accepted that a seven-year-old child may be an employee (see "Hardworking Seven-Year-Old Was Parents' Employee," above) but probably won't believe that children younger than seven are performing any useful work for your business.

In addition, where one spouse solely owns a business (usually as a sole proprietor) and the other spouse works as his or her employee, the spouse who owns the business must substantially control the business in terms of management decisions and the employee-spouse must be under that spouse's direction and control. If the employee-spouse has an equal say in the affairs of the business, provides substantially equal services to the business, and contributes capital to the business, that spouse *cannot be treated as an employee.*

You should keep track of the work and hours your children or spouse perform by having them fill out timesheets or timecards. You can find these in stationery stores or make a timesheet yourself. It should list the date, the services performed, and the time spent performing the services. Although not legally required, it's also a good idea to have your spouse or child sign a written employment agreement specifying his or her job duties and hours. These duties should be related only to your real estate business.

Rule 2: Compensation Must Be Reasonable

When you hire your children, it is advantageous (tax-wise) to pay them as much as possible. That way, you can shift as much of your income as possible to your children, who are probably in a much lower income tax bracket. Conversely, you want to pay your spouse as little as possible, since you get no benefits from income shifting. This is because you and your spouse are in the same income tax bracket (assuming you file a joint return, as the vast majority of married people do). Moreover, your spouse will have to pay a 7.65% Social Security tax on his or her salary—an amount that is not tax deductible. (For 2011 and 2012, the tax rate is 5.65% instead of 7.65%.) As your spouse's employer, you'll have to pay employment taxes on your spouse's salary as well, but these taxes are deductible business expenses. The absolute minimum you can pay your spouse is the minimum wage in your area.

However, you can't just pay any amount you choose: Your spouse's and/or your child's total compensation must be reasonable. Total compensation means the sum of the salary plus all the fringe benefits you provide your spouse, including health insurance and medical expense reimbursements, if any. This is determined by comparing the amount paid with the value of the services performed. You should have no problem as long as you pay no more than what you'd pay a stranger for the same work—don't try paying your child $100 per hour for office cleaning just to get a big tax deduction. Find out what workers performing similar services in your area are being paid. For example, if you plan to hire your teenager to help answer the phone, call an employment agency or temp agency in your area to see what these workers are being paid.

To prove how much you paid (and that you actually paid it), you should pay your child or spouse by check, not cash. Do this once or twice a month as you would for any other employee. The funds should be deposited in a bank account in your child's or spouse's name. Your child's bank account may be a Roth IRA, Section 529 college savings plan, or custodial account that you control until your child turns 21.

Rule 3: Comply With Legal Requirements for Employers

You must comply with most of the same legal requirements when you hire a child or spouse as you do when you hire a stranger.

At the time you hire. When you first hire your child or spouse, you must fill out IRS Form W-4. You, the employer, use it to determine how much tax you must withhold from the employee's salary. A child who is exempt from withholding should write "exempt" in the space provided and complete and sign the rest of the form. You must also complete U.S. Citizenship and Immigration Services (USCIS) Form I-9, *Employment Eligibility Verification*, verifying that the employee is a U.S. citizen or is otherwise eligible to work in the United States. Keep both forms. You must also record your employee's Social Security number. If your child doesn't have a number, you must apply for one. In addition, you, the employer, must have an Employer Identification Number (EIN). If you don't have one, you may obtain it by filing IRS Form SS-4.

Every payday. You'll need to withhold income tax from your child's pay only if it exceeds a specified amount. ("Employing Your Children," above.) You don't need to withhold FICA taxes for children younger than 18. You must withhold income tax and FICA for your spouse, but not FUTA tax. If the amounts withheld, plus the employer's share of payroll taxes, exceed $2,500 during a calendar quarter, you must deposit the amounts monthly by making federal tax deposits at specified banks or electronically depositing them with the IRS.

Every calendar quarter. If you withhold tax from your child's or spouse's pay, you must deposit it with the IRS or a specified bank. If you deposit more than $1,000 a year, you must file Form 941, *Employer's Quarterly Federal Tax Return*, with the IRS showing how much the employee was paid during the quarter and how much tax you withheld and deposited. If you need to deposit less than $2,500 during a calendar quarter, you can make your payment quarterly along with the Form 941 instead of paying monthly. Employers with total employment tax liability of $1,000 or less may file employment tax returns once a year instead of quarterly. Use IRS Form 944, *Employer's Annual Federal Tax Return*. You should be notified by the IRS if you're eligible to file Form 944. If you haven't been notified but believe you qualify to file Form 944, call the IRS at 800-829-0115.

Each year. By January 31 of each year, you must complete and give to your employee a copy of IRS Form W-2, showing how much you paid the employee and how much tax was withheld. You must also file copies with the IRS and the Social Security Administration by February 28. You must include IRS Form W-3 with the copy you file with the Social Security Administration. If your child is exempt from withholding, a new W-4 form must be completed each year. Starting with tax reporting for the 2012 tax year (so in early 2013), employers will be required to report on their W-2 forms the cost of providing group health insurance to their employees. However, for employers that file fewer than 250 Form W-2s, this group health insurance reporting requirement is optional for 2012. The reporting is required purely for informational purposes. Such benefits will remain tax-free to employees.

You must also file Form 940, *Employer's Annual Federal Unemployment (FUTA) Tax Return*. The due date is January 31; however, if you deposited all of the FUTA tax when due, you have ten additional days to file. You must file a Form 940 for your child even though you are not required to withhold any unemployment taxes from his or her pay. If your child is your only employee, enter his or her wages as "exempt" from unemployment tax.

RESOURCE

Need more information? IRS Circular E, *Employer's Tax Guide,* and Publication 929, *Tax Rules for Children and Dependents,* provide detailed information on these requirements. You can download them from the IRS website at www.irs.gov.

Employing Yourself

Most real estate brokers and agents are sole proprietors, partners in a partnership, or members of limited liability companies (LLC) taxed as partnerships. These agents and brokers are not employees of their businesses; They are business owners. However, if you have incorporated your real estate business, whether as a regular C corporation or an S corporation, you must be an employee of your corporation if you actively work in the business. In effect, you will be employing yourself. This has important tax consequences.

Your Company Must Pay Payroll Taxes

Your incorporated business must treat you just like any other employee for tax purposes. This means it must withhold income and FICA taxes from your pay and pay half of your FICA tax itself. It must also pay FUTA taxes for you. It gets a tax deduction for its contributions, the same as any other employer. (See "Hiring Employees," above.) Your corporation—not you personally—must pay these payroll taxes.

You can't avoid having your corporation pay payroll taxes by working for free. You must pay yourself at least a reasonable salary—what similar companies pay for the same services.

Tax Deductions for Your Salary and Benefits

When you're an employee, your salary is deductible by your incorporated business as a business expense. However, you must pay income tax on your salary, so there is no real tax savings.

But being an employee can have an upside. You'll be eligible for all of the tax-advantaged employee benefits discussed in "Hiring Employees," above. This means your corporation can provide you with benefits like health insurance and deduct the expense. (See Chapter 11 for more on deducting medical expenses.) If your corporation is a regular C corporation, you won't have to pay income tax on the value of your employee benefits. However, most employees of S corporations must pay tax on their employee benefits, so you probably won't get a tax benefit. The only exception is for employees of an S corporation who own less than 2% of the corporate stock. It isn't likely you'll have this little stock in your own S corporation.

You Can't Deduct Business Owner's "Draws"

If you're a business owner—sole proprietor, partner, or LLC member—you do not pay yourself a salary, as you do when you are employed by your incorporated business. If you want money from your business, you simply withdraw it from your business bank account. This is called a "draw." Because you are not an employee of your business, your draws are not employee compensation and are not deductible as a business expense.

Your Employee Expenses

You have a couple of options for dealing with expenses you incur while working for your corporation—for example, when you travel on company business.

From a tax standpoint, the best option is to have your corporation reimburse you for your expenses. Whether you've formed a C or an S corporation, the rules regarding reimbursement of employee expenses, discussed above, apply to you. If you comply with the requirements for an accountable plan, your corporation gets to deduct the expense and you don't have to count the reimbursement as income to you. If you fail to follow the rules, any reimbursements must be treated as employee income subject to tax.

Another option is simply to pay the expenses yourself and forgo reimbursement from your corporation. This is not a good idea, however, because as an employee, you may deduct work-related expenses only to the extent they exceed 2% of your adjusted gross income. (See "Reimbursing Employees for Business-Related Expenditures," above.)

CHAPTER

15

Real Estate Professionals Who Own Rental Property

If you're a real estate agent or broker and you own one or more rental properties (or are thinking about buying rental property), you should read this chapter. It explains what many consider to be the real estate pro's tax ace in the hole: the real estate professional exemption to the passive loss rules for rental losses. This special exemption, which is just for real estate pros, allows you to deduct all of your rental estate rental losses from your other income, regardless of the amount. Because many rentals lose money, this can result in substantial tax savings.

Limits on Deducting Rental Property Losses

Many real estate agents and brokers own rental properties or think about acquiring them. It is extremely common for landlords to experience rental losses, especially in the first few years they own a property. Indeed, IRS statistics show that in the year 2000, 4,520,000 of the 8,720,000 Schedule Es that were filed reporting rental income and expenses showed a loss. So if you have a rental loss, you have plenty of company. Often, you'll have a loss for tax purposes even if your rental income exceeds your operating expenses. This is due to the depreciation deduction allowed on the cost of the property.

Under the tax rules that apply to everybody except real estate professionals, rental losses are subject to the passive activity loss (the "PAL") rules. For purposes of the PAL rules, all the income you earn, and losses you incur, during the year are divided into three separate categories:

- **Active income or loss.** Salary or wages you earn from a job; income and deductions from a business you actively manage; self-employment income for personal services; Social Security benefits.
- **Passive income or loss.** Income and deductions from rental properties. Income and deductions from businesses in which you don't materially participate (actively manage). Casualty losses from rental property are not passive losses. (See Chapter 13.)
- **Portfolio income or loss.** Income from investments, such as interest earned on savings, or dividends earned on stocks. Gains or losses when investments are sold. Expenses paid for investments.

You cannot use passive losses to offset active or portfolio income. Nor can you use active or portfolio losses to offset passive income.

Passive income or loss includes income or loss from real estate rentals and income from any business in which the taxpayer does not "materially participate." (Material participation is explained below.) The PAL rules apply to any ordinary rental of a house, duplex, condominium, or apartment building. This is true whether you rent the property month to month or have a lease, no matter what the duration. However, the rules do not apply to short-term rentals, including most time-shares and many vacation homes. Such losses can be deducted from any type of income you earn during the year, provided that you materially participate in (actively manage) the rental activity.

Because of the PAL rules, landlords ordinarily cannot deduct their rental losses from their active or portfolio income.

> EXAMPLE: John is a physician who also owns several rental properties. This year he lost $50,000 from his rentals and had $250,000 in active income from his medical practice. Because John's rental losses are passive losses, he may not deduct them from his $250,000 of active income for the year.

There is a limited exception to these rules. Most landlords with modest incomes may deduct up to $25,000 in rental losses from their nonpassive income each year. But this deduction is phased out if a landlord's adjusted gross income exceeds $100,000. Landlords who have an adjusted gross income over $150,000 get no deduction at all.

Suspended Losses

Passive losses a landlord can't deduct during the current year don't disappear. Such losses, called "suspended losses," may be used in any future year when you have enough passive income for them to offset. In addition, when you sell a rental property, you may deduct your suspended losses from your profits to determine your taxable gain, and from any other income you earn during that year. You must keep track of suspended losses from each of your passive activities from year to year.

Real Estate Professional Exception to Passive Loss Rules

People involved in the real estate industry moaned and groaned so much about the passive loss rules that in 1994 Congress enacted a special exemption just for them. If you qualify, you may deduct any amount of real estate rental property losses you have for the year from your other income regardless of how high your income for the year is. (IRC Sec. 469(c)(7).) This exemption from the passive loss rules gives real estate professionals who invest in real estate an enormous tax advantage over all other investors.

> EXAMPLE: Mary is a real estate agent who owns several rental properties. This year she earned $200,000 in agent commissions and had $50,000 in rental losses. If she qualifies for the real estate professional exemption from the PAL rules, she may deduct the entire $50,000 rental loss from her commission income. This leaves her with just $150,000 in taxable income, instead of $200,000.

This exemption can be used by real estate professionals who are individuals, general partnerships, limited liability companies taxed like partnerships (most are), and S corporations. C corporations qualify only if 51% or more of their gross receipts comes from real property businesses in which they materially participate (see below). The exemption does not apply to limited partnerships, estates, and most types of trusts.

CAUTION

The exemption is not optional. The real estate professional exemption is not optional. If you qualify for it, you must apply it to your income and loss for the year. Usually this is a good thing, but in some cases it can be costly.

Unfortunately, the real estate professional exemption from the passive loss rules is rather complex. You qualify for the exemption, and may treat all your losses from your rental properties as active losses, only if you satisfy all three of the following tests:

- **51% Test:** You (or your spouse, if you file a joint return) spend more than half of your working hours during the year working in one or more real property businesses in which you materially participate.
- **751-Hour Test:** You (or your spouse, if you file a joint return) spend more than 751 hours a year in one or more real property businesses in which you materially participate.
- **Material Participation Test:** You and your spouse materially participate in your rental activity.

For the first two tests, each spouse's time is taken into account separately. Thus, one spouse alone must satisfy the 51% and 751-hour requirements. For the third test, both spouses' time together is counted if they file a joint return. Usually, you'll have no problem satisfying the first two tests, unless you only work part time in real estate. It's the material participation test that can cause big problems.

51% Test

The exemption is for real estate professionals, so it makes sense that you (or your spouse) must spend more than half (51%) of your working hours during the year running a "real property trade or business." Your working hours are the hours you spend personally working in a trade or business. Time you spend working on your personal investments is not counted.

A real property trade or business includes any "real property brokerage business." Any person who engages in one or more of the following activities is in the real estate brokerage business:

- selling, exchanging, purchasing, renting, or leasing real property
- offering to do the activities mentioned above
- negotiating the terms of real estate contracts
- listing real property for sale, lease, or exchange, or
- procuring prospective sellers, purchasers, lessors, or lessees.

It makes no difference whether a person who engaged in these activities is licensed as a real estate broker, agent, or salesperson. In one case, for example, the tax court held that a person licensed as a real estate salesperson in California was engaged in a brokerage business for tax purposes because she sold, exchanged, leased, and rented property, and solicited listings. It made no difference that under California law a person must be licensed as a broker to be in the brokerage business. (*Agarwall v. Comm'r*, T.C. Summ. Op. 2009-29.)

Other real estate business activities also qualify for the 51% test, including real estate development, redevelopment, construction, reconstruction, acquisition, conversion, rental, operation, management, or leasing. (IRC Sec. 469(c)(7)(C).) This covers virtually any real estate business activity.

You must be directly involved in one or more of these real property businesses. Thus, for example, an attorney or accountant is not in the real property business, even if he or she advises people who are in the business. Mortgage brokers, lenders, and bankers probably don't qualify either.

In addition, you cannot just be an employee in someone else's real property business. You must own your own real property business or at least be a part owner, owning more than 5% of the business. If you work as an employee for a corporation, you must own more than 5% of your employer's outstanding stock.

If you only work part time at real estate, and work full time at something else, it may be hard to pass the 51% test. For example, if you work 40 hours per week at a non-real-estate business, you'd have to work an average of 41 hours per week at one or more real estate activities to pass the test. This would require you to put in an 81-hour week. The IRS is not likely to believe you do this unless you have extremely convincing documentation. IRS auditors are instructed to look carefully at W-2 forms when they audit a taxpayer who claims the real estate professional exemption. If the W-2 shows that the taxpayer has a job not dealing with real estate, the auditor will question whether the 51% test has been satisfied.

On the other hand, if you're married, one spouse can work full time at a non-real-property business and still meet the test if the other spouse spends all (or at least over half) of his or her work time managing your rental properties.

> **EXAMPLE:** Leo and Leona are married and file a joint return. Leo is a physician, and spends no time working on real estate. Leona

spends 100% of her annual work time as a real estate salesperson. The test is satisfied because one spouse spends more than half of her time working in a real property business.

If you or your spouse is involved in more than one real property business, you can add the time you spend in each of them to pass the 51% test.

EXAMPLE: John works 800 hours per year as a part-time bookkeeper. He owns rental property on which he works 100 hours per year. He also works 701 hours per year as a real estate broker. John passes the 51% test because he spent 801 hours working in real estate businesses and 800 hours in other activities.

751-Hour Test

It's not enough that you (or your spouse) spend more than half of your work time in a real property business. After all, if you had no other work, you'd spend more than half your work time on real estate if you spent only one hour a year on it. To avoid this result, you or your spouse is required to spend at least 751 hours per year working at your real property business or businesses. 751 hours amounts to only 14.5 hours a week. Again, if you work in more than one real property business, you may combine the time you spend on each.

EXAMPLE: John is a part-time real estate agent who also owns several rental properties He worked 200 hours per year on his rental properties and 601 hours as a real estate broker. By combining both these real estate business activities, John exceeds the 751-hour limit.

Material Participation Test

Material participation is the ketchup of the real estate professional exemption—it has to cover everything. Material participation is what makes an activity active instead of passive for tax purposes. You (or your spouse) must materially participate in:

- your real property business or businesses, and
- in each rental real estate activity you want to treat as nonpassive.

If you fail to materially participate in a real estate business, you can't count the hours you spend working at it for purposes of the 51% or 751-hour tests.

If you fail to participate in a rental real estate activity, it will be a passive activity, even if you otherwise qualify for the real estate professional's exemption from the passive loss rules.

You "materially participate" in a business only if you are *involved with its day-to-day operations on a regular, continuous, and substantial basis.* (IRC Sec. 469(h).)

The IRS has created several tests to determine material participation, based on the amount of time you spend working in real estate activities. You only need to pass one of the tests. Most people use one or more of the first three tests.

501-hour test: You participated in the activity for more than 500 hours during the year.

You did substantially all the work test: You did substantially all the work in the activity during the year. You probably need to have worked at least 71% of the total hours devoted to the activity by all the people involved in it to qualify. This includes hours spent working on the property by co-owners, employees, and independent contractors, such as property managers.

101-hour test: You participated in the business for more than 100 hours during the year, and you participated at least as much as any other person (including employees and independent contractors, such as property managers).

Combo test: You participated in two or more businesses between 100 to 500 hours, so that the total hours are more than 500.

Past performance test: You materially participated in the business for any five of the last ten years.

Facts and circumstances test: The facts and circumstances show that you materially participated. You can't use this test if (1) you didn't participate in the activity for at least 101 hours; (2) anyone worked more than you; or (3) anyone was paid to manage the activity.

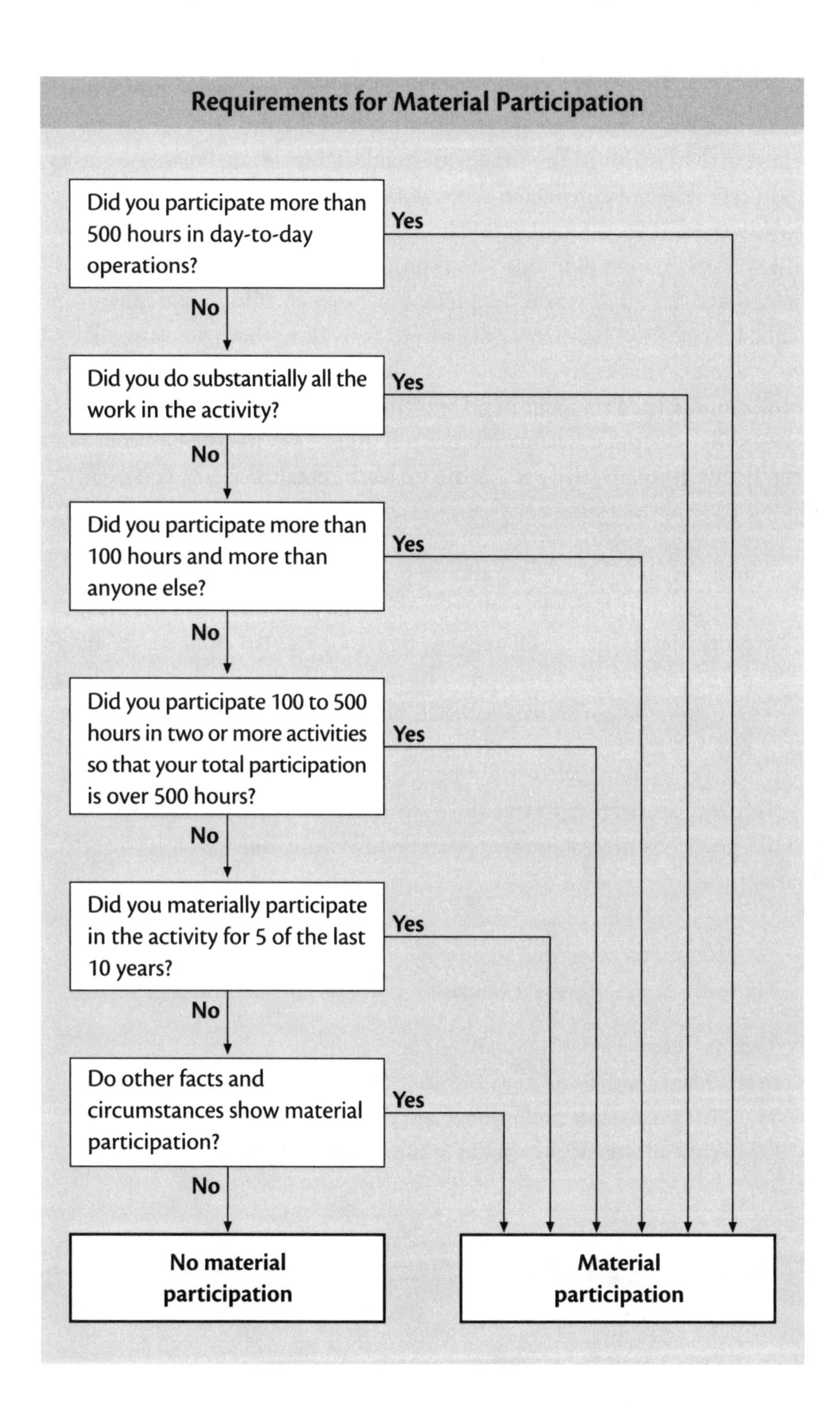
Requirements for Material Participation
Did you participate more than 500 hours in day-to-day operations?
Yes
No
Did you do substantially all the work in the activity?
Yes
No
Did you participate more than 100 hours and more than anyone else?
Yes
No
Did you participate 100 to 500 hours in two or more activities so that your total participation is over 500 hours?
Yes
No
Did you materially participate in the activity for 5 of the last 10 years?
Yes
No
Do other facts and circumstances show material participation?
Yes
No
No material participation
Material participation

You apply these tests separately: first to all your real estate businesses, including your rental real estate activities; and then to your rental real estate activities alone. The time you spend on real estate businesses other than rentals is not considered when you determine if you materially participated in your rental activity.

If you own more than one rental property, each one is a separate "rental activity" unless you designate otherwise by filing a statement (called an election) with your tax return providing that you want all your rental activities to be treated as one, single activity. This way, you can combine the time you spend working on each rental property to satisfy the material participation tests. If you fail to file the election, you'll have to materially participate for each rental property you own.

> EXAMPLE: Dennis owns five rental homes. He works 101 hours a year managing all five, and no one else does any work on the properties. If he files an election with his tax return to treat all his properties as one rental activity, he'll pass the 101-hour material participation test. However, if he fails to file the election, he'll have to materially participate for each house he owns—that is, he'd have to work 101 hours on each house, instead of all five together.

To make an election to treat all your rental activities as one activity, you'll need to draft a statement like the following and attach it to your tax return:

Tax Year: ________ Taxpayer Name: ______________________________

Taxpayer Identification Number: ______________________________

In accordance with Regulation 1.469-9(g)(3), taxpayer states that he/she is a qualifying real estate professional, and elects under IRC Section 469(c)(7)(A) to treat all interests in real estate as a single rental real estate activity.

____

Your Signature

The election can be filed any year you qualify for the real estate professional exemption and only needs to be filed once; it applies to all future years that you qualify for the exemption. It may only be revoked if you have a "material change" in circumstances. The fact that the election is less advantageous to you in a particular year is not a material change in circumstances. (IRS Reg. 1.469-9(g).)

Activities That Don't Count as Participation

Any work you do for a business you own, wholly or in part, counts as participation in the business, unless:

- the work is not customarily done by owners of that type of activity, and
- one of your main reasons for doing the work is to avoid application of the PAL rules. (IRS Reg. 1.469-5(f)(2)(i).)

EXAMPLE: Martha has her own small real estate brokerage business. This year, business is slow. Martha figures that she'll end up spending only 500 hours working at the business for the year. To pass the 751-hour test, she hires her husband Bob to work 251 hours answering phones and doing clerical work for the business. Unfortunately, Bob's time does not count as participation in the real estate activity because answering phones and doing clerical work is not work customarily done by the owner of a real estate broker business.

In addition, you do not treat work you do in your capacity as an investor in an activity as participation. This includes:

- studying and reviewing financial statements or reports on the activity's operations
- preparing or compiling summaries or analyses of the finances or operations of the activity for your own use, and
- monitoring the activity's finances or operations in a nonmanagerial capacity—for example, reviewing rental statements you receive from a rental management company that manages your property for you. (IRS Reg. 1.469-5(f)(2)(ii).)

Courts have held that the time you spend organizing your personal records, preparing your taxes, paying bills, and reviewing monthly statements prepared by a real estate management company constitutes investor activities. (*Barniskis v. Comm'r*, TC Memo 1999-258.) Time you spend doing these tasks cannot be counted in order to pass the material participation tests.

Absentee Landlords

Absentee landlords who hire real property managers to do all the work for them may have difficulty materially participating in their rental real estate activities under any of the tests. To materially participate, a landlord must be involved with the day-to-day operation of the rental property, something absentee landlords often don't do. If you live a substantial distance away from your rental property, the IRS will likely question whether you are really involved in day-to-day operations.

> EXAMPLE: Real estate broker Josephine owns two five-unit apartment buildings in Las Vegas, but lives in Houston. She hires a real property management company to manage the properties. She is not involved with the day-to-day management of the buildings. Her involvement is limited to approving the management company's decisions. This year, she spent 50 hours dealing with her management company. She spent another 25 hours reading financial statements and otherwise dealing with her investment. Josephine has not materially participated in her rental activity. None of the time she spends reading financial statements counts as material participation. This leaves her with just 50 hours of work during the year, not enough to materially participate under any of the tests. She clearly doesn't satisfy the 501-hour or 101-hour tests. Nor does she meet the you-did-all-the-work test because the management company did most of the work.

Spouses Combine Their Work

If you're married, you combine the time your spouse spends materially participating with your own. This is true whether or not you and your spouse file a joint return. (IRS Reg. 1.469-9(c)(4).) This can make it much easier to pass one of the material participation tests.

EXAMPLE: Frank and Felicia are married and file a joint return. They own a four-unit apartment building they manage themselves. Felicia does most of the work, spending 400 hours a year dealing with tenants, showing vacant units, handling bookkeeping chores and so forth. Frank does most of the repair work for the property, spending 120 hours a year. Together, Frank and Felicia spent 520 hours materially participating in their rental real estate activity, more than enough to pass the 501-hour test.

Putting All Three Tests Together

To put it mildly, the rules for the real estate professional exemption are complicated. The easiest way to see if you qualify is to break them down step-by-step.

Determine hours you worked in real estate. Figure the number of hours you and your spouse spent on each of your real property businesses during the year, including your rental activity. Do this separately for each activity—for example, your rental activity, real estate brokerage, and real property management. Only count work performed in a real estate business or rental activity in which you or your spouse are a more than 5% owner.

Determine if you materially participated in each of your real estate activities. Determine if you and your spouse materially participated in each activity by applying the material participation tests. You combine your hours with your spouse to determine material participation in each activity.

Determine non-real-estate activity hours. Determine the total number of hours you and your husband or wife worked in non-real-estate work activities during the year, whether as an employee, or in a non-real-property business you wholly or partly own. Material participation is not considered here. Make separate tallies of the hours for your spouse and yourself.

Determine if you pass the 51% test. Compare the total number of hours you worked on real estate activities, including rental activities, in which you materially participated, with the number of hours you worked on non-real-estate activities. (You don't consider the time you spent working on real estate activities in which you didn't materially participate.) Do the same for your spouse. Either you or your spouse must have spent 51% of your total work hours on real estate activities. If not, you don't qualify for the exemption.

Determine if you pass the 751-hour test. Separately determine the total time you and your spouse each spent working on real property activities during the year in which you materially participated. Don't include the time you or your spouse spent on nonrental real property activities. If you or your spouse spent at least 751 hours on rental real estate activities, you qualify for the real property professional exemption from the PAL rules.

EXAMPLE: Max and Maxine are married and own two duplexes they rent out. They have filed an election with their tax return to treat both properties as a single rental activity for tax purposes. Max works full time (1,800 hours per year) as an accountant. Maxine is a licensed real estate agent. She spends 2,000 hours per year working in this real estate business. Max and Maxine both work at managing their rental property. This doesn't take much time. Max spent 25 hours this year, and Maxine 80 hours. Their total hours are shown in the following charts.

Max's Activities

Real estate activities	Time Spent	Non-real-estate activities	Time Spent
Rental property management	25 hours	Accounting	1,800 hours
Total	25 hours	Total	1,800 hours

Maxine's Activities

Real estate activities	Time Spent	Non-real-estate activities	Time Spent
Real estate agent	1,800 hours	None	
Rental property management	80 hours		
Total	1,880 hours	Total	0

First, how many hours did both Max and Maxine work in real estate activities? Max worked only 20 hours. Maxine worked 1,880 hours.

Did Max and Maxine materially participate in each of their real estate activities? The couple's hours are combined to determine material participation. There are two separate activities—managing rental properties and working as a real estate agent. Maxine spent 1,800 hours working at real estate brokerage—more than enough to materially participate under the 501-hour test. Together, the couple spent 105 hours managing their rental property. This is far too little for the 501-hour material participation test; but they qualify under the 101-hour test because no one else worked on their rentals as much.

Max had 1,800 non-real-estate hours; Maxine had none.

Can either Max or Maxine pass the 51% test? Max can't pass the test. He spent almost all his time working at accounting. Maxine passes the test because she spent 100% of her time working on real property activities.

Can either pass 751-hour test? Max obviously can't pass this test; he spent only 25 hours working at a real property activity. Maxine easily passes: She put in a whopping 1,880 hours on real property activities.

Max and Maxine qualify for the real estate professional exemption.

What Happens If You Qualify for the Exemption

You must qualify for the real estate professional exemption anew each year. Any year you qualify, the income and loss from your rental property is not considered passive: It is now nonpassive income or loss. Any loss you have from the property may be deducted from your active or portfolio (investment) income, but not from any passive income. Likewise, any income from the property may be offset by active or portfolio losses. However, you may not use the exemption to reduce your income for the year to below zero—that is, to create a net operating loss for the year.

What happens if you incurred passive losses from the property in previous years that you weren't able to deduct because you didn't qualify for the exemption or couldn't use the $25,000 offset? These unused passive losses are called "suspended passive losses." They remain passive losses. However, you may deduct them from income from your now exempt rental property. You can also deduct them from passive income for that year, or if you sell the exempt rental property. However, you can't deduct these suspended losses from your active or portfolio income. (IRC Sec. 469(f)(1)(C).)

The real estate professional exemption is mandatory, not optional. If you qualify, you are not allowed to deduct your losses from your exempt rental real property from passive income. The only way to avoid this is to make sure you don't qualify for the exemption. This is not hard to do—for example, you could hire a management company to manage your rentals for you so you would not materially participate in them. Or you could just make sure you work less than 751 hours per year in real estate activities.

Record Keeping for the Real Estate Professional Exemption

To know whether you qualify for the real estate professional exemption you must know how many hours you (and your spouse, if you're married) spent during the year working in (1) real estate businesses of all kinds, (2) rental real estate activities, and (3) all non-real-estate work activities (if any).

If you are audited by the IRS, the key to preserving your real estate professional exemption is good records of your annual work hours. IRS regulations provide that you may use any "reasonable means" to keep track of your work time, including daily time reports, logs, appointment books, calendars, or narrative summaries. (IRS Reg. 1.469-5T(f)(4).) You are not absolutely required to keep contemporaneous records—that is, records made at or near the time you did the work involved—but it is a good practice to do so.

Many taxpayers keep few or no records of their time. When they get audited, they sit down and write a narrative summary of work they did during the year and estimating the time they spent, or they rely on their oral testimony. This is a good way to lose your exemption.

> EXAMPLE: Judy Bailey kept a daily calendar for 1997 that listed the number of visits she made to her many rental properties, but the calendar did not quantify the number of hours that she spent on her rental activities. When she was audited by the IRS, she wrote a summary report, in which she generally explained the activities she performed at the rental properties and estimated the number of the hours she spent on each rental property. Both the IRS and tax court found this summary to be inadequate. The court noted that Bailey's estimates were uncorroborated by any other evidence. She assigned hours to activities years later, based solely on her judgment and experience as to how much time the activities must have taken her. The court concluded, therefore, that the summary was an unreliable "ballpark guesstimate." Bailey lost her exemption. (*Bailey v. Comm'r*, T.C. Memo 2001-296.)

You should learn from Judy Bailey's mistakes. Keep careful track of the actual number of hours you (and your spouse) spend working on each activity during the year. For example, keep track of the time you spend showing properties, marketing your services, and dealing with buyers and sellers.

You can note your time on a calendar, appointment book, log, or timesheet. It doesn't matter, as long as your records are accurate and believable.

Get into the habit of writing down the time you perform any task related to your rental properties. For example, you should include the time you spend:

- traveling for any of the activities listed below
- showing the property for rental
- taking tenant applications
- screening tenants
- preparing and negotiating leases and other rental agreements
- cleaning and preparing units for rent

- doing repairs yourself
- doing improvements yourself or arranging for others to do them
- hiring and supervising a resident manager
- hiring and dealing with a rental management company
- purchasing supplies and materials for your rental business
- inspecting the property
- responding to tenant complaints and inquiries
- collecting and depositing rents
- evicting deadbeat tenants
- writing and placing advertisements, and
- attending seminars or other educational events on how to manage rental property.

If you buy or sell a rental property during the year, keep track of the time involved as well—for example, finding the property, negotiating the purchase, arranging financing, dealing with escrow, and so forth.

CHAPTER

16

Staying Out of Trouble With the IRS

This chapter explains IRS audits and provides tips and strategies that will help you avoid attracting the attention of the IRS—or come out of an audit unscathed, if you find yourself in the government's crosshairs.

RESOURCE

Need more information on dealing with the IRS? For a detailed discussion of audits and other IRS procedures, see *Stand Up to the IRS*, by Frederick Daily (Nolo).

What Every Real Estate Agent Needs to Know About the IRS

Just as you should never go into battle without knowing your enemy, you should never file a tax return without understanding what the IRS plans to do with it.

Anatomy of an Audit

You can claim any deductions you want to take on your tax return—after all, you (or your tax preparer) fill it out, not the government. However, all the deductions you claim are subject to review by the IRS. This review is called a tax audit. There are three types of audits: correspondence audits, office audits, and field audits.

- **Correspondence audits.** As the name indicates, correspondence audits are handled entirely by mail. These are the simplest, shortest, and by far the most common type of IRS audit, usually involving a single issue. The IRS sends you written questions about a perceived problem, and may request additional information or documentation. If you don't provide satisfactory answers or information, you'll be assessed additional taxes. Correspondence audits are often used to question a business about unreported income—income the IRS knows the taxpayer received because an IRS Form 1099 listing the payment has been filed by a client or customer.

- **Office audits.** Office audits take place face to face with an IRS auditor at one of the 33 IRS district offices. These are more complex than correspondence audits, often involving more than one issue or more than one tax year. This is the type of in-person audit you're likely to face.
- **Field audits.** The field audit is the most comprehensive IRS audit, conducted by an experienced revenue officer. In a field audit, the officer examines your finances, your business, your tax returns, and the records you used to create the returns. As the name implies, a field audit is normally conducted at the taxpayer's place of business; this allows the auditor to learn as much about your business as possible. Field audits are ordinarily reserved for taxpayers who earn a lot of money.

How Small Business Owners Get in Trouble With the IRS

When auditing small business owners, including real estate agents, the IRS is most concerned about whether you have done one of the following:

Underreported your income. Unlike employees who have their taxes withheld, business owners who are not employees have no withholding—and many opportunities to underreport how much they earned, particularly if they run a cash business.

Claimed tax deductions to which you were not entitled. For example, you claimed that nondeductible personal expenses, such as a personal vacation, were deductible business expenses.

Properly documented the amount of your deductions. If you don't have the proper records to back up the amount of a deduction, the IRS may reduce it, either entirely or in part. Lack of documentation is the main reason real estate agents and other small business owners lose deductions when they get audited.

Taken business deductions for a hobby. If you continually lose money, the auditor may also question whether you are really in business. If the IRS claims you are engaged in a hobby, you could lose every single deduction for the activity. (See Chapter 3 for more on the hobby loss rule.)

Records Available to Auditors

An IRS auditor is entitled to examine the business records you used to prepare your tax returns, including your books, check registers, canceled checks, and receipts. The auditor can also ask to see records supporting your business tax deductions, such as a mileage record if you took a deduction for business use of your car. The auditor can also get copies of your bank records, either from you or your bank, and check them to see whether your deposits match the income you reported on your tax return. If you deposited a lot more money than you reported earning, the auditor will assume that you didn't report all of your income, unless you can show that the deposits you didn't include in your tax return weren't income. For example, you might be able to show that they were loans, inheritances, or transfers from other accounts. This is why you need to keep good financial records.

The IRS: Clear and Present Danger or Phantom Menace?

A generation ago, the three letters Americans feared most were I-R-S. There was a simple reason for this: The IRS, the nation's tax police, enforced the tax laws like crazy. In 1963, an incredible 5.6% of all Americans had their tax returns audited. Everybody knew someone who had been audited. Jokes about IRS audits were a staple topic of nightclub comedians and cartoonists.

In 2011, an IRS audit was a relatively rare event—only 1.1% of all Americans were audited. The decline in audits was primarily due to budget cuts and hiring freezes which led to a reduction in the IRS workforce. At the same time, the agency's workload vastly increased due to:

- a higher overall number of tax filings each year
- the increasing complexity of the tax code
- frequent changes to the tax code (there were approximately 4,430 changes to the tax code from 2001 through 2010, an average of more than one a day), and
- the IRS's increasing responsibility for administering economic and social policies, including the new health care law.

According to the IRS Oversight Board, the IRS does not have the resources to pursue at least $30 billion worth of known taxes that are incorrectly reported or not paid. In 2005, the nation's "tax gap"—the total inventory of taxes that are known and not paid—was estimated at $345 billion.

Both the IRS and Congress are aware of the IRS's enforcement problems and have taken steps to ameliorate them. The IRS has received moderate budget increases in the past few years and has placed a renewed emphasis on enforcement. Staff has been shifted from performing service functions like answering taxpayer questions to doing audits. Moreover, the IRS appears to be targeting small businesses: Audit rates for all small businesses have gone up for the last five years. Since most real estate professionals run small businesses, they are affected more than most.

Aggressive or Dishonest?

Given the relatively low audit rates in recent years, many tax experts say that this is a good time to be aggressive about taking tax deductions. In this context, "aggressive" means taking every deduction to which you might arguably be entitled. If a deduction falls into a gray area of law, you would decide the question in your favor. This is *tax avoidance,* which is perfectly legal.

However, being aggressive does not mean being dishonest—that is, taking phony deductions that you are clearly not entitled to take or falsely increasing the amount of the deductions to which you are entitled. This is *tax evasion,* which is a crime.

You Are a Prime IRS Target

Although audit rates remain relatively low in historical terms, hundreds of thousands of people still get audited every year. In 2011, the IRS audited 278,092 tax returns filed by Schedule C filers—the category that includes most real estate agents and brokers. This amounted to over

16% of all IRS audits for the year. Such audits can hurt. In 2010, the average recommended additional tax for an audit of a sole proprietor earning $25,000 to $100,000 was $8,776. For those earning $100,000 to $200,000, it was a whopping $31,979.

Every year, the IRS releases statistics about who got audited the previous year. Here are the most recent available audit statistics.

IRS Audit Rates		
	2010 Audit Rate	**2009 Audit Rate**
Sole Proprietors		
Income less than $25,000	1.2%	1.1%
$25,000 to $100,000	2.5%	1.9%
$100,000 to $200,000	4.7%	4.2%
More than $250,000	3.3%	3.2%
Partnerships	0.4%	0.4%
S Corporations	0.4%	0.4%
C Corporations		
Assets less than $250,000	0.8%	0.7%
$250,000 to $1 million	1.4%	1.3%
$1 million to $5 million	1.7%	1.8%
$5 million to $10 million	3.0%	2.7%

This chart shows that in 2010, 4.7% of sole proprietors earning $100,000 to $200,000 were audited. Not even corporations with assets worth between $5 million and $10 million were audited as often.

These statistics undoubtedly reflect the IRS's belief that sole proprietors habitually underreport their income, take deductions to which they are not entitled, or otherwise cheat on their taxes. The lesson these numbers teach is that you need to take the IRS seriously. This doesn't mean that you shouldn't take all the deductions you're legally entitled to take, but you should understand the rules and be able to back up the deductions you do take with proper records.

How Tax Returns Are Selected for Audits

It's useful to understand how tax returns are selected for audit by the IRS. (By the way, if you are audited, you are entitled to know why you were selected. You ordinarily have to ask to find out.)

DIF Scores

One way the IRS decides who to audit is by plugging the information from your tax return into a complex formula to calculate a "discriminate function" score (DIF). Returns with high DIFs have a far higher chance of being flagged for an audit, regardless of whether or not you have done anything obviously wrong. Anywhere from 25% to 60% of audited returns are selected this way. Exactly how the DIF is calculated is a closely guarded secret. Some of the known factors the formula takes into account are:

The nature of your business. Businesses that deal with large amounts of cash are scrutinized more closely than those that don't.

Where you live. Audit rates differ widely according to where you live. In 2000, for example, taxpayers in Southern California were almost five times more likely to be audited than taxpayers in Georgia. The IRS no longer releases information on audit rates by region, but according to the latest available data, the state with the highest audit rate is Nevada; other high-audit states include Alaska, California, and Colorado. Low-audit states include Illinois, Indiana, Iowa, Maryland, Massachusetts, Michigan, New York (not including Manhattan), Ohio, Pennsylvania, and West Virginia.

The amount of your deductions. Returns with extremely large deductions in relation to income are more likely to be audited. For example, if your tax return shows that your business is earning $25,000, you are more likely to be audited if you claim $20,000 in deductions than if you claim $2,000.

Hot-button deductions. Certain types of deductions have long been thought to be hot buttons for the IRS—especially auto, travel, and entertainment expenses. Casualty losses and bad debt deductions may also increase your DIF score. Some people believe that claiming the home office deduction makes an audit more likely, but the IRS denies this.

Businesses that lose money. Businesses that show losses are more likely to be audited, especially if the losses are recurring. The IRS may suspect that you must be making more money than you are reporting—otherwise, why would you stay in business?

Peculiar deductions. Deductions that seem odd or out of character for your business could increase your DIF score—for example, a plumber who deducts the cost of foreign travel might raise a few eyebrows at the IRS.

How you organize your business. Sole proprietors get higher DIF scores than businesses that are incorporated or owned by partnerships or limited liability companies. As a result, sole proprietors generally are most likely to be audited by the IRS. Partnerships and small C corporations are ten times less likely to be audited than sole proprietors.

IRS Matching Program

The IRS matches the payments reported to it each year on IRS Form 1099-MISC with the amount of income reported on tax returns using Social Security and other identifying numbers. Discrepancies usually generate correspondence audits.

Groups Targeted for Audit

Every year, the IRS gives special attention to specific industries or groups of taxpayers that it believes to be tax cheats. IRS favorites include doctors, dentists, lawyers, CPAs, and salespeople.

The IRS also targets taxpayers who use certain tax shelters or have offshore bank accounts or trusts. But you don't have to be rich to be an audit target. The IRS also heavily audits low-income taxpayers who claim the earned income tax credit.

Tips and Referrals

You could get audited as a result of a referral from another government agency, such as your state tax department. The IRS also receives tips from private citizens—for example, a former business partner or an ex-spouse.

Bad Luck

A certain number of tax returns are randomly selected for audit every year. IRS examiners will look for unreported income and overstated deductions or tax credits, focusing on Schedule C filers. If you find yourself in this category, there's not much you can do about it. As long as you have adequate documentation to support your deductions, you should do just fine.

State Tax Audits Grow Increasingly Common

Although most people (and books) focus on IRS audits, audits by state income tax agencies are becoming increasingly common. Many states have increased fines and late-payment penalties. Others have adopted severe—and highly effective—punishments against delinquent taxpayers. For example, some states refuse to issue driver's licenses to people who owe back taxes. Others are hiring private tax collectors and publishing names of tax evaders online.

Ten Tips for Avoiding an Audit

Here are ten things you can do to minimize your chances of getting audited.

Tip #1: Be Neat, Thorough, and Exact

If you file by mail (as you should), submit a tax return that looks professional; this will help you avoid unwanted attention from the IRS.

Your return shouldn't contain erasures or be difficult to read. Your math should be correct. Avoid round numbers on your return (like $100 or $5,000). This looks like you're making up the numbers instead of taking them from accurate records. You should include, and completely fill out, all necessary forms and schedules. Moreover, your state tax return should be consistent with your federal return. If you do your own taxes, using a tax-preparation computer program will help you produce an accurate return that looks professional.

Tip #2: Mail Your Return by Certified Mail

Mail your tax return by certified mail, return receipt requested. In case the IRS loses or misplaces your return, your receipt will prove that you submitted it. The IRS also accepts returns from private delivery services, including Airborne Express, Federal Express, and United Parcel Service. Contact these companies for details on which of their service options qualify and how to get proof of timely filing.

Tip #3: Don't File Early

Unless you're owed a substantial refund, you shouldn't file your taxes early. The IRS generally has three years after April 15 to decide whether to audit your return. Filing early just gives the IRS more time to think about whether you should be audited. You can reduce your audit chances even more by getting an automatic extension to file until October 15. (Partnerships and S corporations receive an automatic extension only until September 15—five months, instead of six.) Note, however, that filing an extension does not extend the date by which you have to pay any taxes due for the prior year—these must be paid by April 15.

Tip #4: Don't File Electronically

The IRS would like all taxpayers to file their returns electronically—that is, by email. There is a good reason for this: It saves the agency substantial time and money. Every year, the IRS must hire thousands of temp workers to enter the numbers from millions of paper returns into its computer system. This is expensive, so the IRS only has about 40%

of the data on paper returns transcribed. The paper returns are then sent to a warehouse where they are kept for six years and then destroyed. The IRS makes its audit decisions based on this transcribed data. By filing electronically, you give the IRS easy access to 100% of the data on your return instead of just 40%. Moreover, if you file electronically, you cannot add written explanations of any deductions the IRS might question (see Tip #6). No one can say for sure whether filing a paper return lessens your chance of an audit, but why make life easier for the IRS if you don't have to? On the other hand, if you're owed a refund, you'll get it much faster if you file electronically.

New IRS rules that went it effect in 2011 require professional tax preparers to file their clients' returns electronically unless the client elects to opt out of electronic filing. To opt out, you must file a special form with your paper tax return. Ask your tax preparer about this.

Tip #5: Form a Business Entity

The IRS audit rate statistics, discussed above, show that partnerships and small corporations are audited far less often than sole proprietors. In 2011, for example, the IRS audited 0.4% of partnerships, 0.4% of S corporations, and only 0.7% of regular C corporations with assets worth less than $250,000. In contrast, 2.9% of sole proprietors earning $25,000 to $100,000 were audited. The majority of real estate agents are sole proprietors, but no law says they have to be. Incorporating your business or forming a limited liability company will greatly reduce your audit risk. However, you must balance this against the time and expense involved in forming a corporation or LLC and having to complete more complex tax returns. Moreover, in some states—most notably California—corporations and LLCs have to pay additional state taxes. (See Chapter 2 for a detailed discussion of choice of business entity by real estate professionals.)

Tip #6: Explain Items the IRS Will Question

If your return contains an item that the IRS may question or that could increase the likelihood of an audit, include an explanation and documentation to prove everything is on the up and up. For example, if your return contains a substantial bad debt deduction, explain the circumstances showing that the debt is a legitimate business expense. This won't necessarily avoid an audit, but it may reduce your chances. Here's why: If the IRS computer gives your return a high DIF score, an IRS classifier screens it to see whether it warrants an audit. If your explanations look reasonable, the screener may decide you shouldn't be audited after all.

Such explanations ("disclosures" in tax parlance) can be made on plain white paper and attached to your return, or you can use special IRS forms. IRS Form 8275, *Disclosure Statement*, can be used to explain or disclose any information that there isn't room to include on your other tax forms. Another IRS form, Form 8275-R, *Regulation Disclosure Statement*, must be used to disclose tax positions that are contrary to IRS regulations or other rules. You shouldn't file Form 8275-R without professional help.

Tip #7: Avoid Ambiguous or General Expenses

Don't list expenses under vague categories such as "miscellaneous" or "general expense." Be specific. IRS Schedule C lists specific categories for the most common small business expenses. If an expense doesn't fall within one of these classifications, create a specific name for it.

Tip #8: Report All of Your Income

The IRS is convinced that many self-employed people, including many real estate agents and brokers, don't report all of their income. Finding such hidden income is a high priority. As mentioned above, IRS computers compare 1099 forms with tax returns to determine whether there are any discrepancies.

Tip #9: Watch Your Income-to-Deduction Ratio

Back in the 1990s, a statistics professor named Amir D. Aczel got audited by the IRS. The experience proved so unpleasant that he decided to conduct a statistical study of how and why people get selected for IRS audits. He carefully examined more than 1,200 returns that were audited and reported his findings in a book (now out of print) called *How to Beat the IRS at Its Own Game* (Four Walls Eight Windows, 1995). He concluded that the key factor leading to an audit was the ratio of a taxpayer's expenses to his or her income.

According to Aczel, if your total business expenses amount to less than 52% of your gross business income, you are "not very likely" to be audited. If your business expenses are 52% to 63% of your business income, there is a "relatively high probability" that the IRS computer will tag you for an audit. Finally, if your expenses are more than 63% of your income, Aczel claims you are "certain to be computer tagged for audit." Of course, this doesn't necessarily mean that you *will* be audited. Less than 10% of returns that are computer tagged for audit are actually audited. But being tagged considerably increases the odds that you'll be audited.

Whether Aczel's precise numbers are correct or not is anyone's guess. However, his basic conclusion—that your income-to-deduction ratio is an important factor in determining whether you'll be audited—is undoubtedly true. (A former IRS commissioner admitted as much in a CNN interview in 1995.)

Tip #10: Beware of Abnormally Large Deductions

It is not just the total amount of your deductions that is important. Very large individual deductions can also increase your audit chances. For example, claiming a $50,000 auto expense deduction might seem abnormally large for a real estate agent and increase your audit chances.

CHAPTER

17

The Boring Stuff: Record Keeping and Accounting

When you incur business expenses, you get tax deductions and save money on your taxes. But those deductions are only as good as the records you keep to back them up. Any expense you forget to deduct (or lose after an IRS audit because you can't back it up) costs you dearly. Every $100 in unclaimed deductions costs the average midlevel-income agent (in a 25% tax bracket) $43 in additional federal and state income and self-employment taxes.

Luckily, it's not difficult to keep records of your business expenses. In this chapter, we'll show you how to document your expenditures so you won't end up losing your hard-earned business deductions.

What Type of Bookkeeping and Accounting System Do You Need?

You may be surprised to discover that the IRS does not require you to use any particular bookkeeping or accounting system. You can use any method that provides a reasonably accurate picture of your income and expenses. There are many different ways to keep track of business income and expenses, from the exceedingly simple to the extremely complex. The type of system you use should depend on:

- the size of your business
- the number of financial transactions you have each month
- whether you have employees
- the experience of the person doing your bookkeeping, and
- whether you use a computerized bookkeeping system.

No one would expect an independent contractor agent with no employees to use the same bookkeeping and accounting system as a large real estate brokerage firm with many agents and employees.

Basic Record Keeping for Tax Deductions

This section explains how to set up a basic system an independent contractor real estate agent or broker with no employees can use to keep track of deductible expenses. All you need is:

- a business checking account
- an appointment book

- an expense journal, and
- supporting documents, such as receipts.

This system will get you started—it is by no means everything you'll need for your business record keeping. For example, every business must keep track of its income. And if you have employees, you must create and keep a number of records, including payroll tax records, withholding records, and employment tax returns.

RESOURCE

For an excellent overall guide to small business bookkeeping, refer to *Small Time Operator,* by Bernard B. Kamoroff (Bell Springs Press).

Business Checkbook and Credit Cards

One of the first things you should do (if you haven't done it already) is to set up a separate checking account for your real estate business. Your business checkbook will serve as your basic source of information for recording your business expenses and income. Deposit all your business receipts (checks you receive from clients, for example) into the account and make all business-related payments by check from the account. Don't use your business account to pay for personal expenses or your personal account to pay for business items.

A separate business checkbook is legally required if you've formed a corporation, partnership, or LLC. Keeping a separate business account is not legally required if you're a sole proprietor, but it will provide these important benefits:

- It will be much easier for you to keep track of your business income and expenses if you pay them from a separate account.
- Your business account will clearly separate your personal and business finances; this will prove very helpful if you're audited by the IRS.
- Your business account will help convince the IRS that you are running a business and not engaged in a hobby. Hobbyists don't generally have separate bank accounts for their hobbies. This is a huge benefit if you incur losses from your business, because losses

from hobbies are not fully deductible. (See Chapter 3 for more on the hobby loss rule.)

Setting Up Your Bank Account

Your business checking account should be in your business name. If you're a sole proprietor, this can be your own name. If you've formed a corporation, partnership, or limited liability company, the account should be in your corporate, partnership, or company name.

You don't need to open your business checking account at the same bank where you have your personal checking account. Shop around and open your account with the bank that offers you the best services at the lowest price.

If you're doing business under your own name, consider opening up a second account in that name and using it solely for your business instead of a separate business account. You'll usually pay less for a personal account than for a business account.

If you're a sole proprietor doing business under an assumed name, you'll likely have to give your bank a copy of your fictitious business name statement.

If you've incorporated your business, call your bank and ask what documentation is required to open the account. You will probably need to show the bank a corporate resolution authorizing the opening of a bank account and showing the names of the people authorized to sign checks. Typically, you will also have to fill out a separate bank account authorization form provided by your bank. You will also need to have a federal employer identification number.

Similarly, if you've established a partnership or limited liability company, you'll likely have to show the bank a resolution authorizing the account.

You may also want to establish interest-bearing accounts for your business in which you place cash you don't immediately need. For example, you may decide to set up a business savings account or a money market mutual fund in your business name.

When You Write Checks

If you already keep an accurate, updated personal checkbook, do the same for your business checkbook. If, however, like many people, you tend to be lax in keeping up your checkbook, you're going to have to change your habits. Now that you're in business, you can't afford this kind of carelessness. Unless you write large numbers of business checks, maintaining your checkbook won't take much time.

When you write business checks, you may have to make some extra notations besides the date, number, amount of the check, and name of the person or company to which the check is written. If it's not clear from the name of the payee what a check is for, describe the business reason for the check—for example, the equipment or service you purchased.

You can use the register that comes with your checkbook and write in all this information manually, or you can use a computerized register. Either way works fine as long as the information is complete and up to date. (See "Records Required for Specific Expenses," below, to find out what information you need for various types of expenses.)

Don't Write Checks for Cash

Avoid writing checks payable to cash, because this makes it hard to tell whether you spent the money for a business purpose. Writing cash checks might lead to questions from the IRS if you're audited. If you must write a check for cash to pay a business expense, be sure to include the receipt for the cash payment in your records.

Use a Separate Credit Card for Business

Use a separate credit card for business expenses instead of putting both personal and business items on one card. Credit card interest for business purchases is 100% deductible, while interest for personal purchases is not deductible at all. Using a separate card for business purchases will make it much easier for you to keep track of how much interest you've paid for business purchases. The card doesn't have to be in your business name. It can just be one of your personal credit cards. Always use your business checking account to pay your business credit card bill.

Calendar or Appointment Book

Another highly useful item is an appointment book, day planner, tax diary, or calendar. You can find inexpensive ones in any stationery store. Many computerized calendars are available as well.

Properly used, this humble item will:

- provide solid evidence that you are serious about making a profit from your business, and thereby avoid having the IRS claim that your real estate activity is a hobby (see Chapter 3 for more on businesses versus hobbies).
- help show that the expenses you incur are for business, not personal purposes
- help verify entertainment, meal, and travel expenses
- enable you to use a sampling method to keep track of business mileage, instead of keeping track of every mile you drive all year (see "Records Required for Specific Expenses," below), and
- if you claim a home office deduction, help show that you use your office for business.

EXAMPLE: Tom, a part-time real estate agent who works out of his Florida home, kept a detailed appointment book. He devoted a page to each day, listing all of his business activities. He also kept a mileage log to record his business mileage. When he was audited by the IRS, the auditor picked out a trip from his mileage log at random and asked him the purpose of the trip. Tom looked at his appointment book entry for that day and was able to truthfully and credibly tell the auditor that the trip was to visit a client. The auditor accepted his explanation and the rest of his business mileage deductions.

Every day you work, you should track in your calendar or appointment book:

- the name of every person you talk to for business
- the date, time, and place of every business meeting
- every place you go for business
- the amount of all travel, meal, and entertainment expenses that are below $75, and

- if you claim the home office deduction, the time you spend working in your office.

Here's a sample page from an appointment book for a self-employed real estate salesperson. (You'll find information in "Records Required for Specific Expenses," below, on what information you need to list for different types of expenses.)

Sunday	Monday	Tuesday	Wednesday	Thursday	Friday	Saturday
	1 Meeting with Earl Crowler	2	3 Show 111 Green St.	4 Answer phones	5 Sales Meeting	6 Prepare for open house—Green St.
7 Open House 111 Green St.	8	9 Sales Meeting	10 Lunch Gibbons	11	12 Meeting Kim Mann	13
14 Open House 222 Blue St.	15	16 Show Gibbons 222 Blue St.	17	18 Lunch Mortgage Broker	19 Sales Meeting	20
21 Open House 456 Main St.	22	23 Sales Meeting	24 Lunch Mortgage Broker	25 Breakfast Kiwanis Club	26 Sales Meeting	27
28 Open House 826 3rd St.	29 Continuing education seminar	30	31			

Expense Journal

You can track your expenses by creating what accountants call a chart of accounts—a listing by category of all your expenses. This will show what you buy for your business and how much you spent. It's very easy to do this. You can write your chart out on paper or you can set up a computer spreadsheet program, such as *Excel*, to do it. Or, if you already have or would prefer to use a financial computer program such as *Quicken*, you can do that instead.

Creating a Paper Expense Journal

You can easily create an expense journal by using paper divided into columns or a professional multicolumn book you can get from any stationery or office supply store. These multicolumn pages are also called "ledger sheets." Get ledger sheets with at least 12 or 14 columns. Devote a separate column to each major category of expenses you have. Alternatively, you can purchase accounting record books with the expense categories already printed on them. These cost more, however, and may not offer categories that meet your needs.

Here are common expense categories used by real estate agents:

- accounting and legal
- advertising
- auto expenses
- bank charges
- board of realtor fees
- client reimbursements
- commissions paid
- continuing education
- conventions and seminars
- depreciation and Section 179 expense deductions
- entertainment
- equipment repairs and maintenance
- insurance (other than health)
- Internet and website
- interest
- licenses and dues
- meals
- MLS fees
- office expenses
- office assistants
- office equipment and furniture
- office supplies
- open house expenses
- postage and delivery
- photos and supplies
- rent
- software
- subscriptions
- supplies
- taxes

- telephone
- travel and lodging
- meals and entertainment.

You should always include a final category called "miscellaneous" for various and sundry expenses that are not easily pigeonholed. However, you should use this category sparingly, to account for less than 10% of your total expenses. Unlike travel or advertising, miscellaneous is not a type of business expense. It's just a place to lump together different types of expenses that don't fit into another category.

In separate columns, list the check number, date, and name of the person or company paid for each payment. If you pay by credit card or cash, indicate it in the check number column.

Once a month, go through your check register, credit card slips, receipts, and other expense records and record the required information for each transaction. Also, total the amounts for each category when you come to the end of the page and keep a running total of what you've spent for each category for the year to date.

The following example shows a portion of an expense journal.

Expense Journal

Date	Check No.	Transaction	Amount	Advertising	Outside Contractors	Utilities	Supplies	Rent	Travel	Equipment	Meals & Entertainment	Misc.
5/1	123	ABC Properties	500					500				
5/1	124	Office Warehouse	150				150					
5/10	VISA	Computer World	1,000							1,000		
5/15	VISA	Cafe´ Ole´	50								50	
5/16	Cash	Sam's Stationery	50				50					
5/18	125	Electric Co.	50			50						
5/30	126	Bill Carter	5,050		500							
Total This Page			6,850		500	50	200	500		1,000	50	
Total Year to Date			7,900	200	2,000	250	400	2,500	300	1,500	250	500

Using Computer Financial Programs

There are many computer programs designed to help people and businesses keep track of their finances. These range from relatively simple checkbook programs like *Quicken* to more complex and sophisticated accounting programs like *QuickBooks*. You can use these in place of the handwritten ledger sheets or simple spreadsheets described above. However, you'll be better off using handwritten ledger sheets, which are easy to create and understand and simple to keep up to date, instead of a complicated computer program that you don't understand or use properly. So, if you're not prepared to invest the time to use a computer program correctly, don't use it!

We won't discuss how to use these programs in detail. You'll need to read the manual or tutorial that comes with the program you choose. There are also books that explain how to use them.

Before You Purchase a Program

You don't want to spend your hard-earned money on a financial program only to discover that you don't like it. Before you purchase a program:

- Talk to others in similar businesses to find out what they use—if they don't like a program, ask them why.
- Think carefully about how many features you need—the more complex the program, the harder it will be to learn and use it.
- Obtain a demo version you can try out for free to see if you like it—you can usually download one from the software company's website.

The simplest financial programs are those like *Quicken* that work off of a computerized checkbook. When you buy something for your business, you write a check using the program. It automatically inputs the data into a computerized check register, and you print out the check using your computer (payments can also be made online). You'll have to input credit card and cash payments separately.

You create a list of expense categories just like you do when you create a ledger sheet or spreadsheet. The expense category is automatically noted in your register when you write a check.

The program can then take this information and automatically create income and expense reports—that is, it will show you the amounts you've spent or earned for each category. This serves the same purpose as the expense journal. It can also create profit and loss statements. You can even import these amounts into tax preparation software, such as *TurboTax*, when it's time to do your income taxes.

Quicken provides all the tools many real estate agents need. However, if you have employees, you'll need a more sophisticated program. Other programs (such as *QuickBooks* by Intuit) can accomplish more complex bookkeeping tasks, such as double-entry bookkeeping, payroll, invoicing, handling accounts receivable, and maintaining fixed asset records.

Supporting Documents

The IRS lives by the maxim that "figures lie and liars figure." It knows very well that you can claim anything in your books and on your tax returns, because you create or complete them yourself. For this reason, the IRS requires that you have documents to support the deductions you claim on your tax return. In the absence of a supporting document, an IRS auditor may conclude that an item you claim as a business expense is really a personal expense, or that you never bought the item at all. Either way, your deduction will be disallowed.

The supporting documents you need depend on the type of deduction involved. However, at a minimum, every deduction should be supported by documentation showing what, how much, and who. That is, your supporting documents should show:

- what you purchased for your business
- how much you paid for it, and
- whom (or what company) you bought it from.

Additional record keeping requirements must be met for deductions for local transportation, travel, entertainment, meal, and gift deductions, as well as for certain long-term assets that you buy for your business. ("Records Required for Specific Expenses," below, covers these rules.)

You can meet the what, how much, and who requirements by keeping the following types of documentation:

- canceled checks
- sales receipts
- account statements
- credit card sales slips
- invoices, or
- petty cash slips for small cash payments.

Make Digital Copies of Your Receipts

According to an old Chinese proverb, the palest ink is more reliable than the most retentive memory. However, when it comes to receipts, ink is no longer so reliable. Receipts printed on thermal paper (as most are) fade over time. By the time the IRS audits your return, you may find that all or most of the paper receipts you've carefully retained in your files are unreadable.

Because of the fading problem, you should photocopy your receipts if you intend to rely on hard copies. Obviously, this is time consuming and annoying. But there is an easier alternative: Make digital copies of your receipts and throw away the hard copies.

Making a digital copy of a receipt used to require a scanner, which could be cumbersome and inconvenient. This is no longer necessary. If you have an iPhone or other smartphone with a camera, you can use that to take digital photographs of receipts. Because you are likely to have your phone with you anyway, this is easy and convenient. After a business dinner, simply make a digital copy of your receipt and then throw it away. You don't have to worry about losing it or storing it.

There are many inexpensive smartphone applications you can use to copy and keep track of receipts. Two of the most popular are Shoeboxed.com and Expensify.com. Using these and other similar apps, you can add notes and then upload the digital photos to an online account for permanent storage. These apps can even automatically categorize your expenses, and you can export your data to Quickbooks, Quicken, Excel, Freshbooks, and other accounting software.

Keep your supporting documents in a safe place. If you don't have a lot of receipts and other documents to save, you can simply keep them all in a single folder. If you have a lot of supporting documents to save or are the type of person who likes to be extremely well organized, separate your documents by category—for example, income, travel expenses, or equipment purchases. You can use a separate file folder for each category or get an accordion file with multiple pockets.

Canceled Check + Receipt = Proof of Deduction

Manny, a real estate agent, buys a $500 digital camera for his business from the local electronics store. He writes a check for the amount and is given a receipt. How does he prove to the IRS that he has a $500 business expense?

Could Manny simply save his canceled check when it's returned from his bank? Many people carefully save all their canceled checks (some keep them for decades), apparently believing that a canceled check is all the proof they need to show that a purchase was a legitimate business expense. This is not the case. All a canceled check proves is that you spent money for something. It doesn't show what you bought. Of course, you can write a note on your check stating what you purchased, but why should the IRS believe what you write on your checks yourself?

MANNY FARBER
123 SHADY LANE
ANYTOWN, IL 12345

2345

Date Feb. 1, 20xx

12-34/5780

Pay to the order of Acme Camera Store $ 500.00

Five hundred and 100/100 Dollars

Piggy Bank
100 Main Street
Anytown, IL 12345

Memo Digital Camera Manny Farber

⑆ 578000358⑆ 5355⑈05556⑈05555⑈

Does Manny's sales receipt prove he bought his camera for his business? Again, no. A sales receipt only proves that somebody purchased the item listed in the receipt. It does not show who purchased it. Again, you could write a note on the receipt stating that you bought the item. But you could easily lie. Indeed, for all the IRS knows, you could hang around stores and pick up receipts people throw away to give yourself tax deductions. There are also websites that, for a fee, will create legitimate-looking fake receipts.

509257

CUSTOMER'S ORDER NO. 14601					DATE February 1, 20xx	
NAME						
ADDRESS						
CITY, STATE, ZIP						
SOLD BY SF	CASH	C.O.D.	CHARGE	ON ACCT.	MDSE. RETD.	PAID OUT

	QUAN.	DESCRIPTION	PRICE	AMOUNT
1	1	Minolta Digital Camera	500	500
2				
3				
4				
5				
6				
7				
8				
9				
10				
11			Total	500
12				

RECEIVED BY

KEEP THIS SLIP FOR REFERENCE

However, when you put a canceled check together with a sales receipt (or an invoice, a cash register tape, or a similar document), you have concrete proof that you purchased the item listed in the receipt. The check proves that you bought something, and the receipt proves what that something is.

This doesn't necessarily prove that you bought the item for your business, but it's a good start. Often, the face of a receipt, the sales slip, or the payee's name on your canceled check will strongly indicate that the item you purchased was for your business. But if it's not clear, note what the purchase was for on the document. Such a note is not proof of how you used the item, but it will be helpful. For some types of items that you use for both business and personal purposes—cameras are one example—you might be required to keep careful records of your use. (See "Records Required for Specified Expenses," below.)

Credit Cards

Using a credit card is a great way to pay business expenses. The credit card slip will prove that you bought the item listed on the slip. You'll also have a monthly statement to back up your credit card slips. You should use a separate credit card for your business.

Account Statements

Sometimes, you'll need to use an account statement to prove an expense. Some banks no longer return canceled checks, or you may pay for something with an ATM card or another electronic funds transfer method. Moreover, you may not always have a credit card slip when you pay by credit card—for example, when you buy an item over the Internet. In these events, the IRS will accept an account statement as proof that you purchased the item. The chart below shows what type of information you need on an account statement.

Proving Payments With Bank Statements

If payment is by:	The statement must show:
Check	Check number Amount Payee's name Date the check amount was posted to the account by the bank
Electronic funds transfer	Amount transferred Payee's name Date the amount transferred was posted to the account by the bank
Credit card	Amount charged Payee's name Transaction date

Records Required for Specific Expenses

The IRS is particularly suspicious of business deductions people take for local transportation, travel, meals, gift, and entertainment expenses. It knows that many people wildly inflate these deductions—either because they're dishonest or because they haven't kept good records and make estimates of how much they think they must have spent. For this reason, special record keeping requirements apply to these deductions. Likewise, there are special requirements for long-term assets that can be used for both personal and business purposes. If you fail to comply with the requirements discussed below, the IRS may disallow the deduction, even if it was legitimate.

Automobile Mileage and Expense Records

If you use a car or other vehicle for business purposes other than just commuting to and from work, you're entitled to take a deduction for gas and other auto expenses. You can either deduct the actual cost of your gas and other expenses or take the standard rate deduction based on the number of business miles you drive. (See Chapter 4 for more on car expenses.)

Either way, you must keep a record of:

- your mileage
- the dates of your business trips
- the places you drove for business, and
- the business purpose for your trips.

The last three items are relatively easy to keep track of. You can record the information in your appointment book, calendar, or day planner. Or, you can record it in a mileage logbook—you can get one for a few dollars from any stationery store and stash it in your car glove compartment.

Calculating your mileage takes more work. The IRS wants to know the total number of miles you drove during the year for business, commuting, and personal driving other than commuting. Commuting is travel from your home to your office or other principal place of business. If you work from a home office, you'll have no commuting mileage. (See Chapter 4 for more on commuting and automobile expenses.) Personal miles other than commuting include all the driving you do other than from home to your office—for example, to the grocery store, on a personal vacation, or to visit friends or relatives.

Claiming a Car Is Used Solely for Business

If you use a car 100% for business, you don't need to keep track of your personal or commuting miles. However, you can successfully claim to use a car 100% for business only if you:

- work out of a tax-deductible home office
- have at least two cars, and
- use one car just for business trips.

If you don't work from a home office, your trips from your home to your outside office are nonbusiness commuting, so the car you take from your home to your office is not used 100% for business, even if you drive it only for business after you get to your office and then drive straight home.

To keep track of your business driving you can use either a paper mileage logbook that you keep in your car or an electronic application. Logbooks are available in any stationery store while there are dozens of apps you can use with an iPhone or similar device.

Whichever you choose, there are several ways to keep track of your mileage; some are easy, and some are a bit more complicated.

52-Week Mileage Log

The hardest way to track your mileage—and the way the IRS would like you to do it—is to keep track of every mile you drive every day, 52 weeks a year, using a mileage logbook or business diary. This means you'll list every trip you take, whether for business, commuting, or personal reasons. If you enjoy record keeping, go ahead and use this method. But there are easier ways.

Tracking Business Mileage

An easier way to keep track of your mileage is to record your mileage only when you use your car for business. If you record your mileage with an electronic app, check the manual to see how to implement this system. If you use a paper mileage logbook, here's what to do:

- Note your odometer reading in the logbook at the beginning and end of every year that you use the car for business. (If you don't know your January 1 odometer reading for this year, you might be able to estimate it by looking at auto repair receipts that note your mileage.)
- Record your mileage and note the business purpose for the trip every time you use your car for business.
- Add up your business mileage when you get to the end of each page in the logbook. (This way, you'll have to add only the page totals at the end of the year instead of all the individual entries.)
- If you commute to your office or other workplace, figure out how many miles you drive each way and note in your appointment book how many times you drive to the office each week.

Below is a portion of a page from a mileage logbook.

Date	Business Purpose	Beginning Odometer Reading	Ending Odometer Reading	Business Miles
5/1	Open house—111 Main St., Any town	10,111	10,186	75
5/2	View properties with Art Andrews	10,200	10,255	55
5/2	Attend sales seminar	10,255	10,275	20
5/3	Lunch—Sam Simpson	10,275	10,311	36

At the end of the year, your logbook will show the total business miles you drove during the year. You calculate the total miles you drove during the year by subtracting your January 1 odometer reading from your December 31 reading.

If you use the actual expense method, you must also calculate your percentage of business use of the car. You do this by dividing your business miles by your total miles.

> **EXAMPLE:** Yolanda is a real estate agent who uses her car extensively for business. At the beginning of the year her odometer reading

was 34,201 miles. On December 31, it was 58,907 miles. Her total mileage for the year was therefore 24,706. She recorded 62 business trips in her mileage logbook for a total of 9,280 miles. Her business use percentage of her car is 37% (9,290 ÷ 24,706 = 0.366). Yolanda commuted to her office every day, 50 weeks a year. She determined that her office was ten miles from her home. So Yolanda had 5,000 miles of commuting mileage for the year.

Record Your Mileage Electronically

If writing your mileage down in a paper mileage logbook seems too primitive, you can keep your records in electronic form with an electronic device such as an iPhone or computer. There is special software available for recording business mileage. However, be warned: Although the IRS's official policy is that electronic records are acceptable, many IRS auditors are old-fashioned. They like to see paper-and-ink mileage records because they are much harder to alter, forge, or create in a hurry than electronic records.

Sampling Method

There is an even easier way to track your mileage: use a sampling method. Under this method, you keep track of your business mileage for a sample portion of the year and use your figures for that period to extrapolate your business mileage for the whole year.

This method assumes that you drive about the same amount for business throughout the year. To back up this assumption, you must scrupulously keep an appointment book showing your business appointments all year long. If you don't want to keep an appointment book, don't use the sampling method.

Your sample period must be at least 90 days—for example, the first three months of the year. Alternatively, you may sample one week each month—for example, the first week of every month. You don't have to use the first three months of the year or the first week of every month;

you could use any other three-month period or the second, third, or fourth week of every month. Use whatever works best—you want your sample period to be as representative as possible of the business travel you do throughout the year.

You must keep track of the total miles you drove during the year by taking odometer readings on January 1 and December 31 and deducting any atypical mileage before applying your sample results.

> EXAMPLE: Tom, a real estate broker, uses the sample method to compute his mileage, keeping track of his business miles for the first three months of the year. He drove 6,000 miles during that time and had 4,000 business miles. His business use percentage of his car was 67%. From his January 1 and December 31 odometer readings, Tom knows he drove a total of 27,000 miles during the year. However, Tom drove to the Grand Canyon for vacation, so he deducts this 1,000 mile trip from his total. This leaves him with 26,000 total miles for the year. To calculate his total business miles, he multiplies the year-long total by the business use percentage of his car: 67% × 26,000 = 17,420. Tom claims 17,420 business miles on his tax return.

Keeping Track of Actual Expenses

If you take the deduction for your actual auto expenses instead of the standard rate (or are thinking about switching to this method), keep receipts for all of your auto-related expenses, including gasoline, oil, tires, repairs, and insurance. You don't need to include these expenses in your ledger sheets; just keep them in a folder or envelope. At tax time, add them up to determine how large your deduction will be if you use the actual expense method. Also add in the amount you're entitled to deduct for depreciation of your auto. (See Chapter 4 for more on calculating automobile deductions.)

Costs for business-related parking (other than at your office) and for tolls are separately deductible whether you use the standard rate or the actual expense method. Get and keep receipts for these expenses.

Use a Credit Card for Gas

If you use the actual expense method for car expenses, use a credit card when you buy gas. It's best to designate a separate card for this purpose. The monthly statements you receive will serve as your gas receipts. If you pay cash for gas, you must either get a receipt or make a note of the amount in your mileage logbook.

Entertainment, Meal, Travel, and Gift Expenses

Deductions for business-related entertainment, meals, and travel are hot-button items for the IRS because they have been greatly abused by many taxpayers. You need to have more records for these expenses than for almost any others, and they will be closely scrutinized if you're audited.

Whenever you incur an expense for business-related entertainment, meals, gifts, or travel, you must document the following five facts:

- **The date.** The date the expense was incurred will usually be listed on a receipt or credit card slip; appointment books, day planners, and similar documents have the dates preprinted on each page, so entries on the appropriate page automatically date the expense.
- **The amount.** How much you spent, including tax and tip for meals.
- **The place.** The nature and place of the entertainment or meal will usually be shown by a receipt, or you can record it in an appointment book.
- **The business purpose.** Show that the expense was incurred for your business—for example, to obtain future business, encourage existing business relationships, and so on. What you need to show depends on whether the business conversation occurred before, during, or after entertainment or a meal. (See Chapter 6 for more on deducting meal expenses.)
- **The business relationship.** If entertainment or meals are involved, show the business relationship of people at the event—for example, list their names and occupations and any other information needed to establish their business relation to you.

The IRS does not require that you keep receipts, canceled checks, credit card slips, or any other supporting documents for entertainment, meal, gift, or travel expenses that cost less than $75. However, you must still document the five facts listed above. This exception does not apply to lodging—that is, hotel or similar costs—when you travel for business. You do need receipts for these expenses, even if they are less than $75.

CAUTION

The $75 rule applies only to travel, meals, gifts, and entertainment. The rule that you don't need receipts for expenses less than $75 applies only to travel, gift, meal, and entertainment expenses. It does not apply to other types of business expenses. For example, if you go to the office supply store and buy $50 worth of supplies for your business and then spend $70 for lunch with a client, you need a receipt for the office supplies, but not the business lunch. If you find this rule hard to remember, simply keep all of your receipts.

All this record keeping is not as hard as it sounds. You can record the five facts you have to document in a variety of ways. The information doesn't have to be all in one place. Information that is shown on a receipt, canceled check, or other item need not be duplicated in a log, appointment book, calendar, or account book. Thus, for example, you can record the five facts with:

- a receipt, credit card slip, or similar document alone
- a receipt combined with an appointment book entry, or
- an appointment book entry alone (for expenses less than $75).

However you document your expense, you are supposed to do it in a timely manner. You don't need to record the details of every expense on the day you incur it. It is sufficient to record them on a weekly basis. However, if you're prone to forget details, it's best to get everything you need in writing within a day or two.

Receipt or Credit Card Slip Alone

An easy way to document an entertainment, gift, travel, or meal expense is to use your receipt, credit card slip, invoice, or bill. A receipt or credit card slip will ordinarily contain the name and location of the place where the expense was incurred, the date, and the amount charged. Thus, three of the five facts you must document are taken care of. You just need to describe the business purpose and business relationship if entertainment or meals are involved. You can write this directly on your receipt or credit card slip.

> EXAMPLE: Real estate agent Mary has lunch with Harold to discuss listing his home for sale. Her restaurant bill shows the date, name, and location of the restaurant, the number of people served, and the amount of the expense. Mary just has to document the business purpose for the lunch and identify who it was with. She writes on the receipt: "Lunch with Harold Lipshitz. Discussed signing listing agreement." All five facts Mary must prove to document her meal expense are on the receipt. This is all she needs. She need not duplicate the information elsewhere—for example, in an appointment book or day planner.

Receipt Plus Appointment Book

You can also document the five facts you need to prove an expense by combining the information on a receipt with entries in an appointment book, day planner, calendar, diary, or similar record.

> EXAMPLE: Assume that Mary from the above example saves her receipt from the restaurant where she had her business lunch. She writes nothing on the receipt. She still needs to document the five facts. Her receipt contains the date, name, and location of the restaurant, and the amount of the lunch. She records who the lunch was with and the business purpose by writing a note in her appointment book: "Lunch—Harold Lipshitz. Discussed signing listing agreement."

Appointment Book Alone

If your expense is for less than $75, you don't need to keep a receipt (unless the expense is for lodging). You may record the five facts in your appointment book, day planner, daily diary, calendar, or on any other sheet of paper.

EXAMPLE: Assume that Mary from the above example doesn't keep her receipt from her lunch. Because lunch cost less than $75, she does not need it. Instead, she documents the five facts she needs to record in her appointment book. She writes: "Lunch—Greens Restaurant, with Harold Lipshitz, Discussed signing listing agreement. $74." This short entry records the place of the lunch, who it was with, the business purpose, and the amount. She doesn't need to add the date because this is already shown by her appointment book.

Receipts to Keep

Type of Expense	Receipts to Save
Travel	Airplane, train, or bus ticket stubs; travel agency receipts; rental car; and so on.
Meals	Meal check, credit card slip.
Lodging	Statement or bill from hotel or other lodging provider. Your own written records for cleaning, laundry, telephone charges, tips, and other charges not shown separately on hotel statement.
Entertainment	Bill from entertainment provider; ticket stubs for sporting event, theater, or other event; credit card slips.

Listed Property

Listed property refers to certain types of long-term business assets that can easily be used for personal as well as business purposes. Listed property includes:

- cars, boats, airplanes, motorcycles, and other vehicles
- computers, and
- any other property generally used for entertainment, recreation, or amusement—for example, VCRs, cameras, and camcorders.

Because all listed property is long-term business property, it cannot be deducted like a business expense. Instead, you must depreciate it over several years or deduct it in one year under Section 179. (See Chapter 9 for more on deducting long-term assets.)

Special Record-Keeping Requirements

With listed property, the IRS fears that taxpayers might claim business deductions but really use the property for personal reasons instead. For this reason, you're required to document how you use listed property. Keep an appointment book, logbook, business diary, or calendar showing the dates, times, and reasons for which the property is used—both business and personal. You also can purchase logbooks for this purpose at stationery or office supply stores.

> EXAMPLE: Real estate agent Bill purchases a computer he uses 50% for business and 50% to play games. He must keep a log showing his business use of the computer. Following is a sample from one week in his log.

Usage Log for Personal Computer

Date	Time of Business Use	Reason for Business Use	Time of Personal Use
5/1	4.5 hours	Worked on new property listing for 5 Main Street	1.5 hours
5/2			3 hours
5/3	2 hours	Worked on new property listing for 5 Main Street	
5/4			2 hours

Exception to Record-Keeping Rule for Computers

You usually have to document your use of listed property even if you use it 100% for business. However, there is an exception to this rule for computers: If you use a computer or computer peripheral (such as a printer) only for business and keep it at your business location, you need not comply with the record keeping requirement. This includes computers that you keep at your home office if the office qualifies for the home office deduction. (See Chapter 7.)

EXAMPLE: Real estate broker John works out of his home office, which he uses exclusively for his real estate business. The office is clearly his principal place of business and qualifies for the home office deduction. He buys a $4,000 computer for his office and uses it exclusively for his real estate business. He does not have to keep records showing how he uses the computer.

This exception applies only to computers and computer peripheral equipment. It doesn't apply to other items such as calculators, copiers, fax machines, or typewriters.

How Long to Keep Records

You need to have copies of your tax returns and supporting documents available in case you are audited by the IRS or another taxing agency. You might also need them for other purposes—for example, to get a loan, mortgage, or insurance.

You should keep your records for as long as the IRS has to audit you after you file your returns for the year. These statutes of limitations range from three years to forever—they are listed in the table below.

To be on the safe side, you should keep your tax returns indefinitely. They usually don't take up much space, so this is not a big hardship. Your supporting documents probably take up more space. You should keep these for at least six years after you file your return. If you file a fraudulent return, keep your supporting documents indefinitely (if you have any). If you're audited, they will show that at least some of your deductions were legitimate. Keeping your records this long ensures that you'll have them available if the IRS decides to audit you.

Keep your long-term asset records for three years after the depreciable life of the asset ends. For example, keep records for five-year property (such as computers) for eight years.

You should keep your ledger sheets for as long as you're in business, because a potential buyer of your business might want to see them.

IRS Statutes of Limitations	
If:	**The limitations period is:**
You failed to pay all the tax due	3 years
You underreported your gross income for the year by more than 25%	6 years
You filed a fraudulent return	No limit
You did not file a return	No limit

What If You Don't Have Proper Tax Records?

Because you're human, you may not have kept all the records required to back up your tax deductions. Don't despair, all is not lost—you may be able to fall back on the *Cohan* rule. This rule (named after the Broadway entertainer George M. Cohan, involved in a tax case in the 1930s) is the taxpayer's best friend. The *Cohan* rule recognizes that all businesspeople must spend at least some money to stay in business and so must have had at least some deductible expenses, even if they don't have adequate records to back them up.

If you're audited and lack adequate records for a claimed deduction, the IRS can use the *Cohan* rule to make an estimate of how much you must have spent and allow you to deduct that amount. However, you must provide at least some credible evidence on which to base this estimate, such as receipts, canceled checks, notes in your appointment book, or other records. Moreover, the IRS will allow you to deduct only the least amount you must have spent, based on the records you provide. In addition, the *Cohan* rule cannot be used for travel, meal, entertainment, or gift expenses, or for listed property.

If an auditor claims you lack sufficient records to back up a deduction, you should always bring up the *Cohan* rule and argue that you should still get the deduction based on the records you do have. At best, you'll probably get only part of your claimed deductions. If the IRS auditor disallows your deductions entirely or doesn't give you as much as you think you deserve, you can appeal in court and bring up the *Cohan* rule again there. You might have more success with a judge. However, you can't compel an IRS auditor or a court to apply the *Cohan* rule in your favor. Whether to apply the rule and how large a deduction to give you is within their discretion.

Reconstructing Tax Records

If you can show that you possessed adequate records at one time, but now lack them due to circumstances beyond your control, you may reconstruct your records for an IRS audit. Circumstances beyond your control would include acts of nature such as floods, fires, earthquakes, or theft. (Treas. Reg. 1.275.5(c)(5).) Loss of tax records while moving does not constitute circumstances beyond your control. Reconstructing records means you create brand-new records just for your audit or obtain other evidence to corroborate your deductions—for example, statements from people or companies from whom you purchased items for your business.

Accounting Methods

An accounting method is a set of rules used to determine when and how your income and expenses are reported. Accounting methods might sound like a rather dry subject, but your choice about how to account for your business expenses and income will have a huge impact on your tax deductions. You don't have to become as expert as a CPA on this topic, but you should understand the basics.

You choose an accounting method when you file your first tax return. If you later want to change your accounting method, you must get IRS approval. You are free to choose the method you want, as long as it clearly shows your income and expenses. If you operate two or more separate businesses, you can use a different accounting method for each. (A business is separate for tax purposes only if you keep a separate set of books and records for it.)

There are two basic methods of accounting: cash basis and accrual basis.

Cash Method

The cash method is by far the simplest method. It is used by individuals who are not in business and by most real estate agents. The cash method is based on this commonsense idea: You haven't earned income for tax purposes until you actually receive the money, and you haven't incurred an expense until you actually pay the money. Thus, for example, if a sale closes in February, but you don't receive your commission check until March, the commission is accounted for as March revenue.

Using the cash basis method, then, is like maintaining a checkbook. You record income only when the money is received and expenses only when they are actually paid. If you borrow money to pay business expenses, you incur an expense under the cash method only when you make payments on the loan.

The Cash Method of Paying Expenses

Although it's called the cash method, this method for paying business expenses includes payments by check, credit card, or electronic funds transfer, as well as by cash. If you pay by check, the amount is deemed paid during the year in which the check is drawn and mailed—for example, a check dated December 31, 2012 is considered paid during 2012 only if it has a December 31, 2012 postmark. If you're using a check to pay a substantial expense, you may wish to mail it by certified mail so you'll have proof of when it was mailed.

Constructive Receipt

Under the cash method, payments are "constructively received" when an amount is credited to your account or otherwise made available to you without restrictions. Constructive receipt is as good as actual receipt. If you authorize someone to be your agent and receive income for you, you are considered to have received it when your agent receives it.

EXAMPLE: Interest is credited to your business bank account in December 2012, but you do not withdraw it or enter it into your passbook until 2013. You must include the amount in gross business income for 2012.

No Postponing Income

You cannot hold checks or other payments from one tax year to another to avoid paying tax on the income. You must report the income in the year the payment is received or made available to you without restriction.

EXAMPLE: On December 1, 2012, Helen receives a $5,000 commission check. She holds the check and doesn't cash it until January 10, 2013. She must still report the $5,000 as income for 2012, because she constructively received it that year.

No Prepayment of Expenses

The general rule is that you can't prepay expenses when you use the cash method—you can't hurry up the payment of expenses by paying them in advance. An expense you pay in advance can be deducted only in the year to which it applies.

EXAMPLE: Real estate broker Helen pays $1,000 in 2012 for a business insurance policy that is effective for one year, beginning July 1, 2012. She can deduct $500 in 2012 and $500 in 2013.

However, there is an important exception to the general rule, called the 12-month rule. Under this rule, you may deduct a prepaid expense in the current year if the expense is for a right or benefit that extends no longer than the earlier of:

- 12 months, or
- until the end of the tax year after the tax year in which you made the payment.

EXAMPLE: You are a calendar year taxpayer and you pay $10,000 on July 1, 2012 for a business insurance policy that is effective for one year beginning July 1, 2012. The 12-month rule applies because the benefit you've paid for—a business insurance policy—extends only 12 months into the future. Therefore, the full $10,000 is deductible in 2012.

There is one small catch: If you previously followed the old rule under which expenses prepaid beyond the calendar year were not currently deductible, you must get IRS approval to use the 12-month rule. Approval is granted automatically by the IRS upon filing of IRS Form 3115, *Application for Change in Accounting Method.* You should attach one copy of the form to the return for the year of change and then send another copy to the IRS national office (not the service center where you file your return). The address is on the instructions for the form.

It is a good idea to get a tax pro to help you with this form because it may require some adjustment of the deductions you've taken for prepaid expenses in previous years under the old rule.

Accrual Method

In accrual basis accounting, you report income or expenses as they are earned or incurred, rather than when they are actually collected or paid. With the accrual method, income is counted when a sale occurs and expenses are counted when you receive the goods or services. You don't have to wait until you see the money or actually pay money out of your checking account. The accrual method can be difficult to use because there are complex rules to determine when income or expenses are accrued.

When Expenses Are Incurred

Under the accrual method, you generally deduct a business expense when:

- You are legally obligated to pay the expense.
- The amount you owe can be determined with reasonable accuracy.
- You have received or used the property or services involved.

EXAMPLE: Real estate broker Bill borrows $10,000 from his bank to help pay his business operating expenses. He signs a promissory note on December 15, 2012 and receives the money the same day but doesn't start making payments to the bank until the following January. Bill can deduct the expense in 2012 because he became legally obligated to pay the expense upon signing the note, the amount of the expense can be determined from the note, and he received the money that day.

Thus, when you use the accrual method, you can take a deduction for an expense you incur even if you don't actually pay for it until the following year. You can't do this under the cash basis method. There are obvious advantages to getting a tax deduction this year without actually having to shell out any money until a future year.

When Income Is Received

While the accrual method lets you deduct expenses that you haven't paid for yet, it also requires that you report as income payments you haven't yet received. Transactions are counted as income when an order is made or services are provided, regardless of when the money for them (receivables) is actually received or paid.

EXAMPLE: Real estate broker Andrea closes a home sale in December 2012, and becomes legally entitled to payment of her $50,000 commission. However, Andrea doesn't actually receive the commission check from escrow until January of 2013. She uses the accrual method of accounting so Andrea must count the $50,000 commission as income in December 2012 because that's when she became legally entitled to the money. This income must be reported on her 2012 tax return even though she did not receive the money that year.

Businesses That Must Use the Accrual Method

Any business, however small, may use the accrual method. Some types of businesses are required to use it, including C corporations with average annual gross receipts exceeding $5 million and partnerships with average annual gross receipts exceeding $5 million that have C corporations as partners. (See IRS Publication 538, *Accounting Periods and Methods*, for more details.)

Which Is Better: Accrual or Cash Method Accounting?

There is no single best accounting method. Each method has its advantages and disadvantages. The cash basis method is much simpler to use and easier to understand. The accrual method is more complicated than the cash basis method and harder to use, but it shows the ebb and flow of business income and debts more accurately than the cash basis method. You get a truer picture of your net profits for any given time period with the accrual method, because income earned in one time period is accurately matched against the expenses for that period

Tax Years

You are required to pay taxes for a 12-month period, also known as the tax year. Sole proprietors, partnerships, limited liability companies, S corporations, and personal service corporations are required to use the calendar year as their tax years—that is, January 1 through December 31.

However, there are exceptions that permit some small businesses to use a tax year that does not end in December (also known as a fiscal year). You need to get the IRS's permission to use a fiscal year. The IRS doesn't like businesses to use a fiscal year, but it might grant you permission if you can show a good business reason for it.

To get permission to use a fiscal year, you must file IRS Form 8716, *Election to Have a Tax Year Other Than a Required Tax Year.*

Index

D

E

F

G

H

I

K

L

M

P

Q

R

S

T

U

V

W

Z

Keep Up to Date

Go to Nolo.com/newsletters to sign up for free newsletters and discounts on Nolo products.

- **Nolo's Special Offer.** A monthly newsletter with the biggest Nolo discounts around.
- **Landlord's Quarterly.** Deals and free tips for landlords and property managers.

Don't forget to check for updates. Find this book at Nolo.com and click "Legal Updates."

Let Us Hear From You

Register your Nolo product and give us your feedback at Nolo.com/customer-support/productregistration.

- Once you've registered, you qualify for technical support if you have any trouble with a download (though most folks don't).
- We'll send you a coupon for 15% off your next Nolo.com order!

DEAR2